INTRODUCTION TO PASCAL

Second Edition

by

JIM WELSH

The University of Manchester Institute of Science and Technology, England

and

JOHN ELDER

Queen's University of Belfast, Northern Ireland

Prentice/Hall PHI International

ENGLEWOOD CLIFFS, N.J.   LONDON   NEW DELHI   SINGAPORE
SYDNEY   TOKYO   TORONTO   WELLINGTON

Library of Congress Cataloging in Publication Data

WELSH, JIM, 1943-
  Introduction to Pascal.

  Includes index.
  1. PASCAL (Computer program language)
  I. Elder, John, 1949– . II. Title.
  QA76.73.P2W44 1982   001.64'24   81–15335
  ISBN 0–13–491530–5 (pbk.)   AACR2

British Library Cataloguing in Publication Data

WELSH, JIM
  Introduction to Pascal.—Rev. ed.
  1. PASCAL (Computer program language)
  I. Title   II. Elder, John
  001.64'24   QA76.73.P2
  ISBN 0–13–491530–5

© 1982, 1979
by PRENTICE-HALL INTERNATIONAL INC., LONDON

PRENTICE-HALL INTERNATIONAL, INC., *London*
PRENTICE-HALL OF AUSTRALIA PTY. LTD., *Sydney*
PRENTICE-HALL CANADA, INC., *Toronto*
PRENTICE HALL OF INDIA PRIVATE LIMITED, *New Delhi*
PRENTICE-HALL OF JAPAN, INC., *Tokyo*
PRENTICE-HALL OF SOUTHEAST ASIA PTE., LTD., *Singapore*
PRENTICE-HALL, INC., *Englewood Cliffs, New Jersey*
WHITEHALL BOOKS LIMITED, *Wellington, New Zealand*

ISBN 0-13-491530-5

Printed in the United States of America

10 9 8 7 6

INTRODUCTION TO PASCAL

Second Edition

Prentice-Hall International
Series in Computer Science

C. A. R. Hoare, Series Editor

Published

BACKHOUSE, R. C., *Syntax of Programming Languages: Theory and Practice*
de BAKKER, J. W., *Mathematical Theory of Program Correctness*
DROMEY, R. G., *How to Solve it by Computer*
DUNCAN, F., *Microprocessor Programming and Software Development*
GOLDSCHLAGER, L. and LISTER, A., *Computer Science: A Modern Introduction*
HENDERSON, P., *Functional Programming: Application and Implementation*
JONES, C. B., *Software Development: A Rigorous Approach*
REYNOLDS, J. C., *The Craft of Programming*
TENNENT, R. D., *Principles of Programming Languages*
WELSH, J. and ELDER, J., *Introduction to PASCAL, Second Edition*
WELSH, J. and McKEAG, M., *Structured System Programming*

Contents

CHAPTER TEN :   **RECORDS,** 166

CHAPTER ELEVEN :   **SETS,** 192

CHAPTER TWELVE :   **FILES,** 210

Preface to the Second Edition

Since the first edition of this book was published in 1979 a new definition of PASCAL has been agreed by representatives of the appropriate national and international standards organizations. This definition, which is known as ISO draft international standard(DIS) 7185, is now in the process of formal ratification as an international standard.

For the most part, this new definition eliminates minor loopholes in the previous definition of PASCAL, but in two areas additional language features have been introduced. These affect the use of procedures and functions as parameters, and of arrays as parameters. The changes significantly enhance the security and effectiveness of PASCAL in these areas, and have already been incorporated in many major implementations of the language.

The second edition of this book describes PASCAL exactly as defined by the new standard, and includes descriptions of the new features and their proper use. Through the text the terms "the definition of PASCAL" and "the PASCAL standard" are used to refer to DIS 7185.

The programming language PASCAL was developed in the late 1960s by Professor Niklaus Wirth at the Eidgenössische Technische Hochschule, Zürich, Switzerland. His aim was to produce a language containing a small number of fundamental programming concepts that would be suitable for teaching programming as a logical and systematic discipline, and also be capable of efficient implementation on most computers. His success in achieving this goal can be measured by the rapid and widespread increase in the use of PASCAL, both as a language for teaching the principles of computer programming and as a practical language for writing systems and applications programs.

This book provides a comprehensive introduction to PASCAL and is suitable for use by novice programmers and by those with a knowledge of other programming languages. The complete language is described and the use of all the features of PASCAL is fully illustrated. The language which we describe does not contain any features peculiar to any particular implementation—indeed great care is taken to isolate and stress the implementation-dependent features of PASCAL. More general principles of programming are illustrated implicity in the text. In fact, the style of programming used is consistent with the current methods of structured programming and stepwise refinement.

The material is based on various courses given at The Queen's University of Belfast over nine years by the authors, who have wide experience in the teaching, use, and implementation of PASCAL. The teaching sequence of the book is that used on those courses and is suitable for a reader learning PASCAL, or indeed learning to program, for the first time. The other aspects of computers and computer organization of which a first-time programmer must be aware are not covered in detail, but Chap. 1 presents a summary of the knowledge and terminology on which subsequent chapters depend. Chapters 3–6 introduce the basic data types and statements of PASCAL. Chapter 7 deals with procedures and functions, the use of which we consider fundamental in the program-construction process. In Chaps. 9–13 PASCAL's data-structuring facilities—arrays, strings, records, sets, files and pointers—are introduced.

The features of PASCAL are presented in turn, by

(a) defining the feature using the notation and terminology of the standard PASCAL definition;
(b) explaining its use, and any limitations and practical problems of which the user must be aware;
(c) illustrating its use by small, tested, program fragments imbedded within the explanatory text.

A distinguishing feature of the book is the inclusion, where appropriate, in each chapter of one or more complete case-study programs. In all the book contains seventeen such case studies illustrating the use of various PASCAL facilities, and basic computing algorithms, in a significant practical context. For each case study the design of the program is developed by means of a step-wise refinement of the problem, and a final listing of the PASCAL program and the results it produces is reproduced directly from its computer-printed output.

Most chapters end with a set of programming exercises which involve further use of the language features described in the chapter. These exercises require modifications or extensions to be made to earlier case-study programs as well as the construction of new programs. Solutions to a selection of these exercises are given as Appendix 2.

The book is intended for use in both learning and reference mode. To facilitate its use in reference mode the book includes an Appendix of syntax diagrams, and a comprehensive index. The syntax diagrams provide a concise summary of the language features in a form which is easily used by someone familiar with the basic framework of the language. The index lists all formal and informal terms used in the text showing the defining occurrence of each, together with other occurrences which may help to clarify its significance.

We wish to thank Professor Tony Hoare who first encouraged us to write the book, and to thank all those people who read drafts of the manuscript, pointed out our mistakes, and made constructive suggestions. In particular, we thank Tony Addyman for his assistance in ensuring that this second edition is consistent with the new definition of PASCAL. Any discrepancies that remain are entirely our responsibility.

JIM WELSH
JOHN ELDER

1

Computers and Programming

Computer programming requires an understanding of the nature of computers, of computer programs and of the programming languages in which programs may be expressed. Subsequent chapters of this book explain how computer programs may be written in the programming language PASCAL. This first chapter summarizes the general concepts of computers and their programming on which the subsequent chapters depend.

For those readers who have already programmed computers in other languages the chapter may provide a summary of the terminology, and perhaps a hint of the programming philosophy, used in the following chapters.

For those learning to program for the first time this chapter provides a very brief summary of the facts and concepts which they must come to appreciate while programming in PASCAL or any other language. A course instructor may provide a more detailed treatment of these topics before or during study of the material covered in the following chapters.

THE COMPUTER

A *computer* is a machine which can carry out long, complex and repetitive sequences of operations at very high speed. These operations are applied to *information* or *data* supplied by the user to produce further information or *results* which the user requires. The sequence of operations required to produce the desired results in any particular computing task is specified as a *computer program* prepared for that task.

The essential components of a computer are a *processor*, a *memory*, and some *input and output devices*.

The *processor* is the work horse which carries out the sequence of operations specified by the program. The individual operations provided by the processor are very simple but are carried out at very high speed—perhaps one million or more operations per second.

The *memory* is used to store the information to which the processor's operations are applied. Memory is of two kinds—*primary* or *main store*, and *secondary* or *backing store*. The main store enables the processor to fetch and to store units of information at a speed which is comparable to its speed of operation, in fact each operation normally involves at least one store access. To enable the processor to proceed from one operation to the next without delay the sequence of program instructions which specifies these operations is also held in the main store. The main store thus holds both *instructions* and *data*, on which the processor operates.

The amount of main store available to the processor is limited, and is used to hold only the programs and data on which the processor is operating at that time. It is not used for any permanent storage of data. In some cases the main store may not even be large enough to hold all the instructions or data involved in the execution of one program. For these reasons computers are also equipped with secondary storage devices such as magnetic tapes, disks or drums. The essential characteristics of these devices are:

(a)   their capacity is normally much greater than that of the main store;
(b)   information can be held by them permanently, e.g. from one program execution to another.

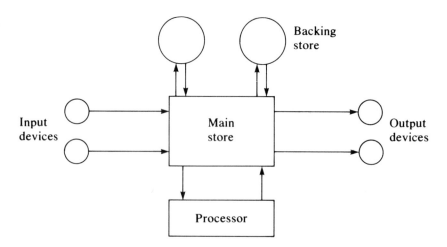

Fig. 1.1   Organization of a computer.

However, the speed at which information can be transferred to and from secondary storage is much lower than for main store.

Input and output devices are used to transfer information from the outside world to the computer's main store (*input*) and from the main store to the outside world (*output*). Familiar input devices are card readers, which read information punched on cards into the computer's store, and terminal keyboards which transfer the characters indicated by key depressions into the computer store. Familiar output devices are line printers and typewriters which print information on continuous paper, and visual display screens which display textual or graphic information on the screen of a cathode ray tube.

The logical organization of a computer may thus be depicted as in Fig. 1.1.

WRITING A COMPUTER PROGRAM

The use of a computer for a particular task involves three essential steps:

(a) specifying the task the computer is to carry out, in terms of the input data to be supplied and the output data or results to be produced;

(b) devising an *algorithm* or sequence of steps, by which the computer can produce the required output from the available input;

(c) expressing this algorithm as a computer program in a programming language such as PASCAL.

Step (a), the specification, is not normally considered as part of the programming process but a precise specification is an essential prerequisite for a successful program.

It has been common practice in the past to separate steps (b) and (c), first defining the algorithm in a notation convenient for its design, and then translating or encoding this design into the chosen programming language. However, the language PASCAL provides a notation which may be used both for the design and for the final coding of the program required. With PASCAL, therefore, steps (b) and (c) are not usually separated, but merged as a continuous design/programming process. This approach is well illustrated by the case-study programs considered in the following chapters of this book.

In principle, once the computer program has been written, the programmer's task is complete, since execution of this program by the computer should produce the required results. In practice, because the task to be carried out by the computer is complex, and the human programmer's ability is limited, the first program written may not produce the required results. The programmer, therefore, engages in a cycle of checking and correcting his program until he is satisfied that it meets its specification completely. This process of detecting and correcting errors in a program is known as *debugging*. Debugging is commonly accomplished by running the program on the computer with suitable test data.

RUNNING A COMPUTER PROGRAM

In a "high-level" language such as PASCAL the program is expressed as a sequence of elementary steps which are convenient to the programmer. Likewise the program is prepared in a form which is convenient for the programmer to generate—as a piece of text written or printed on paper, punched on a sequence of cards, or typed at a computer-terminal keyboard.

However, the program which the computer's processor executes must be expressed as a sequence of the much simpler "low-level" operations available to the processor, and must be held in the computer store as a sequence of encoded instructions each of which is immediately executable by the processor. Preparation of a program in this form is an extremely tedious and painstaking task for a human programmer.

Fortunately, however, the translation of a program text expressed in a high-level language into an equivalent sequence of processor-executable instructions within the computer store is itself a routine task which can be carried out by a computer program. Such a program is provided for each high-level language which may be used on a computer, and is known as the *compiler* for that language.

Thus a program written in a high-level language in text form is first input to the computer as data for an execution of the compiler program for that language. The compiler produces an equivalent executable program in the computer store, which may then be executed or run to produce the desired effect. Figure 1.2 shows this two-stage process in schematic form.

In translating a high-level language program the compiler may detect many of the simple mistakes which the programmer has made in expressing his program in that language. The compiler reports these errors to the programmer by outputting a *program listing*, i.e., a printout of the original program input together with messages identifying any error detected during its compilation. Program errors detected in this way are known as *compile-time errors*.

In running the executable program produced by the compiler, further

Stage 1: *Compilation*

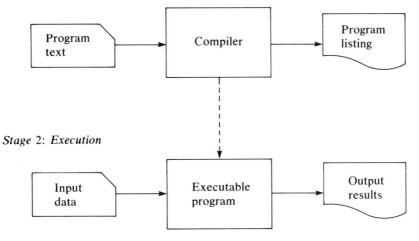

Fig. 1.2   Stages in running a program.

situations, which are not permitted by the language rules, may be detected—such errors are known as *run-time errors.*

A program which produces no compile-time errors during its compilation, and no run-time errors during its execution, may still not produce the correct results, due to some flaw in the chosen algorithm or in its expression in the program. Such errors are known as *logical errors.*

Debugging therefore requires the elimination of all compile-time, run-time and logical errors from the program. To do so the programmer must have an understanding of the language, and of the *implementation* which he is using.

LANGUAGE IMPLEMENTATIONS

One advantage of using a high-level programming language, such as PASCAL, is that a program written in the language may be used on any computer for which a compiler of the language has been provided. In principle the language, and hence the programs written in it, are independent of the actual computer—they are said to be *machine independent.*

In practice many widely different computers are available. The provision of a compiler for a given language and a given computer is called an *implementation* of the language. For practical reasons implementations must impose language restrictions additional to those specified by the language definition. Likewise implementations sometimes require a slightly different representation of the program text to that described by the language definition. The PASCAL standard identifies such aspects of the language as being *implementation defined* or *implementation dependent*, and they are similarly identified in this book. In preparing or using a program for a given implementation, a programmer must ensure that the program conforms to any particular requirements of that implementation, as well as the language rules themselves.

Besides the ability to compile a program an implementation may provide other aids to the programmer. For example, the detection of a run-time or logical error in a program does not necessarily identify its cause. Implementations may provide specific aids to help the programmer in doing so. As such features are wholly dependent on the implementation, they are not discussed in this book, but again a programmer should establish what additional features his available implementation provides.

PROGRAMMING OBJECTIVES

In preparing a program a programmer may have to choose between alternative solutions at many points. Each choice must be made to meet the objectives and constraints of the particular programming task. In this book the following are assumed to be objectives appropriate to every programming task.

Correctness

An obvious objective in writing any computer program is that it should meet its specification exactly. All too often, however, because of the complexity of the program's task, and inadequate understanding or care on the part of the programmer, a program fails to meet some part of its specification. A programmer must be mindful at all times of the correctness or adequacy of the program for its specified purpose.

A key factor in achieving correctness is *simplicity.* By choosing the simplest algorithm or technique available a programmer is more likely to see whether or not it meets the requirements of the program specification, and is less likely to describe it incorrectly in his program. Unnecessary complexity serves no purpose in computer programming.

Some programs are, of course, inherently complex. For such programs the programmer must adopt a systematic approach which controls and limits the complexity he has to deal with at each stage. Such an approach is illustrated in the case-study programs presented in this book.

Clarity

A program is necessarily as complex as the algorithm which it describes. However, it is important that the way in which the algorithm is described by the program text be no more complicated than is necessary. Program clarity is an important aid to the programmer himself, in the design and debugging of the program; and to others who may have to read and amend the program at some later stage.

Program clarity is achieved in much the same way as for any written text, such as an essay or a book. It requires

(a) a logical separation of the text into meaningful parts (chapters, sections, etc.) which reflect the distinction between the subjects they describe, and their presentation in a logical sequence which reflects the relationships between them;
(b) a careful choice of the language features used within each part to express its intended meaning as precisely as possible;
(c) a further careful choice of the words used to denote the objects and concepts involved;
(d) the inclusion of additional comments and preambles to clarify the main text when necessary;
(e) an exploitation of text-layout devices, such as blank lines and indentation, to emphasize the relationship between the text's component parts.

A programmer should be as assiduous in the use of these techniques for achieving clarity as the author of any text. In many cases the usefulness of a program is as much determined by the clarity of its text, as by the qualities of the algorithm which it describes.

Efficiency

The cost of executing a computer program is normally measured in terms of

(a) the *time* taken by the computer to carry out the sequence of operations involved;
(b) the amount of computer *store* used in doing so.

In many environments the program will compete with other programs for the use of these computer resources, and it is therefore logical to minimize the program's requirements of each.

The time taken to execute the program is directly proportional to the number of operations which the processor has to carry out in doing so. The programmer should therefore choose an algorithm which minimizes the operations involved, and take care to avoid any redundant operations in expressing the algorithm as a computer program.

The store used by the program during its execution is determined by the amount of data which must be held and by the number of processor instructions required to define the program, since these too must be held in the store. To minimize the storage used by his program a programmer must therefore consider both the data manipulated, and the number of operations specified by the program.

For some programs, or parts of programs, the efficient use of time or storage may be critical, for others less so. The programmer must be aware of any such efficiency requirements when writing his program. Where a distinction exists in the efficiency of alternative PASCAL features it is explained in this book, so that a programmer may make the proper choice according to the requirements of his program.

2

Notations and Fundamental Concepts

EXTENDED BACKUS–NAUR FORM

A computer program is first constructed as a sequence of symbols or characters which form the program "text". (1) is a simple program written in the programming language PASCAL.

```
program add (input, output) ;
var first, second, sum : integer ;
begin
    read (first, second) ;                          (1)
    sum := first + second ;
    write (sum)
end.
```

As with natural languages, every programming language has a strictly defined set of rules associated with it which describes how a valid program may be constructed in the language. These rules are necessary firstly so that the programmer may be sure of the correctness and effect of the program he writes and, secondly, so that his program may be understood both by the computer system and anyone who reads the program.

The language rules are made up of two parts, known as the *syntax* and *semantics* of the language. The syntax rules define how the words (or *vocabulary*) of the language may be put together to form "sentences". The semantic rules ascribe meaning and significance to these combinations of words. These semantic rules are usually stated less formally than the syntax rules which, for the language PASCAL, are described by means of a formalism known as *Extended Backus–Naur Form*, or simply EBNF.

For example, the form of a PASCAL program is defined by the following EBNF rule

> *program = program-heading   block   "."* .

This rule is read as "A *program* is defined as a *program-heading* followed by a *block* followed by a period *"."*". Further EBNF rules then define the allowable forms for a *program-heading* and a *block*. In the example program given above the first line of symbols is the *program-heading*. The following symbols from **var** to **end** form a *block*. In an EBNF rule the appearance of a language symbol within quote marks, e.g., *"."*, denotes the symbol itself. Each rule is terminated by a period.

Sometimes a syntactic category may have several alternative forms. For example, the rule

> *digit = "0" | "1" | "2" | "3" | "4" | "5" | "6" | "7" | "8" | "9"* .

defines a *digit* in PASCAL as one of the ten characters 0,1,...,9 by means of a list of alternatives. The above rule is read as "A *digit* is defined as either a *"0"* or a *"1"* or a *"2"* or . . . .".

Enclosure of a syntax construct by the brackets { and } is used to denote repetition of the enclosed construct zero or more times. For example, the rule

> *unsigned-integer = digit { digit }* .

defines an *unsigned-integer* as a sequence of one or more of the digits defined above. Thus the following are examples of *unsigned-integers* :

> 1   27   97300

Enclosure of a syntax construct by the brackets [and] denotes that the enclosed construct is optional, e.g., the rules

> *integer = [sign] unsigned-integer* .
> *sign = "+" | "−"* .

define an *integer* as an *unsigned-integer* preceded, optionally, by either a *"+"* or *"−"* symbol.

Parentheses (and) may be used, where necessary, to group syntactic categories together, e.g., the rules for *integer* above may be re-expressed as

> *integer = signed-integer | unsigned-integer* .
> *signed-integer = ("+" | "−") unsigned-integer* .

In general the syntactic categories defined by EBNF rules are denoted by single (possibly hyphenated) words giving suitable English descriptions.

Throughout this book we shall introduce, along with new features of the language, their EBNF definitions. These define concisely the full range of constructions for each syntactic category. Some constructions may include other syntactic categories not yet fully defined at the point of introduction. A student learning the language may ignore these undefined categories at that point as they will be dealt with in due course. The index of syntax definitions given at the end of the book enables the definition and explanation of all syntactic categories to be located.

The syntax of PASCAL is sometimes defined by means of *syntax diagrams*. These give a concise graphic specification of the sequences of symbols allowed in each of the major constructs of PASCAL, and are useful to those familiar with the language for checking the validity or allowable form of particular constructs.

Appendix 1 summarizes the syntax of PASCAL in this form.

THE VOCABULARY OF PASCAL

Every language, whether it is a spoken language or a computer-programming language, makes use of a vocabulary. English, for instance, in its written form, consists of words, numbers, and punctuation symbols. The vocabulary of the programming language PASCAL consists of letters, digits, and special symbols. Sentences of the language are then constructed out of this vocabulary according to the syntax of PASCAL.

According to the standard definition of PASCAL a letter may be any one of the 26 letters in the Roman alphabet in either upper-case or lower-case form, i.e., there are 52 alternatives in the syntactic category *letter*.

$$
\begin{aligned}
letter = \ & "A" | "B" | "C" | "D" | "E" | "F" | "G" | "H" | "I" | "J" | "K" | "L" | \\
& "M" | "N" | "O" | "P" | "Q" | "R" | "S" | "T" | "U" | "V" | "W" | "X" | \\
& "Y" | "Z" | "a" | "b" | "c" | "d" | "e" | "f" | "g" | "h" | "i" | "j" | "k" | "l" | \\
& "m" | "n" | "o" | "p" | "q" | "r" | "s" | "t" | "u" | "v" | "w" | "x" | "y" | "z" \ .
\end{aligned}
$$

In practice, however, some of the computers on which PASCAL has been implemented provide only letters of one case, in which case the use of letters of the other case is not available to the programmer. In this book we shall freely use lower-case letters, purely for typographical clarity and easy reading of the text. The resultant programs can be made acceptable to PASCAL implementations that accept only upper-case by replacing all lower-case letters by their upper-case equivalents. The final versions of the programs used as case studies in subsequent chapters have been photographically reproduced from computer-printed listings, which show the upper-case representation.

A *digit* in PASCAL is any one of the ten Arabic digits, i.e.,

$$digit \ = \ "0" \mid "1" \mid "2" \mid "3" \mid "4" \mid "5" \mid "6" \mid "7" \mid "8" \mid "9" \ .$$

Note that the letter $"O"$ and the digit $"0"$ are two quite distinct characters.

The number of special symbols required by PASCAL for punctuation and various other purposes is quite high. Many of these special symbols are represented as words rather than special characters, as shown in (2).

$$
\begin{aligned}
special\text{-}symbol \ = \ & "+" \mid "-" \mid "*" \mid "/" \mid "=" \mid "<>" \mid "<" \mid ">" \mid \\
& "<=" \mid ">=" \mid "(" \mid ")" \mid "[" \mid "]" \mid ":=" \mid "." \mid \\
& "," \mid ":" \mid ";" \mid ".." \mid " \uparrow " \mid \textbf{"div"} \mid \textbf{"mod"} \mid \\
& \textbf{"nil"} \mid \textbf{"in"} \mid \textbf{"or"} \mid \textbf{"and"} \mid \textbf{"not"} \mid \textbf{"if"} \mid \textbf{"then"} \mid \\
& \textbf{"else"} \mid \textbf{"case"} \mid \textbf{"of"} \mid \textbf{"repeat"} \mid \textbf{"until"} \mid \qquad (2) \\
& \textbf{"while"} \mid \textbf{"do"} \mid \textbf{"for"} \mid \textbf{"to"} \mid \textbf{"downto"} \mid \textbf{"begin"} \mid \\
& \textbf{"end"} \mid \textbf{"with"} \mid \textbf{"goto"} \mid \textbf{"const"} \mid \textbf{"var"} \mid \textbf{"type"} \mid \\
& \textbf{"array"} \mid \textbf{"record"} \mid \textbf{"set"} \mid \textbf{"file"} \mid \textbf{"function"} \mid \\
& \textbf{"procedure"} \mid \textbf{"label"} \mid \textbf{"packed"} \mid \textbf{"program"} \ .
\end{aligned}
$$

In this text the words used to represent special symbols are distinguished by the use of bold face type, like **this**. However, the definition of PASCAL states that they are reserved words which may not be used for any other purpose, and can thus be written without underlining or any other distinguishing marks. The photographically reproduced program listings illustrate this practical alternative.

NUMBERS

Numbers in PASCAL may be represented in either of two forms— integers or real numbers.

An *integer-number* is a whole number which may be positive, negative, or zero. The number is written as a sequence of digits of any length, which may or may not be preceded by a sign (+ or −).

integer-number = [*sign*] *unsigned-integer* .
sign = "+" | "−" .
unsigned-integer = *digit* { *digit* } .

Examples of valid integers:

6
0
−6
+7000000

The following are invalid integers for the reasons specified:

6,437,271   integer must not contain non-digits,
−6.0   integer must not contain a decimal point.

Although the above definition allows integers of any size, in practice each implementation of PASCAL will define a limited range of integers that it permits. This is necessary because the maximum number of digits that can be used in an integer depends on the size of the memory location in the computer that will store the integer.

Numbers outside the permitted range of integers, or numbers with fractional parts, may be represented as *real* numbers. A real number can be written in two different forms. In the first form the number is written with a decimal point, and the number may be preceded by a sign. However, the decimal point must be preceded by at least one digit and followed by at least one digit.

Examples of valid real numbers:

0.0
0.873
−74.1
73.36789

The following are invalid numbers for the reasons indicated:

0.   no digit after the decimal point,
.736   no digit before the decimal point,
2,736.45   comma not allowed.

In the second form of representation the real number is expressed as an integer or decimal number multiplied by an integral power of 10 (this is known as the scientific or exponential form). The integer or decimal number is followed immediately by the letter E (in either upper or lower case) and a signed or unsigned integer (known as the exponent or *scale-factor*).

Examples of valid real numbers:

0E0
8.73E+02
−741E−1
0.7336789E2

The following are all acceptable ways of writing the real number 253.0 :

253.0   2.53E2   25.3E+01   253E0   2530E−1

The syntactic definition of a real number is thus as shown in (3).

> *real-number* = [*sign*] *unsigned-real* .
> *unsigned-real* = *unsigned-integer* "." *digit-sequence* ["E" *scale-*
> *factor*] | *unsigned-integer* "E" *scale-factor* .   (3)
> *digit-sequence* = *digit* { *digit* } .
> *scale-factor* = *integer* .

The range of real numbers permitted by implementations is also restricted, but is usually very much greater than that of integers. However, the representation of real numbers on a computer is only an approximation whereas integers are represented exactly. Thus, whenever possible, a number should be represented as an integer to gain maximum accuracy in operations involving the number. A fuller discussion of real numbers follows in Chap. 3.

IDENTIFIERS

PASCAL requires that various quantities used in a program, such as data items and pieces of program text, be given names by which they can be identified. These names are known as *identifiers*, and are created by the programmer.

PASCAL provides a large degree of flexibility in the choice of identifiers by the programmer. An identifier consists of a letter followed by any number of letters and digits, i.e.,

> *identifier* = *letter* { *letter* | *digit* } .

Thus, in theory, an identifier may be of any length (and we shall encourage the use of meaningful and hence, possibly, long identifiers) but, in practice, many implementations of PASCAL impose a restriction on the length of each line of program text, and hence on the length of identifiers. On implementations which provide both upper and lower case, letters of either case may be used in identifiers but the PASCAL standard requires that the meaning of a program is not altered by changing the case of any such letter. Hence the following identifiers are considered identical:

> *somename*   SOMENAME   *SomeName*

Examples of valid identifiers:

> *I*
> *ufo*
> *PC*49
> *averylongnameindeed*

The following are illegal identifiers for the reasons indicated :

1*abc*	an identifier must begin with a letter,
TO-MORROW	an identifier must not contain a hyphen,
$100	an identifier must begin with a letter.

As mentioned previously, some of the special symbols of PASCAL are reserved words which cannot be used for other purposes. Thus words such as **array** and **begin** cannot be used as identifiers.

Although the programmer has an otherwise unlimited choice of possible identifier names at his disposal, it is accepted practice to choose identifiers whose meaning in the program is suggested by their names. If a program makes use of values describing temperatures and pressures then it is much more meaningful to the reader of the program if these values are represented by identifiers such as *temperature* and *pressure*, rather than the shorter, but less obvious, *t* and *p*.

However meaningfully its name has been chosen, an identifier does not by itself determine the quantity which it identifies, as far as the language rules are concerned. This information must be given in the form of a *declaration*. The allowable forms of identifier declaration will be explained as we describe the various quantities which an identifier may denote in PASCAL.

Certain identifiers, known as *standard identifiers*, are predeclared in every implementation of standard PASCAL. These describe standard quantities and facilities provided by the language, such as trigonometric and arithmetic functions. Table 2.1 gives a full list of standard identifiers. In contrast with the reserved words which may not be used at all as identifiers, the programmer may re-use any of the standard identifiers to describe a quantity which he wishes to introduce into his

abs	*ln*	*reset*
arctan	*maxint*	*rewrite*
boolean	*new*	*round*
char	*odd*	*sin*
chr	*ord*	*sqr*
cos	*output*	*sqrt*
dispose	*pack*	*succ*
eof	*page*	*text*
eoln	*pred*	*true*
exp	*put*	*trunc*
false	*read*	*unpack*
get	*readln*	*write*
input	*real*	*writeln*
integer		

Table 2.1 Standard identifiers

program. However, by doing so he removes from himself the capability to use the standard PASCAL facility named by that identifier, and creates a potential confusion for any subsequent reader of the program. The practice is not recommended.

STRINGS

A sequence of characters enclosed by quotes forms what is known as a *string*. It is used within a program to denote the sequence of characters themselves. If the string of characters is to include a quote then that quote should be written twice. Thus the syntactic definition of a *string* is

string = *"'"* *string-character* { *string-character* } *"'"* .
string-character = *any-character-except-quote* | *"'''"* .

Some examples of strings are

'This is an example of a string.'
'?'
'His name is O''Brien'
''''

COMMENTS

A PASCAL program is expressed as a sequence of identifiers, numbers, strings and special symbols, as described in the preceding sections. In preparing a program text the programmer has considerable freedom in how these identifiers, numbers, and symbols are positioned within and across lines of text.

In general an arbitrary number of blank characters or ends of line may occur between the identifiers, numbers, and symbols. However, blanks or ends of line may not occur within any identifier, number, or special symbol, and at least one blank or end of line must occur between those identifiers, numbers and reserved word symbols which would be otherwise indistinguishable.

We shall attempt to show in the program examples in this book that a considered layout of the program text and a careful choice of identifiers help to make a PASCAL program largely self-explanatory. However, it is still necessary or desirable that the programmer should provide additional explanatory text, or *comment*, to explain some of the actions carried out within his program to a subsequent reader.

In standard PASCAL any sequence of characters enclosed by the symbols { and }, and not containing a } , form what is known as a *comment*. Comments may appear anywhere that a blank or end of line may appear, but have absolutely no significance as far as the execution of the program is concerned. They serve solely as a means whereby the programmer can make the meaning of his program clearer by the inclusion of explanatory remarks in natural language.

      example: { this is a comment written in ordinary English }

    There is no limit on the length of a comment—it may range from a few characters to many hundreds of lines of the program text.

ALTERNATIVE SYMBOLS

On many computers the symbols { and } are not available, in which case PASCAL allows the use of (* instead of {, and *) instead of } as an alternative comment convention. The use of this convention is illustrated by the photographically reproduced program listings in subsequent chapters.

    On some computers other symbols used in the standard representation of PASCAL are also unavailable. To overcome this problem, the following alternatives are acceptable substitutes for the standard symbols on all implementations whose character sets include the characters involved.

SYMBOL	ALTERNATIVE
↑	ˆ or @
{	(*
}	*)
[	(.
]	.)

In many cases implementations will, therefore, accept more than one representation of each symbol, and programs using a mixture of representations are possible. In general, however, it is good practice to use only the standard symbol representation if available and to avoid mixing different representations of the same symbol at all times.

BASIC PROGRAM STRUCTURE

    We finish this chapter with a short look at the basic structure of PASCAL programs so that the reader may appreciate the context and significance of the concepts introduced in the next few chapters.

    A computer program must describe the nature of the data or information to be manipulated, and the actions which are to be performed upon those data. These two aspects of the function of a program are reflected in the syntax which most programming languages provide for programs. In PASCAL, a program is formally defined as in (1).

program = *program-heading   block   "."* .
program-heading = *"**program**" identifier "(" identifier-list ")" ";"* .
block = *declaration-part statement-part* .
declaration-part = *[label-declaration-part]*
                     [constant-definition-part]   (4)
                     [type-definition-part]
                     [variable-declaration-part]
                     procedure-and-function-declaration-part.
identifier-list = *identifier { "," identifier }* .

That is, a *program* consists of a *program-heading* followed by a *block* and terminated by a full stop (period), where a *block* consists of a *declaration-part* followed by a *statement-part*. The precise roles of the various parts of the *declaration-part* will be explained in subsequent chapters. In its simplest form the *declaration-part* of a program defines the data items which are used by the program. The *statement-part* then defines the actions to be executed on these data items.

Consider again the very simple program introduced at the beginning of this chapter, reproduced for convenience as (5). Its purpose is to read in two whole numbers and print out their sum. The first line is the *program-heading*, which gives the program the name *add* and indicates that it will perform both input (reading-in of information from some medium external to the program) and output (writing-out of information to an external medium). The second line is the *declaration-part*, which names the three data items used in the program and states that they will be whole numbers.

```
program add (input,output);
var first,second,sum:integer;
begin                                                 (5)
    read (first,second);
    sum:=first+second;
    write(sum)
end.
```

The *statement-part* of the program consists of the description of three actions enclosed by the pair of reserved words **begin** and **end**. Firstly, two whole numbers are read in and their values recorded as the data items *first* and *second*. These two values are then added and their sum recorded as the data item *sum*. Finally, the sum is written out. The program text is terminated by a period.

EXERCISES

2.1 Consider the following numbers :

275	3,475	7.4	.1475	6000
6E3	275.0	0.001	27365982	0
10E−4	0.074E3	0.1E999	275.	0.0620

Which are valid integers in PASCAL?
Which are valid real numbers in PASCAL?
Which denote the same values in PASCAL?
Which of those valid in PASCAL are also acceptable on the implementation to which you have access?

2.2 Which of the following are valid identifiers in PASCAL ?

H2SO4	X-RAY	alphabetic	ALPHABETIC
ALPHA	McDougall	BEGIN	ALPHABETICAL
omega	X99999	round	INPUT

Which of the valid identifiers are also acceptable on your implementation?

2.3 Which of the following lines are valid strings in PASCAL?

```
'JACK SPRATT'
'six + one = ninetyseven'
'SPRATT''S WIFE'
'HIS WIFE''S DOG'
'''''''''''''
```

2.4 The following is a valid sequence of PASCAL symbols:

if input ↑ = ' '
then { *skip the blank* } get (*input*)
else { *count its occurrence* } c[*input* ↑] := c[*input* ↑] +1

Can it be written in this form on your implementation?
If not, what changes are necessary?

3

Data Types and Declarations

DATA TYPES

A computer program manipulates information, or *data*, to obtain some desired effect or result. The data operated upon by a program are ultimately represented as a sequence of electrical signals within the hardware of the computer. However, high-level programming languages such as PASCAL enable the programmer to ignore the actual machine representation and express the nature of data in terms of *data types*.

A data type defines a set of values. PASCAL, in common with most other high-level languages, requires that every data item in a program must have a *type* associated with it, based on the following assumptions:

(a) the type of a data item determines the *range of values* which it may take, and the *range of operations* which may be applied to it;
(b) each data item has a single type;
(c) the type of a data item in a program can be deduced solely from its form or context, without any knowledge of the particular values which it may take during execution of the program;
(d) each *operator* in the language requires *operands* of specified types and produces a result of specified type.

The significance and effect of these rules will be described and illustrated throughout the next two chapters.

By providing a range of readily available types, together with appropriate operators, the language enables the programmer to describe the manipulation of his data in terms natural to the data, rather than the underlying machine representation. Also, by enforcing the above four constraints, the language protects the programmer from forming illogical combinations of data and operators, a protection which is not available at the machine level.

It will be seen in later chapters that PASCAL allows the definition of highly structured and complex data types; indeed this is the feature of PASCAL that sets it apart from the more commonly used programming languages. Ultimately, however, all data types are structured out of *unstructured* types. In PASCAL an unstructured type is either defined by the programmer or else it is one of the four standard pre-defined types provided (sometimes known as the *primitive* types of the language), namely, the *integer, real, char* and *boolean* types.

We begin our treatment of unstructured data types by looking at the properties of each of the four primitive types.

The Type *integer*

This type represents the set of whole numbers and any value of this type is therefore a whole number. However, as was mentioned in Chap. 2, all computers have a limit to the size of the largest whole number which they can store conveniently and so each implementation of PASCAL restricts integer values to a subset of the whole numbers. Thus the integer type in practice is the set of whole numbers defined by a given implementation. A value of the integer type is one of the whole numbers in the implementation-defined subset. The representation of integer numbers was described in the previous chapter.

PASCAL defines a number of arithmetic operators which take integer operands and return integer results, i.e.,

+	add
−	subtract
*	multiply
div	division with truncation
mod	modulo

These are *dyadic infix operators*, i.e., they are used with two operands written one on each side of the operator, thus $a+b$. However, + and − may also be used as *monadic prefix operators*, thus $+a$ and $-a$, to denote sign identity and sign inversion (negation). Some examples of integer operations are given in Table 3.1.

When the operands a and b have the same sign the operation a **div** b gives familiar integer division results, e.g.,

7 **div** 3 = 2
(-7) **div** (-3) = 2

Operation	Result
7+3	10
7−3	4
7∗3	21
7 **div** 3	2
7 **mod** 3	1
−3	−3
+3	3

Table 3.1   Some examples of integer operations.

When the operands differ in sign, and therefore the true quotient is negative, "truncation" means towards zero, so that

$$(-7) \textbf{ div } 3 = -2$$
$$7 \textbf{ div } (-3) = -2$$

If b is zero an error occurs.

The modulo operation a **mod** b is defined only for positive b; if b is zero or negative an error occurs. For positive b the value of a **mod** b is defined to be the smallest non-negative integer which may be subtracted from a to give an integral multiple of b. Thus

$$6 \textbf{ mod } 3 = 0$$
$$7 \textbf{ mod } 3 = 1$$
$$(-6) \textbf{ mod } 3 = 0$$
$$(-7) \textbf{ mod } 3 = 2$$

Note that for positive a and b the value a **mod** b is the remainder corresponding to the integer division a **div** b, but for negative a it is not.

Care must be taken to ensure that the result of adding, subtracting or multiplying two values does not produce a result outside the integer range defined by the implementation. If it does an *overflow* error is said to occur. Likewise division by zero is an error, as is a modulo operation whose second operand is zero or negative. Most implementations of PASCAL provide some means whereby the occurrence of these errors during the execution of a program may be detected.

Besides the infix and prefix operators listed above PASCAL provides a number of *standard functions* which may be applied to integer values.

Two of these are as follows

> *abs*   if x is an integer value then the standard function $abs(x)$
>   denotes the absolute integer value of x
> *sqr*   the square of an integer value x may be written as $sqr(x)$

e.g.,

$abs(7)$	gives	7
$abs(-6)$	gives	6
$sqr(3)$	gives	9
$sqr(-4)$	gives	16.

The square of an integer value x can clearly be written as $x*x$. However, use of $sqr(x)$ improves the clarity of the program at all times, and may also improve its efficiency in some implementations.

A number of other standard functions which relate to integers and other data types are introduced in the following sections.

In common with other unstructured types (other than *real*) in PASCAL the type *integer* defines an ordered succession of values—from a least value to a greatest value, both of which are defined by the particular implementation of the language. Each value except the least has a *predecessor*, and each value except the greatest has a *successor*. Such types are called *ordinal* types. For integers the successor of any value can be obtained by adding 1, and the predecessor by subtracting 1. For all ordinal types PASCAL provides standard functions *succ* and *pred* which are defined as follows

> $succ(x)$ gives the immediate successor of x, if it exists
> $pred(x)$ gives the immediate predecessor of x, if it exists

Thus, for an integer x,

> $succ(x) = x+1$
> $pred(x) = x-1$

The Type *real*

The values of this type are the set of real numbers. However, once again, there is a limit to the size of such numbers that a computer can conveniently represent and so, in each implementation of PASCAL, the type *real* consists of the real values in some implementation-defined range. The representation of real numbers was described in the previous chapter.

PASCAL provides a number of arithmetic operators which take real operands and produce real-valued results, i.e.,

  \+   add
  \−   subtract
  *   multiply
  /   divide.

As with the integer operators these are dyadic infix operators but + and − may also be used as monadic prefix operators to denote sign identity and inversion. Some examples of real operations are given in Table 3.2.

Operation	Result
2.1+1.4	3.5
2.1−1.4	0.7
2.1*1.4	2.94
2.1/1.4	1.5

Table 3.2   Some examples of real operations

It should be noted that the representation of real numbers within a computer is not exact and the execution of operations upon these approximate values may produce consequent and greater inaccuracies. The study of the estimation and effect of such inaccuracies belongs to numerical mathematics and will not be discussed further here. However, the reader is warned that, for instance, for real values x and y the relation

$(x/y)*y = x$

may not always hold in computer arithmetic.

The standard functions *abs* and *sqr* which were introduced in the previous sub-section for integer arguments, may also be used with real arguments to give real results, e.g.,

  abs(−6.4)   gives   6.4
  sqr(3.1)   gives   9.61

Note that *real* is not an ordinal type and so the standard functions *succ* and *pred* are not defined for real arguments.

PASCAL also provides six standard mathematical functions, all of which take real arguments and give real results. These are as follows:

  ln(x)   gives the natural logarithm of x, i.e., $\log_e x$ for $x>0.0$
  exp(x)   gives the exponential of x, i.e., e^x

sqrt(*x*)	gives the square root of *x*, for *x* ⩾ 0.0
sin(*x*)	⎰ give the trigonometric functions sine and cosine of *x*,
cos(*x*)	⎱ where *x* is expressed in radians
arctan(*x*)	gives the angle, in radians in the range 0 to π, whose tangent is *x*.

The result of using *ln* with a non-positive argument or *sqrt* with a negative argument is an error.

The values of type *integer* may be thought of as having equivalent values of type *real*. As a general rule in PASCAL an integer value may be used wherever a real value is expected.

Thus the dyadic operators +, − and * may be used with one integer operand and one real operand, to give a real result. Likewise the standard mathematical functions may be used with integer arguments to give real results, e.g.,

4.7*2	gives	9.4
4−1.5	gives	2.5
sqrt(9)	gives	3.0

Of course if both operands of the operators +, − and * are integers an integer result is produced, as defined in the previous sub-section. Note however that the real division operator, /, always produces a real result, even when both its operands are integer, e.g.,

13 / 5	gives	2.6

In effect each integer value which occurs where a real value is required by the rules of PASCAL is automatically converted to the equivalent real value. However the converse is never true—if an integer value is required a real value cannot be used instead.

Two standard functions are provided in PASCAL for converting real values to integer values. (Functions which convert a value of one type into a value of another type are termed *transfer functions*.) These are the *truncation* and *rounding* functions, defined as follows:

trunc(*x*)	takes a real value *x* as its argument and produces as its result the whole, or integer, part of the value.

Thus,

trunc(7.1)	gives	7
trunc(−7.1)	gives	−7
round(*x*)	takes a real value *x* as its argument and gives the nearest integer as result.

For non-negative *x*, *round*(*x*) is equivalent to *trunc*(*x*+0.5) while, for negative x, it is equivalent to $trunc(x-0.5)$, e.g.,

round(7.6)	gives	8
round(7.1)	gives	7
round(−7.6)	gives	−8
round(−7.1)	gives	−7

In using the functions *trunc* and *round* care must be taken that the desired result does not lie outside the allowed range of integers—if it does an error occurs. Although the range of real values is much greater than that allowed for integers it must also be remembered that limits still apply and that overflow, i.e., an attempt to calculate a real value outside this range, may still occur. Implementations usually provide some means of detecting such overflow during execution of real operations.

The Type *char*

Every computer system has an associated set of characters by means of which it communicates with its environment, i.e., these characters are usually available on the input and output devices (such as readers and printers) which are used to transfer readable character information to and from the computer. Unfortunately, many computers provide slightly differing character sets, although they generally support a standard subset consisting of the 26 letters, 10 digits, the space character, and other punctuation symbols.

In PASCAL the type *char* is defined as the set of characters available on the computer system which executes the program. The documents defining a particular PASCAL implementation will normally specify the available character set.

Within a PASCAL program a particular value of type *char* is denoted by enclosing the character in single quotes (apostrophes), e.g.,

   '*a*'   '4'   '?'   ' '   '+'

To represent the single quote character it is written twice, i.e.,

   ''''

Thus the values of the type *char* are denoted by strings containing a single character (or two quotes). Strings were discussed in Chap. 2.

Two standard transfer functions are provided by PASCAL to map the character set onto a set of consecutive non-negative integer values starting at zero (called the *ordinal numbers* of the character set), and vice-versa.

ord(c)   is the ordinal number of the character *c* in the character set

chr(i)   is the character value which has ordinal number *i*, if it exists; if no character value with ordinal number *i* exists, an error occurs.

Obviously *ord* and *chr* are inverse functions, and

chr (ord(c)) = c
ord (chr(i)) = i

will always hold.

The mapping between characters and ordinal numbers is implementation defined, and will in general vary from one implementation to another. The PASCAL standard requires that in all implementations the characters denoting decimal digits are given an ordered coherent set of ordinal numbers, so that

$$ord ('0') = ord('1') - 1$$
$$ord ('1') = ord('2') - 1$$
$$\vdots$$
$$ord ('8') = ord('9') - 1$$

In many implementations the upper-case and lower-case letters of the alphabet (when available) also have coherent ordered sets of ordinal numbers, so that

$$ord ('A') = ord ('B') - 1 \qquad ord ('a') = ord ('b') - 1$$
$$ord ('B') = ord ('C') - 1 \qquad ord ('b') = ord ('c') - 1$$
$$\vdots \qquad\qquad\qquad\qquad \vdots$$
$$ord ('Y') = ord ('Z') - 1 \qquad ord ('y') = ord ('z') - 1$$

However, the PASCAL standard does not require that this is so, and users should check that it is for their implementation before writing any program that depends upon it. The standard does require that the ordinal values of letters are ordered, i.e. that

$$ord ('A') < ord ('B') \qquad ord ('a') < ord ('b')$$
$$ord ('B') < ord ('C') \qquad ord ('b') < ord ('c')$$
$$\vdots \qquad\qquad\qquad\qquad \vdots$$

This condition is sufficient to explain the ordered comparison of letter characters as explained in the next section.

The mapping of the values of type *char* onto a set of consecutive integer values enables it to be designated an ordinal type, and the standard functions *pred* and *succ* are defined for arguments of type *char*, as follows:

$$pred(c) = chr (ord(c) - 1)$$
$$succ(c) = chr (ord(c) + 1)$$

The Type *boolean*

A *boolean* value is one of the logical truth values represented by the standard PASCAL identifiers *true* and *false*.

PASCAL provides standard operators which take boolean values as operands and produce a boolean result. These operators include

and   logical *and*
or   logical *inclusive or*
not   logical *negation*.

p	*q*	*p* **and** *q*	*p* **or** *q*	**not** *p*
false	*false*	*false*	*false*	*true*
false	*true*	*false*	*true*	*true*
true	*false*	*false*	*true*	*false*
true	*true*	*true*	*true*	*false*

Table 3.3   Action of **and** , **or** and **not** operators.

Table 3.3 shows the results of applying these operators to boolean arguments *p* and *q*.

Boolean values may also be produced by applying *relational operators* to operands of other types. PASCAL provides the six relational operators of mathematics, which are as follows:

$=$ equal to
$<>$ not equal to
$<$ less than
$<=$ less than or equal to
$>$ greater than
$>=$ greater than or equal to.

A relation consists of two operands separated by a relational operator. If the relation is satisfied it has the value *true*, otherwise the value *false*, i.e., the result of a relation is a boolean value. The above operators may be applied to any two operands of the same unstructured type. (Their use with operands of other types is discussed further in this and later chapters.)

For integer and real operands the relational operators have their usual meaning. Thus,

$7 = 11$ gives   *false*
$7 < 11$ gives   *true*
$3.4 <= 5.9$ gives   *true*

For operands of type *char* the result is determined by applying the mathematical relation to the ordinal numbers corresponding to the operands. Thus for any relational operator R and operands $c1$, $c2$ of type *char*

$$c1 \; R \; c2$$

is equivalent to

$$ord(c1) \; R \; ord(c2)$$

Note that the restrictions specified by the PASCAL standard for the ordinal numbers of the type *char* ensure that the following character relations are true:

$'0' < '1'$	$'A' < 'B'$	$'a' < 'b'$
$'1' < '2'$	$'B' < 'C'$	$'b' < 'c'$
⋮	⋮	⋮

A similar ordering convention is adopted for the type *boolean* itself, which is defined to be an ordinal type such that

$ord\;(false) = 0$	$false = pred\;(true)$
$ord\;(true) = 1$	$true = succ\;(false)$

With this convention other *boolean* operators can be expressed in terms of the relational operators, e.g.,

the *implication* operator is expressed by the $<=$ operator;
the *equivalence* operator is expressed by the $=$ operator;
the *exclusive or* operator is expressed by the $<>$ operator.

Table 3.4 confirms that these relational operators correspond to the named logical operators.

p	q	$p <= q$	$p = q$	$p <> q$
false	*false*	*true*	*true*	*false*
false	*true*	*true*	*false*	*true*
true	*false*	*false*	*false*	*true*
true	*true*	*true*	*true*	*false*

Table 3.4   Further boolean operators

PASCAL provides three standard functions which yield boolean results—such functions are known as *predicates*. Two of these, *eoln* and *eof*, are discussed in Chap. 5. The third is defined as follows:

$odd(x)$ for an integer argument x, $odd(x)$ gives the result *true* if x is odd, *false* otherwise.

Enumerated Types

We have now considered the four standard, or primitive, types provided by PASCAL. These data types can be used primarily for the description of numerical, character and logical data. However, the programmer may find that none of these types provide values suitable for description of the data which he wishes to introduce into his program. For instance, he may wish to construct a program whose data items are the four suits of a pack of cards (clubs, diamonds, hearts and spades) or the seven days of the week (Sunday to Saturday). Neither of these is naturally describable in terms of the standard types of PASCAL. Fortunately, PASCAL allows the programmer to define his own data types in a form suitable to the particular application.

An *enumerated-type* is defined simply by listing the identifiers by which the values of the type are to be denoted. The identifiers are enclosed in parentheses and separated by commas

> *enumerated-type* = "(" *identifier-list* ")" .
> *identifier-list* = *identifier* { "," *identifier* } .

The suits in a pack of cards could thus be defined as an enumerated type:

> (*club* , *diamond* , *heart* , *spade*)

Items of this type can take only the values denoted by the identifiers *club* , *diamond* , *heart* , *spade* .

The days of the week could be defined as an enumerated type

> (*Sunday* , *Monday* , *Tuesday* , *Wednesday* , *Thursday* , *Friday* , *Saturday*)

The order in which the values of the type are enumerated also defines their ordering for the purposes of applying relational operators, thus

> *club* < *diamond*   gives   *true*
> *Monday* >= *Friday*   gives   *false* .

All six relational operators described previously can be applied to values of enumerated types producing, as always, boolean-valued results.

All enumerated types are defined to be ordinal types, and the standard functions *succ* and *pred* are defined on their values. The successor of an enumerated type value is the next value in the ordered enumeration (if that value exists), while the predecessor is the preceding value in the enumeration (if that value exists).

For example, with the types defined earlier, the following relations are true:

> $succ(Monday) = Tuesday$
> $pred(Monday) = Sunday$.

In the case of the maximum value of an enumerated type *succ* is not defined—likewise, *pred* is not defined for the minimum value, e.g., *pred(Sunday)* and *succ(Saturday)* produce undefined results.

The standard function *ord* (previously defined for the type *char*) is also applicable to arguments which are values of an enumerated type. This function maps the values of the enumerated type, in order, onto the integers 0 to $N-1$ (where N is the number of values, or *cardinality*, of the enumerated type). Thus,

ord(club)	gives the result 0,
ord(diamond)	gives the result 1,
ord(heart)	gives the result 2,
ord(spade)	gives the result 3.

Note that the standard type *boolean* is equivalent to an enumerated type of the form

> (*false* , *true*)

Subrange Types

When a data item takes a range of values which is a subrange of the values described by some existing ordinal type, its type may be defined as a *subrange* of that *host* type. The subrange type is defined by indicating the lower and upper *bounds* of the values in the subrange, separated by the symbol "..".

> *subrange-type = constant "..." constant* .

The full range of possible forms of a *constant* is defined in the next section. Thus,

'A'..'Z'	is a subrange of the type *char*;
Monday .. Friday	is a subrange of the enumeration introduced in the previous sub-section ;
0 .. 9	
1900 .. 1999	are subranges of the type *integer* .

In fact the PASCAL type *integer* is itself really a subrange—the implementation-defined subset of the infinite range of whole numbers.

Note (a):   it is not permitted to define a subrange of the type *real* since it is
              not an ordinal type;

    (b):   on most implementations the subrange 'A' .. 'Z' defines the
              twenty-six upper-case letters of the alphabet as its only values
              but, for the reasons explained earlier, this is not necessarily so.
              On some implementations this subrange may define more than
              twenty-six values, and include non-alphabetic characters.

A subrange type is a means of indicating that the values taken by specific
data items lie in a certain subrange. However, each value taken is regarded
as being of the host type, and thus the operators and functions defined for
the host type are applicable to (the value of) a data item of a subrange type.
For example, the integer arithmetic operators may be applied to operands
of integer subrange types, and *succ* and *pred* may be applied to operands of
any subrange type. In general, however, the value produced by applying an
operation to operands of a subrange type does not necessarily lie within the
same subrange. The result of such an operation is always considered to be
of the parent host type.

DATA DECLARATIONS

The data items which a program manipulates may be divided into *two*
classes—those whose values remain fixed during execution of a program, and those whose values are changed by the execution. The former
are known as *constants*, the latter are known as *variables*. Items of
either class share the properties of type as described in the previous
section. However, the way in which the items are introduced in a
PASCAL program depends on their class, as the following sub-sections
explain.

Constants and Constant Definitions

In previous sub-sections we have seen how particular values of
unstructured data types may be denoted. For example,

    123   denotes a particular value of type *integer* ;
    12.75   denotes a particular value of type *real* ;
    'A'   denotes a particular value of type *char* ;
    true   denotes a particular value of type *boolean* ;
    heart   denotes a particular value of an enumerated type.

A constant data item of an unstructured type may thus be denoted by explicitly writing its value at each point in the program which refers to it. However, this is not always the most satisfactory solution, as the following example will show:

A mathematical program may make frequent use of the real value 3.1415926, which is an approximation to the value of the mathematical constant π. Writing this value explicitly at each point has the following disadvantages:

(a) the actual sequence of digits is much less meaningful than the symbol π;
(b) writing out this digit sequence repeatedly is tedious, and prone to error—one may write 3.1415926 or 3.1415962 or 3.1451926 without the discrepancies being detected;
(c) a decision to change, say, the precision of the value used for π involves changing each occurrence of the digit sequence.

An ideal solution for the programmer is to use the symbol π itself, defining the value which it denotes at one point only in the program. Given that Greek letters such as π are not provided on computer systems, the use of a meaningful mnemonic identifier, such as *pi*, is an acceptable substitute—a solution permitted by PASCAL.

In PASCAL an identifier may be defined to denote a particular constant value, by means of a *constant-definition*. Thereafter each occurrence of the identifier is equivalent to an explicit occurrence of the value itself at that point. Constant definitions are grouped together in the *constant-definition-part* which has the following form:

constant-definition-part = "**const**" constant-definition ";"
                          { constant-definition ";" } .

constant-definition = identifier "=" constant .

constant = integer-number | real-number | string |
            [sign] constant-identifier .

The following is an example *constant-definition-part*:

const   pi = 3.1415926 ;
        e = 2.7182 ;
        asterisk = '*' ;

PASCAL provides three standard identifiers which may be used without prior definition, and which denote standard constant values. Two of these, *false* and *true*, denote the only values of the standard type *boolean*. The third is an implementation-defined constant

maxint

such that every integral value in the closed interval from $-maxint$ to $+maxint$ is a value of the predefined type *integer* on that implementation.

Throughout this book the term *constant-identifier* is used to mean one of the following:

(a)   an identifier defined by a *constant-definition*, or
(b)   an identifier introduced as one of the values of an enumerated type, or
(c)   one of the standard identifiers *false, true, maxint.*

The syntax category

constant-identifier = identifier .

is introduced simply to denote the class of identifiers so defined.

Type Definitions

The primitive types of PASCAL may be used in a program without prior definition—each reference to one of them being indicated by the corresponding identifier *integer, real, char* or *boolean.* It is often necessary, or convenient, that types defined in the program itself are also denoted by identifiers, so-called *type identifiers.*

Each type identifier is introduced by means of a *type-definition.* Type definitions are grouped together in a *type-definition-part*, which has the following form

   *type-definition-part = "**type**" type-definition ";"*
                              { type-definition ";" } .

   type-definition = identifier "=" type .

   type = simple-type | structured-type | pointer-type | type-identifier .

   simple-type = enumerated-type | subrange-type.

The possible forms of *structured* and *pointer types* are explained in later chapters. (1) is an example of a *type-definition-part* involving simple types.

   type   *daysofweek* = (*Sunday, Monday, Tuesday, Wednesday,*
                              Thursday, Friday, Saturday) ;
         daysofmonth = 1..31 ;   (1)
         year = 1900..1999 ;
         workday = *Monday..Friday* ;

Thereafter the types may be denoted by the identifiers *daysofweek, daysofmonth, year* and *workday,* in the same way as the standard types are denoted by *integer, real, char* and *boolean.*

Throughout this book the term *type-identifier* is used to mean either

(a)   an identifier introduced by a type definition, or
(b)   one of the standard identifiers provided in PASCAL to denote standard types, viz., *integer, real, char, boolean* and *text.* (The type *text* is explained in Chap. 12.)

The syntax category

   type-identifier = identifier .

is used to denote the class of identifiers so defined.

The syntax of *type-definition* allows one type identifier to be defined in terms of another defined elsewhere, thus

> **type** $t1 = \ldots\ldots$;
>   ⋮
> $t2 = t1$;

With such a definition the type identifier $t2$ is said to denote the same type as that denoted by $t1$.

Variable Declarations

Variables, those data items whose values are changed by execution of the program, are always denoted by identifiers. Each *variable-identifier* is introduced by a *variable-declaration,* which also specifies the type of the values which the variable may take. Variable declarations are grouped in a *variable-declaration-part,* which has the following form:

> *variable-declaration-part = "***var***" variable-declaration ";"*
>   *{ variable-declaration ";" } .*
> *variable-declaration = identifier-list ":" type .*

Given the type definitions of the preceding sub-section, the following is an example of a *variable-declaration-part* :

> **var**   *today : daysofweek* ;
>   *thisyear , nextyear : year* ;
>   *daysworked : 0. .5* ;
>   *onleave : boolean* ;

Thereafter the identifier *today* denotes a variable data item which at any moment may take one of the seven values *Sunday, Monday, ..., Saturday* ; *thisyear* and *nextyear* denote distinct data items which may take integer values in the range 1900. .1999 .

Note that

(a)   several variables may be declared by the same declaration, pro-
      vided they are to share the same type;
(b)   the type of the variables declared may be defined explicitly in the
      variable declaration itself—if this is the only point in the program
      where the type is to be used then it is superflous to introduce an
      identifier naming the type in a type definition;
(c)   two variables are said to have the same type if they are declared in the
      same variable declaration, or if they are declared (in different variable
      declarations) using the same type identifier, or using different type
      identifiers that denote the same type.

Hereafter the syntax category

variable-identifier = *identifier* .

is used to denote the class of identifiers introduced by variable declarations.

UNIQUENESS AND ORDER OF
IDENTIFIER DEFINITIONS

Constant definitions, enumerated types, type definitions and variable
declarations all have the effect of associating identifiers with the constants, types or variables which they are used to denote. (Further means
of associating identifiers with other program quantities are described in
following chapters.)

PASCAL requires that the association of each identifier with the
quantity which it denotes must be unique throughout its *scope*, or range
of use within the program. The concept of identifier scope is discussed
fully in Chap. 7. For the moment it may be assumed that the association
of each identifier must be unique throughout the program.

Thus the definitions

type   *range* = 1 .. 100 ;
var   *x* , *y* : *range* ;
          y , *z* , *range* : *real* ;

are invalid, since the identifiers *range* and *y* are each defined twice (in
the same scope).

The syntax of PASCAL also requires that the *constant-definition-part*, *type-definition-part* and *variable-declaration-part* of a *program*, or *block*, must appear in exactly that order (referring to the definition in Chap. 2), i.e., as in (2).

> *block* =   ...
>   [*constant-definition-part*]
>   [*type-definition-part*]   (2)
>   [*variable-declaration-part*]
>   . . . .

This has the effect that constant identifiers are defined before they can be used in the *type-definition-part*, that type identifiers are defined before they can be used in declaring variables, that variable identifiers are declared before they can be used in describing any actions to be taken on the variables, etc. This property of each identifier being defined before it is 'used' in the program text adds considerably to program clarity. However, the syntactic definition-before-use requirement is not complete—one constant identifier may be used to define another in the same *constant-definition-part*, one type identifier may be used to define another in the same *type-definition-part*. PASCAL therefore imposes a general definition-before-use requirement for all identifiers, with a specific exception for defining pointer types, where we shall see that such a rule would be impossible to observe. Thus the following definitions are not allowed:

> **const**   *xmin* = −*xmax* ;
>   *xmax* = 100 ;
> **type**   *yrange* = *xrange* ;
>   *xrange* = *xmin* .. *xmax* ;

since *xmax* and *xrange* are each used before they are defined, whereas the following equivalent definitions are acceptable:

> **const**   *xmax* = 100 ;
>   *xmin* = −*xmax* ;
> **type**   *xrange* = *xmin* .. *xmax* ;
>   *yrange* = *xrange* ;

EXERCISES

3.1 Which of the following combinations of operators and operands are valid
in PASCAL?

67 **div** 8	12*2.75	67 **mod** 8	(−3) **div** 8
succ (66.3)	*sqr* (2.5)	'*A*' < '*Z*'	*pred* ('7')
67 / 8	6.7 **div** 8	*sqr* (10E4)	*sqr* (100001)
sqrt (6.25)	*sqrt* (4)	*succ* (*true*)	*exp* (1.0E60)

Write down the result of each valid combination. Are all the results
defined on your implementation?

3.2 Study the following sequence of PASCAL definitions and declarations:

```
const  linemax = 64 ;
       printwanted = true ;
type   lineposition = 1 .. linemax ;
       spacing = (single, double, treble) ;
var    thischar, lastchar : char ;
       thisposition : lineposition ;
       spacingnow : spacing ;
```

List all the *constant-identifiers*,
 all the *type-identifiers*,
 all the *variable-identifiers*, which occur.

3.3 Write a *constant-definition-part* which defines the following constant
identifiers with appropriate values:

   inchespermetre   *currencysymbol*
   degreesperradian   *speedlimit*

3.4 Write a *type-definition-part* which defines types suitable for the values of
the age, sex, height, weight and marital status of a person.

3.5 A typical estate agent's description of a house reads
"Three bedrooms, two reception rooms, oil-fired central heating, garage,
. . .".
Write a *variable-declaration-part* which declares the variables involved,
with an appropriate type for each.

4

Statements, Expressions and Assignments

STATEMENTS

In Chaps. 2 and 3 the concepts of data and data types were introduced, together with the means of defining constant and variable data items in PASCAL programs—the *declaration-part*. The manipulation which the program performs on its data items is defined by its *statement-part*.

The *statement-part* defines the actions to be carried out as a sequence of *statements*, where each statement specifies one corresponding action. PASCAL is a *sequential* programming language in that statements are executed sequentially in time, one after the other, and never simultaneously.

This sequential execution of statements is reflected in the structure of the *statement-part*, which is as follows:

statement-part = "**begin**" *statement* { ";" *statement* } "**end**" .

Chapter 2 introduced an example program which included a simple example of a *statement-part*, consisting of three statements to be executed in the order given, as shown in (1).

```
begin
    read (first,second);
    sum:=first+second;                          (1)
    write(sum)
end
```

PASCAL provides a variety of statement forms, both simple and structured, by which program actions may be specified:

statement = [*label* ":"] (*simple-statement* | *structured-statement*) .

Statement *labels* play a minor role in the construction of PASCAL programs and, until we meet labels in Chap. 8, their existence is ignored. *Structured-statements* are used to describe composite actions in terms of other component statements, and are discussed in Chap. 6. For the moment we concentrate on the *simple-statement*, of which four possible forms are provided

> *simple-statement* = [*assignment-statement* | *procedure-statement* |
> *goto-statement*] .

A statement which consists of no symbols is known as an *empty-statement* and denotes no action. As we shall see, it is used at certain points in a program to denote that no action is to be taken.

Procedure- and *goto-statements* are discussed in later chapters.

An *assignment-statement* is used to assign a particular value to a variable. The value is specified by means of an *expression*, whose form we first consider.

EXPRESSIONS

An *expression* is a rule for computing a value. It consists of one or more operands combined by means of the operators already defined in Chap. 3. An operand may be any of the following:

> a constant value;
> the current value of a variable;
>
> the result of a function call;
> a set.

For the present the only function calls we consider are those involving the standard functions defined in Chap. 3. The use of conformant array bounds is discussed in Chap. 9 and the use of sets is discussed in Chap. 11.

As with normal mathematical expressions a PASCAL expression is evaluated according to the notion of *operator precedence*. Each of the operators is assigned a *precedence*. The precedence of the PASCAL operators is given in Table 4.1.

The rules of evaluation of an expression are then:

(a) if all the operators in an expression have the same precedence the evaluation of the operations proceeds strictly from left to right;

(b) when operators of different precedences are present then the highest precedence operations are evaluated first (on a left-to-right basis), then the next highest precedence operations are evaluated, and so on;

Precedence	Operators
4	**not**
3	* / **div mod and**
2	+ − **or**
1	= <> > < >= <=

Table 4.1   Operator precedences.

(c)   rules (a) and (b) can be overridden by the inclusion of parentheses in an expression—in this case those operations within the parentheses are evaluated first, with the above precedence rules being applied inside the parentheses;

(d)   the order of evaluation of the operands of a dyadic operator i.e. one with two operands, is implementation dependent—as we shall see in Chapter 7, this must be remembered when using some functions.

The effect of these rules of evaluation is best described by means of some examples.

(a)   6*2+4*3

Since the * operators are of highest precedence, this expression is equivalent to (6*2)+(4*3), which gives a result of 24.

(b)   If one wishes to add 4 and 2, and multiply the result by 3, then the following expression

(4+2)*3

may be used. Note that

4+2*3

does not produce the correct result since the * operation, being of higher precedence, would be performed first.

(c)   10 **mod** 3 * 4

Here the two operators **mod** and * are of equal precedence and so are evaluated from left to right, to give the result 4.

Some boolean operations involving **and** and **or** can be evaluated without evaluating both the operands. For example

false **and** *b*
b **or** *true*

give the values *false* and *true*, respectively, regardless of the value of *b*.

However, the definition of PASCAL does not specify whether both operands are evaluated in such cases. In some implementations the second operand *b* in expressions such as

> *a* **and** *b*
>
> *a* **or** *b*

is evaluated even if the first, *a*, is *false* or *true* respectively; in other implementations it is not. As we shall see in subsequent programs, care must be taken to avoid expressions which depend on the method of evaluation used.

The rules given in Chap. 3 determine the type of the result of each operator within an expression, from the types of its operands. The type of a complete expression is determined by applying these rules to each operator and its operands in the order in which the operations are to be carried out. For example,

(e) $2 + sqrt(sqr(3)+11*5)$

> The contents of the outer parentheses are evaluated first. Within these parentheses *sqr*(3) is first evaluated to give an integer result, then 11*5 again giving an integer result, and these two results are added to give an integer result (of 64).
>
> Then *sqrt*(64) is evaluated to give a real result (8.0) and, finally, 2 is added to 8.0 to give a real result (of 10.0).

(f)   In some cases the omission of parentheses leads not to incorrect values but in fact produces illegal expressions, e.g.,

> (3>0) **and** (3<10)

gives the value *true*. However, if the parentheses are omitted, i.e.,

> 3>0 **and** 3<10

then we have an ill-formed expression. Precedence requires that

Expression	Value
3*17−193 **mod** 19	48
193 **mod** 19 **div** 3*127	127
(−4 + 23*2) **div** 3	14
(7+3)<=10	*true*
((3>7) **or** (3<=7)) **and** (7<>10)	*true*
(37 + 15 **mod** 4)/*sqr*(5)	1.6
trunc(3.2*4) **div** 3	4

Table 4.2 Some expressions and their values.

the **and** operation be performed first, but 0 **and** 3 is an illegal operation since **and** requires boolean-valued operands.

The reader should study the expressions in Table 4.2 and convince himself, by applying the rules for evaluation of expressions, that they produce the indicated values.

The PASCAL notation for expressions is less flexible than that used in mathematics, and care must be taken in translating mathematical expressions into PASCAL. In Table 4.3 we give some mathematical expressions and show how they are expressed in PASCAL.

Mathematical Expression	PASCAL Expression
$\dfrac{x+2}{y+4}$	$(x+2)/(y+4)$
$x(y+w(3-v))$	$x*(y+w*(3-v))$
$\dfrac{xy}{w+2}$	$x*y/(w+2)$
$a+\dfrac{b}{c}$	$a+b/c$

Table 4.3   Some mathematical expressions and their PASCAL counterparts.

Some important points should be noted concerning expressions:

(a) every variable used in an expression must already have been given a value in some way, otherwise an error will occur on evaluating the expression;

(b) two arithmetic operators must never be written side by side, e.g., $a* -b$ is an illegal expression and must be written $a*(-b)$;

(c) the multiplication sign should never be omitted when a multiplication operation is required;

(d) there is no harm in using possibly redundant parentheses. Therefore, when in doubt about the precedence rules, use parentheses to construct expressions.

The method of construction of expressions and the operator precedence rules governing their evaluation are defined by the syntax (2) (these syntax definitions merely summarize the rules we have given and are presented in (2) only for reference purposes).

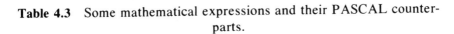
The occurrence of a variable in an expression indicates that the current value of the variable is to be used as an operand in evaluating

$$expression = simple\text{-}expression\ [\ relational\text{-}operator$$
$$simple\text{-}expression\ ]\ .$$
$$simple\text{-}expression = [\ sign\ ]\ term\ \{\ adding\text{-}operator\quad term\ \}\ .$$
$$term = factor\ \{\ multiplying\text{-}operator\quad factor\ \}\ .$$
$$factor = variable\ |\ unsigned\text{-}constant\ |\ function\text{-}designator\ |$$
$$bound\ |\ set\ |\ ''('' \ expression\ '')''\ |\ ''\mathbf{not}''\ factor\ .\qquad(2)$$
$$unsigned\text{-}constant = unsigned\text{-}integer\ |\ unsigned\text{-}real\ |\ string\ |$$
$$constant\text{-}identifier\ |\ ''\mathbf{nil}''\ .$$
$$relational\text{-}operator = ''=''\ |\ ''<>''\ |\ ''<''\ |\ ''>''\ |\ ''<=''\ |\ ''>=''\ |\ ''\mathbf{in}''\ .$$
$$adding\text{-}operator = ''+''\ |\ ''-''\ |\ ''\mathbf{or}''\ .$$
$$multiplying\text{-}operator = ''*''\ |\ ''/''\ |\ ''\mathbf{div}''\ |\ ''\mathbf{mod}''\ |\ ''\mathbf{and}''\ .$$

the expression. As we saw in Chap. 3, a variable is denoted by an identifier introduced in a *variable-declaration*. The identifiers that are introduced by declarations of variables of the data types considered in Chap. 3 denote what are known as *entire-variables*. The full syntactic definition of a *variable* as denoted within the *statement-part* is

$$variable = entire\text{-}variable\ |\ component\text{-}variable\ |$$
$$referenced\text{-}variable\ .$$
$$entire\text{-}variable = variable\text{-}identifier\ .$$

In subsequent chapters we see that variables sometimes consist of a number of *components*, each of which may be considered as a variable in its own right with a corresponding notation.

THE ASSIGNMENT STATEMENT

An *assignment-statement* has the following form:

$$assignment\text{-}statement = (\ variable\ |\ function\text{-}identifier\ )\ '':=''$$
$$expression\ .$$

The second form of assignment is used in the construction of functions, a topic which is discussed in Chap. 7. The two-character symbol ":=" is known as the *assignment operator* and is usually read as "becomes".

The effect of executing an *assignment-statement* is to evaluate the expression on the right of the assignment operator and to assign the resultant value to the variable on the left.

For example,

$$i := 3$$

means replace the current value of the variable i by the value 3;

$$i := j$$

means replace the current value of the variable *i* by the current value of the variable *j*.

Variables of any of the types we have introduced so far, be they of the primitive types, an enumerated type, or a subrange type, may be assigned new values. However, a variable may only be assigned a value of an appropriate type. Thus, the variable on the left-hand side of the assignment operator and the value of the expression on the right-hand side must be of identical type, with the following qualifications:

(a) an expression consisting solely of a variable of a subrange type is considered to be of the corresponding host type;
(b) a variable of a subrange type may be assigned a value of the corresponding host type, provided the value lies within the required subrange;
(c) a real variable may be assigned an integer value, as permitted by the integer-for-real substitution rule of Chap. 3.

A value meeting these conditions is said to be *assignment compatible* with the type of the variable to be assigned. Assignment compatibility for string and set types is discussed in Chaps. 9 and 11 respectively.

The result of assigning a value which is outside the required subrange to a variable of subrange type is an error. Most implementations provide some means of detecting such range errors during execution

Consider the following sequence of assignment statements:

```
a := 3.52 ;
a := b*b*b ;
j := j+1 ;
p := (j>0) or (c<>' ') ;
c := '.'
```

For these to be legal assignment statements the variable *a* must be of type *real*, *b* and *j* may be *integer* or *real*, *p* must be *boolean*, and *c* must be of type *char* (or subranges thereof).

As an exercise the reader should confirm that the following sequence of assignment statements applied to integer variables *x,y,* and *w* leaves all three variables with the final value 100:

```
x := 27 ;
y := 343 ;
w := x + y - 300 ;
x := w div 10 + 23 ;
y := (x+w) div 10 * 10 ;
x := x + 70 + y mod 10 ;
w := w + x - 70
```

EXERCISES

4.1　Insert brackets to clarify the meaning of the following expressions, and then calculate the value of each:

6.75 − 12.3 / 3
6∗11 − 42 **div** 5
175 **mod** 15 **div** 3 ∗ 65
13 + 7 ∗ 5 −4 ∗ 5 **div** 2
11 **mod** 4 **div** 2 <> 0
(*'A'* >= *'Z'*) **or** (*'9'* >= *'8'*) **and** (*'A'* < *'I'*)

4.2　Assuming X, Y, and Z are integer variables, what values will they have after execution of the following sequence of statements?

X := 50 ;
Y := 340 ;
Z := X + Y − 190 ;
X := 17 ;
Y := X + Z ;
Z := X + 200 ;
Z := X + Z − 200 ;

4.3　Write down boolean expressions which determine whether

(a) the value of an integer variable i lies in the range 1 to 100 inclusive;
(b) either of the values of two integer variables j and k is a multiple of the other;
(c) the year y in the twentieth century is a leap year.

4.4　(a)　Using any additional variables necessary, write a sequence of assignment statements which exchanges the values of two real variables x and y.

(b)　X, Y, and Z are integer variables. Write down assignment statements to assign their sum, product, and average to variables named *sum*, *product*, and *average*.
What types have you assumed for the variables *sum*, *product* and *average*?

(c)　H, T, and U are variables declared as follows:

H, T, U : *'0'* .. *'9'*

i.e., they take character values t, h, and u which are decimal digits. Write down an assignment statement which will assign to an integer variable I the decimal number denoted by the characters

htu

in that order.

5

Simple Input and Output of Data

TRANSFERRING INFORMATION TO AND FROM THE PROGRAM

It is the purpose of every program to manipulate data—a payroll program operates on data describing the employees and the hours they have worked; a program for solving systems of linear equations needs to know the coefficients of each of the equations. These data could actually be built into the program but then, in order to compute the next week's payroll or solve another system of equations, it would be necessary to alter the program. What is really required is some means of informing the program of the data to be manipulated on this particular occasion, i.e., a means of entering the data into the program during its execution, from some device outside the computer. Then the same programs could be used to carry out each week's payroll calculation, or to solve many sets of linear equations.

Many such external devices exist—card readers read information punched on cards, tape readers read information punched on paper tapes, typewriter keyboards act as a means of presenting the information typed to the computer. These, and many others, are means of inputting data to a program.

Similarly, we wish to see the results produced by a program—a payroll program must print pay slips for the employees to inspect, and cheques for them to cash; it will be necessary to examine the solution to a set of linear equations. Therefore a means is required of communicating the results of a program to the outside world. Once again devices exist, such as line printers, typewriter printers, and video screens, on which information can be displayed. These devices are means of outputting data from a program.

All the devices mentioned so far have two properties in common. Firstly, they provide all the characters in the character set of the computer with which they communicate and, secondly, their information is structured as a sequence of lines (e.g., a punched card constitutes a line).

In PASCAL input and output are not considered in terms of actual devices such as readers and printers. Instead the program is considered to be a process which obtains information from an *input stream* and delivers information to an *output stream*, both of which are held on external devices whose nature is immaterial. Every implementation of PASCAL assumes the existence of these two streams, organized as sequences of lines of characters. Thus a PASCAL program itself contains no indication of the actual devices being used—this depends entirely on the implementation environment.

The reader may have noticed that the program heading of the example program in Chap. 2 contains references to input and output in the form

program *add* (*input,output*) ;

This merely indicates that the program makes use of the input and output streams provided by the standard input and output devices of the computer installation.

A similar heading will be used for every program in this book until Chap. 12, where more complex means of input and output, involving a more complex program heading, will be discussed.

It was mentioned above that the organization of the input and output streams is as sequences of lines of text, each line containing characters from the available character set. For some devices the separation of one line from the next is denoted by special "control" characters which are not values of the character set described by the PASCAL primitive type *char*. However, PASCAL does enable the line-by-line structure of the input and output streams to be controlled by special language facilities.

INPUT IN PASCAL

An input statement in PASCAL takes one of the following two forms:

read (*variable-list*)
read (*input, variable-list*)

where a *variable-list* is a series of one or more *variable-identifiers*, separated by commas, thus

variable-list = *variable* { "," *variable* } .

Each variable in the *variable-list* must be of type *integer*, *real* or *char*, or of a type which is a subrange of *integer* or *char*. Note that direct input of values of an enumerated type, or of the type *boolean*, is not permitted.

The action on execution of either form of the statement is to obtain from the standard input data stream the required number of data values (i.e., as many values as there are variables in the variable list) and to assign these values, in order, to the variables in the list. For example, the statement

   read (a)

will obtain the next value from the standard input stream and assign this value to the variable *a*. The statement

   read (alpha, beta, gamma)

will obtain three values from the standard input stream and assign them to the variables *alpha*, *beta* and *gamma*, in that order. These two statements may be written

   read (input, a)
   read (input, alpha, beta, gamma)

and will have exactly the same effect. Thus

   read (v1, v2, v3, . . . ,vn)

is equivalent to

   read (v1) ; read (v2) ; read (v3) ; . . . ; read (vn)

The statement *read (v)* or *read (input, v)* may be thought of as an assignment statement which obtains the value to be assigned to *v* from the input stream rather than from an expression. Therefore, the value obtained must be assignment compatible with the type of the variable to which it is to be assigned. How the value is represented in the input stream depends on the type of *v*.

Each integer value or real value in the input stream may be represented as a sequence of characters in any of the forms allowed for such numbers (see Chap. 2) and may be immediately preceded by a plus or minus sign. Each integer or real value may be preceded by any number of blank characters or ends of line, but there must be no blanks or ends of line between the sign and the number.

A character value in the input stream is represented simply by the single character to be assigned. For character input blank characters are significant and are not ignored. Likewise ends of line are significant during character input—each end of line is treated as one character, but the value assigned to the character variable is the blank character.

The input data for a program are treated as a continuous stream. Each input statement executed begins to obtain data values from the point in

the stream immediately following the last value obtained by the pre
viously executed input statement. The reading of an integer value causes
any blanks in the input stream to be skipped. The next data item, which
must be a valid integer number, is then read. The reading of real values
causes scanning of the input stream for a valid integer or real number. In
the case of reading a character value the effect is simply to take the next
character from the input stream. Thus the values in the data stream must
be synchronized with the variables in the variable list of the input
statement. No value in the input stream can be read more than once.

As an example of the possible forms of the input data consider the
following input statement

> read (realvalue, c1, c2, c3, intvalue)

where realvalue is a variable of type real,
$\qquad$ c1, c2, c3 are variables of type char,
$\qquad$ intvalue is a variable of type integer.

The following four data streams will all cause the same values (640.0,
'X', 'Y', 'Z', 104) to be assigned to the five variables.

(a)   640.0XYZ104
(b)   64E1XYZ 104
(c)   +6.4E+02XYZ
$\qquad$ 104
(d)   640XYZ 104

The effect of the read statement using any of these data streams is thus
equivalent to the five assignment statements

> realvalue:=640.0 ;   c1:='X' ;   c2:='Y' ;   c3:='Z' ;
> intvalue:=104

Whenever the reading of the input stream reaches the end of a line,
then the value made available for the character input is a blank. In some
cases the program must be aware that the end of a line has been
reached. To this end PASCAL provides a standard predicate, or boolean
function, which is written

> eoln

or

> eoln (input)

This yields the value true when the last actual character of the current
line of input has been read, otherwise it is false. Thus, if an attempt to
read a character is made when eoln (input) is true, the value obtained is
the blank character, and eoln (input) becomes false (unless of course

the next line consists of zero characters in which case *eoln* (*input*) becomes *true* once again).

A special form of the *read* statement is provided to permit the skipping over of the contents of a line of input. This is the statement

  readln

or

  readln (*input*)

which scans over the remainder of the current line in the input stream. After a *readln* statement has been executed the next available character in the input stream is the first character of the next line. If it is required to read the values of variables $v1,\ldots,vn$ *and then* skip to the start of the next line, one may write

  readln ($v1,\ldots,vn$)

or,

  readln (*input*, $v1,\ldots,vn$)

This is equivalent to

  read ($v1,\ldots,vn$) ; *readln*

Note that the reading of $v1,\ldots,vn$ may itself cause the scanning of several lines, and that the skip to the start of a new line is performed *after* the reading of the variables.

For example, suppose we have three lines in the input stream, each line containing at least two integer values. We wish to assign the *second* integer on each line to variables x, y, and z respectively and ignore all the other values. This can be achieved by introducing another integer variable, say w, and writing

  readln (w, x) ; *readln* (w, y) ; *readln* (w, z)

The input data stream for any program is usually of finite length. Clearly a program cannot read more data than its input stream provides. In some programs therefore it is necessary to be able to detect when the end of the input data stream has been reached. To this end PASCAL provides a standard predicate, or boolean function,

  eof

or,

  eof (*input*)

which returns the value *true* if, and only if, the end of the input data has been reached, otherwise its value is *false.*

The input stream is always an integral number of input lines. Thus, it is in general sufficient to test the *eof* function

(a) before any input has taken place (in case no input is provided), and
(b) after each *readln* operation, or
(c) after reading a blank character input when *eoln* is true.

An error occurs if a *read, readln* or *eoln* operation is attempted when *eof* is true. The use of *eof* and *eoln* is illustrated in various example programs in subsequent chapters.

OUTPUT IN PASCAL

The basic output statement in PASCAL takes one of two forms:

    write (output-list)
    write (output , output-list)

where the *output-list* is a list of values to be output. Its action on execution is to deliver these values, in order, to the standard output stream. For example

    write (2∗x+7)

will output one value, and

    write (a, b, c+1)

will output three values.

As with input data the output generated by a PASCAL program is treated as a continuous stream. However, the program may structure this output into lines for display on the actual output device. New lines in the output stream may be generated by means of the statements

    writeln (output)

or, simply

    writeln

If it is required to output a given list of values (on the current output line), *and then* take a new line, the statements

    writeln (output, output-list)

or

    writeln (output-list)

may be used.

Consider the sequence of statements

> *writeln ('A', 'B')* ;
> *write ('C')* ;
> *writeln ('D')* ;
> *writeln* ;
> *writeln ('E')*

The output resulting from execution of this sequence would be as follows:

AB
CD

E

On some output devices the lines of information may be grouped as pages, and it is possible to ensure that the next line of output is printed as the first line of the next page. To exploit this facility PASCAL provides one further statement in the two alternative forms

> *page*
> *page (output)*

whose effect is to cause a skip to the top of a new page on the output device.

The *output-list* in a *write* or *writeln* statement lists the values to be output, separated by commas, thus:

> *output-list = output-value {"," output-value }* .

Each output value must be of type *integer, real, boolean, char,* or a string.

The output stream itself, like the input stream, is a sequence of characters. Outputting a value of type *char* simply adds that character to the sequence output so far. Outputting a string adds the sequence of characters making up the string to the sequence output so far. A boolean value is output either as the string *'True'* or the string *'False'*.

An integer or real value is output as an appropriate sequence containing digits, sign, decimal point etc., which denotes the value. For example, the statement

> *write (27+3, '=', 30, ' IS', 27+3=30)*

which involves an output list consisting of an integer value, a char value, another integer value, a string, and a boolean value, might add the sequence of characters

> $30=$ *30 IS TRUE*

to the output stream.

The exact number of characters output for each value, which is called the *field-width*, is determined by the way in which the value is denoted in the output list. In its simplest form an *output-value* is simply an *expression* which determines the value to be output. However, this expression may be qualified by either one or two further expressions, separated by colons, which control the field width and format in which the value is output. Thus we have

> *output-value = expression* [*":" field-width* [*":" fraction-length*]] .
> *field-width = expression* .
> *fraction-length = expression* ..

where the first expression, which determines the value to be output, must be of type *integer, real, boolean, char* or a string. The *field-width* and *fraction-length* must be expressions which produce positive integer results, otherwise an error will occur.

When an output value is written without a field-width specification a default field width is assumed. This default value is defined by each PASCAL implementation according to the type of the output value. However, the default field width for the type *char* is 1 in all implementations.

The field width determines the exact number of characters which are written to the output stream. If the actual value to be output requires less than the number of characters specified, an appropriate number of blanks are output before the value itself.

If the actual value to be output requires more than the number of characters specified by the field width, the minimum increased field width required to represent the value is used for an integer or real, but a string is truncated to the specified width by removal of its rightmost characters.

The third form of output value, which includes a fraction-length specification, may be used only when outputting real values. If no fraction length is specified a real value is output in floating-point form, e.g.,

> 0.9761000E+03

However, if a fraction length n is specified the value will be output in fixed-point form with n digits after the decimal point, e.g., with $n=2$ the same value as above would be output as

> 976.10

The advantages of using character strings and format specifications can be seen from Table 5.1, which compares various statements with the output which they produce.

The input and output facilities described in this chapter are in fact particular cases of more general language facilities provided by

Statement	Output
write (a)	−0.357000000E+02
write (a:10)	−0.357E+02
write (a:5:1)	−35.7
write ('a = ', a:5:1)	a = −35.7

Table 5.1 Some output statements and their effects.

PASCAL. The *read, readln, write* and *writeln* statements are actually examples of the use of *procedures* (see Chap. 7) provided as standard facilities in all PASCAL implementations, and their use with the standard input and output streams is just a particular case of PASCAL facilities for handling text files (see Chap. 12).

PROGRAM 1 (Calculating time of arrival)

A program is required to read in three integers representing the blast-off time of a rocket expressed in hours, minutes and seconds on the 24-hour clock, to read another integer giving the rocket's flight time in seconds, to use these data values to calculate the time of day at which the rocket will return to Earth, and to print out this time in a readable format.

The method used in designing the program for this and all other case studies in this book is to break the specified problem down into a number of sub-problems expressed in concise, ordinary English. This same approach is then used to break down each sub-problem into further sub-problems. The method is repeatedly applied until each of the sub-problems can be readily and easily expressed in PASCAL. This technique is often referred to as "programming by stepwise refinement".

Noting that it is good practice to write out any data read in by a program (so that any errors in the preparation of the input data may be detected), the solution to the problem may be stated informally as in (1).

```
begin
      read in and print out data ;
      calculate time of arrival ;                              (1)
      print out time of arrival
end.
```

The first action, *read in and print out data* , consists of two actions:

```
read in and print out blast off time ;
read in and print out flight time
```

The introduction of three positive integer variables *hours*, *minutes* and *seconds* allows the first of these two actions to be expressed using *read* and *write* statements. The read statement required is simply

> read (*hours*, *minutes*, *seconds*)

The *write* statement will output a string *'TAKE-OFF TIME IS '* and the blast-off time in the format hh/mm/ss. This is to appear on a line by itself, and we shall leave a blank line between each of the lines of significant output produced by the program. Thus,

> writeln ('*TAKE-OFF TIME IS '*, *hours*:2, '/', *minutes*:2, '/',
>   *seconds*:2) ;
> writeln

Note that a field width of 2 has been used to obtain the required format.

Similarly, *read in and print out flight time* can be programmed as a simple series of input and output statements involving a variable *flighttime*:

> read (*flighttime*) ;
> writeln ('*FLIGHT-TIME = '*, *flighttime*:7, ' *SECONDS'*) ;
> writeln

Next we deal with the sub-problem *calculate time of arrival*. The problem requires the time of day at which the rocket returns to Earth to be found. This is computed by means of the six assignment statements listed below. Note that the order of the assignments is critical and another order might produce erroneous results.

> *seconds* := *seconds* + *flighttime* ;
> *minutes* := *minutes* + *seconds* **div** 60 ;
> *seconds* := *seconds* **mod** 60 ;
> *hours* := *hours* + *minutes* **div** 60 ;
> *minutes* := *minutes* **mod** 60 ;
> *hours* := *hours* **mod** 24

Finally, *print out time of arrival* consists of outputting a suitable caption followed by the values of the variables *hours*, *minutes* and *seconds*, suitably formatted. The required output statement is

> writeln ('*EXPECTED TIME OF ARRIVAL = '*, *hours*:2, '/',
>   *minutes*:2, '/', *seconds*:2)

The final PASCAL program can now be put together. It consists of a program heading, variable declarations and the statement part. The program heading must indicate that the program uses both the standard input and output streams. The variables are all of the integer subrange type 0..*maxint* and note that they have been given meaningful identifiers. The statement part contains the statements we have developed above, enclosed in **begin** and **end** and followed by a period to denote the end of the program. The resulting program and sample output are shown in Listing 1.

LISTING 1

```
PROGRAM ROCKET (INPUT,OUTPUT) ;

(* THIS PROGRAM READS IN THREE NUMBERS REPRESENTING
   THE BLAST-OFF TIME OF A ROCKET EXPRESSED IN HOURS,
   MINUTES AND SECONDS ON THE 24-HOUR CLOCK. IT THEN
   READS A FOURTH NUMBER GIVING THE FLIGHT-TIME IN
   SECONDS, AND PRINTS OUT THE ESTIMATED TIME OF
   ARRIVAL *)

VAR   HOURS, MINUTES, SECONDS, FLIGHTTIME : 0..MAXINT ;

BEGIN

    (* READ IN AND PRINT OUT DATA *)

    READ (HOURS,MINUTES,SECONDS);
    WRITELN ('TAKE-OFF TIME IS ',HOURS:2,'/',MINUTES:2,'/',SECONDS:2);
    WRITELN;
    READ (FLIGHTTIME);
    WRITELN ('FLIGHT-TIME = ',FLIGHTTIME:7,' SECONDS');
    WRITELN;

    (* CALCULATE TIME OF ARRIVAL *)

    SECONDS:=SECONDS+FLIGHTTIME;
    MINUTES:=MINUTES+ SECONDS DIV 60;
    SECONDS:=SECONDS MOD 60;
    HOURS:= HOURS + MINUTES DIV 60;
    MINUTES:=MINUTES MOD 60;
    HOURS:=HOURS MOD 24;

    (* PRINT OUT TIME OF ARRIVAL *)

    WRITELN ('EXPECTED TIME OF ARRIVAL = ', HOURS : 2,
             '/',MINUTES:2,'/',SECONDS:2);

END.



TAKE-OFF TIME IS  3/47/32

FLIGHT-TIME =   45678 SECONDS

EXPECTED TIME OF ARRIVAL = 16/20/50
```

EXERCISES

5.1 Given 3 lines of input data

```
12.75              24.7
    -33E10
0.075
```

and variables declared as follows

X, Y, Z : *real* ;
I, J, K : *integer* ;
c : *char* ;

what is the effect of executing each of the following sequences of input statements?

(a) *read (X, Y, Z)*
(b) *readln (X) ; readln (Y, Z)*
(c) *readln (X, Y, Z) ; read (I)*
(d) *readln (I) ; readln (J) ; readln (K)*
(e) *read (I, c, J, K)*

5.2 Given integer variables *count*, *min* and *max*, and a real variable *mean*, write a sequence of output statements to print their values in the following form:

NUMBER	*RANGE*	*MEAN*
xxx	*xx. .xx*	*xx.x*

5.3 Write a program which reads a sum of money written in the form

ddd.dd

increases it by 8%, and prints out the original and increased sums. Would your program work if the input was in the form

ddd:dd

If not, how would you modify your program?

5.4 Write a program which reads in the cost of an item sold, and the amount of money tendered by the customer, and prints out the following:

AMOUNT DUE	$*xxx.xx*
AMOUNT TENDERED	$*xxx.xx*
CHANGE DUE	$*xxx.xx*

6

Basic Control Structures

The basic power of a computer lies in its ability to carry out sequential, repetitive, and selective actions at great speed. PASCAL provides for the expression of such actions by a variety of *structured-statements*

> *structured-statement = compound-statement |*
> *repetitive-statement |*
> *conditional-statement |*
> *with-statement .*

The *with-statement* is a special purpose construct whose use we will not consider further at this stage, but the remaining structured statements will all be explained in this chapter.

COMPOUND STATEMENTS

A *compound-statement* has the form

> *compound-statement = "begin" statement-sequence "end" .*
>
> *statement-sequence = statement { ";" statement } .*

i.e., it consists of a sequence of *statements* separated by semicolons, preceded by **begin**, and followed by **end**. Execution of a *compound-statement* simply involves the execution of its component statements in the order in which they are written.

For example,

> **begin** $a := b$; $b := c$; $c := a$ **end**

is a compound statement consisting of three assignment statements. We have already seen examples of compound statements in the example programs of previous chapters—the *statement-part* of each PASCAL program is itself a compound statement.

Figure 6.1 shows the sequence of actions resulting from a compound statement

> **begin** $S1$; $S2$; $S3$ **end**

in the form of a flow diagram. Although we shall use flow diagrams in this chapter to show the flow of control which PASCAL's structured statements imply we do not recommend their use as a tool for program design as they permit an undisciplined approach to program construction.

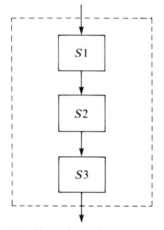

Fig. 6.1 Execution of a compound statement.

The significant role of the compound statement brackets **begin** and **end** is to reduce the enclosed sequence of statements to a single syntactic statement. Thus the *statement-part* of a program is syntactically a single statement. More commonly the brackets are used to place the enclosed sequence of statements under the control of one of PASCAL's repetitive or conditional statements, as we shall see in the following sections.

Within the compound statement the semi-colon acts as a statement separator. Thus the final statement need not be followed by a semi-colon. If it is, then the existence of a null or "empty" statement immediately before the **end** symbol is assumed. An *empty-statement* is a statement consisting of no symbols and having no effect. Thus

> **begin** $a:=b$; ; $b:=c$; $c:=a$; **end**

is a valid compound statement, consisting of an assignment statement, an empty statement, two more assignment statements, and a final empty statement.

REPETITIVE STATEMENTS

An important class of action in computer programs is the *loop*, which enables the repetition of some statement, or group of statements, subject normally to some terminating condition.

PASCAL provides three repetition constructs which reflect the needs of loop construction in most programming situations, viz.,

$$repetitive\text{-}statement \;=\; while\text{-}statement \;|$$
$$repeat\text{-}statement \;|$$
$$for\text{-}statement \;.$$

The *while-statement*

This has the syntactic form

$$while\text{-}statement \;=\; \textbf{"while"} \; expression \; \textbf{"do"} \; statement \;.$$

The *expression* must produce a value of type *boolean*. The expression is repeatedly evaluated and, while it remains true, the *statement* is executed following expression evaluation. The repetition terminates as soon as the value of the expression becomes false.

The flow of control produced by a statement

while *e* **do** *S*

is thus as shown in Fig. 6.2.

Some examples of while-statements are as follows:

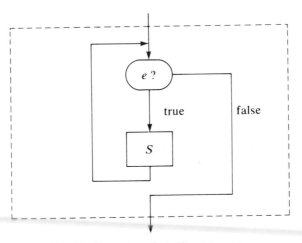

Fig. 6.2 Execution of a while-statement.

(a)   **while** $c=' '$ **do begin** *count*:=*count*+1 ; *read(c)* **end**
(b)   **while** $abs(x-a/x)>1E-6$ **do** $x:=0.5*(x+a/x)$

Note that, if the expression is initially false, the statement is not executed at all. Also, note the use of the compound statement brackets **begin** and **end** in example (a) to put a sequence of statements under the control of the *while-statement*.

The program (1) reads in two positive integers and divides the first integer by the second integer, using only subtraction and addition operations.

> **program** *division* (*input,output*);
> **var** *x,y,quotient,remainder*: 0. .*maxint* ;
> **begin**
>   *read(x,y)*;
>   *remainder*:=*x*; *quotient*:=0;
>   **while** *remainder*>=*y* **do**
>   **begin**   (1)
>   *quotient*:=*quotient*+1 ;
>   *remainder*:=*remainder*−*y*
>   **end**;
>   *writeln* (*x,'   divided by',y,' equals',quotient,*
>   *' ,remainder',remainder*)
> **end**.

The *repeat-statement*

A *repeat-statement* has the form

repeat-statement = "**repeat**" *statement-sequence* "**until**" *expression* .

Once again the *expression* must produce a value of type *boolean*. The action upon execution of a *repeat-statement* is as follows. The sequence of statements between the **repeat** and **until** symbols is executed and the boolean expression is evaluated. If its value is true then the repeat-statement is terminated and execution continues at the next statement of the program, otherwise execution of the *statement-sequence* is repeated until the expression becomes true.

The flow of control resulting from a statement

repeat $S1$; $S2$; ... ; Sn **until** e

is thus as shown in Fig. 6.3.

Some examples of repeat-statements are as follows:

(a)   **repeat** *count*:=*count*+1 ; *read(c)* **until** $c<>' '$
(b)   **repeat** $x:=0.5*(x+a/x)$ **until** $abs(x-a/x)<=1E-6$

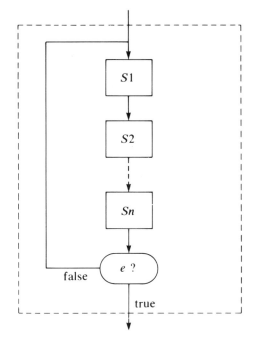

Fig. 6.3 Execution of a repeat statement.

Note that the loop body need not be formed into a *compound-statement* (using **begin** and **end**) since the syntax states that the loop body is the sequence of statements bracketed by the symbols **repeat** and **until**.

The essential difference between repeat- and while-statements is that in the repeat-statement the loop body (i.e., statements to be repeatedly executed) is performed at least once, before the first evaluation of the terminating condition, whereas in the while-statement the terminating condition is evaluated first and so the loop body may not be executed at all. It is sometimes argued that this difference is insufficient to justify two distinct loop constructs and that one, the while-statement, is adequate for both situations. However, besides making explicit the fact that the loop body is executed once, the repeat-statement plays a useful role in avoiding potential programming errors. In repeat loop situations it is often the case that the values of variables contributing to the terminating condition are either indeterminate or positively misleading before the first execution of a loop body. To express the loop using a while-statement the programmer must first arrange some artificial setting of these variables such that the terminating condition is false, a task which is too often done wrongly, or not at all. For example,

     repeat *read*(*ch*) **until** *ch* = '.'

would have to be expressed as

$ch:=';'$; **while** $ch<>'.'$ **do** $read(ch)$

where ch is initially set to some value other than '.' .

The *for-statement*

The while- and repeat-statements are the primary constructs for expressing repetitions in most programming situations. However, the *for-statement* may be used for operations which are to be carried out a pre-determined number of times.

A *for-statement* takes the form

> *for-statement* = "**for**" *variable-identifier* ":=" *initial-expression*
>   ("**to**" | "**downto**") *final-expression* "**do**" *statement* .
> *initial-expression* = *expression* .
> *final-expression* = *expression* .

The *variable-identifier* is known as the *control variable* and must be declared as a variable of some ordinal type in the block immediately containing the for-statement. The *initial-expression* and *final-expression* must yield values of the same ordinal type as the control variable.

The initial and final values determine an ascending succession of values (if **to** is used) or a descending succession of values (in the **downto** case). The action of the *for-statement* is to assign each value to the control variable in turn and execute the statement following **do** after each assignment. If the initial value is greater than the final value in the case of **to**, or less than the final value in the case of **downto**, the statement is not executed at all.

In interpreting this definition the following points should be noted:

(a)   The initial and the final values determined by the initial expression and final expression are evaluated once only, on entry to the *for-statement*. They are not re-evaluated on each cycle, and changes during the repetitive execution in the values of any variables involved in these expressions do not in any way affect the sequence of values assigned to the control variable.

(b)   The value of the control variable is changed implicitly by each cycle of the repetition and no action to change its value may appear within the body of the *for*-loop, or within any procedure or function (see ch. 7) that *could* be called from the body.

(c)   After completion of a *for-statement* the value of the control variable is not defined, and programs should not make any assumption as to its value.

Examples:

1. **for** $i:=$ *lineswritten* **to** *pagesize* **do** *writeln*
2. **for** $j:=$ *m* **downto** *n* **do** *writeln(j,j*j*j)*
3. **for** *day:=* *monday* **to** *friday* **do**
   begin
       read(hoursworked); *totalhours:= totalhours+hoursworked*
   end

The four programs (2)–(5) perform similar actions in that each reads in a series of positive integers and computes their sum, but, due to the slightly different conditions in each case, a different repetitive structure is used.

(a) For (2), the length of the sequence is unknown but the last integer is followed by a negative integer. It is possible that there are no integers in the positive sequence.

```
program sum 1 (input,output);
var i,sum : integer;
begin
    sum:=0; read(i);
    while i>=0 do begin                        (2)
                    sum:=sum+i;
                    read(i)
                end;
    writeln(sum)
end.
```

(b) For (3) the same conditions hold as for (2), except that it is guaranteed that there is at least one positive integer in the sequence.

```
program sum2 (input,output);
var i,sum : integer;
begin
    sum:=0; read(i);
    repeat                                     (3)
        sum:=sum+i;
        read(i)
    until i<0;
    writeln(sum)
end.
```

(c) For (4), the sequence is preceded by an integer specifying the number of integers in the sequence.

```
program sum3 (input,output);
var length,k,i,sum : integer;
begin
    read(length); sum:=0;
    for k:= 1 to length do
    begin                                              (4)
        read(i); sum:=sum+i
    end;
    writeln(sum)
end.
```

(d) For (5), the sequence consists of one integer on each input line. Use
     of *readln* to read each value allows the function *eof* to be used to
     detect the end of the input sequence. Note that *eof* cannot other-
     wise be used during numeric input as the end-of-file condition is not
     established until the blanks trailing the last number have been read.

```
program sum4 (input, output);
var i, sum : integer ;
begin
    sum := 0 ;
    while not eof (input) do
    begin                                              (5)
        readln (i) ;
        sum := sum + i
    end ;
    writeln (sum)
end.
```

The statement(s) controlled by a repetitive statement may be any of
the allowable statement forms defined at the start of this chapter. In
particular, the body of the repetitive statement may itself contain
another repetitive statement, in which case the repetitive statements are
said to be *nested*. This nesting of repetitive statements is illustrated in
(6), which reads an integer *n* and calculates the sum of the series

$$1^1 + 2^2 + 3^3 + \cdots + n^n .$$

```
program sumofpowers (input,output);
var n,x,power,i,sum : 0..maxint ;
begin
    read(n); sum:=0;
    for x := 1 to n do
```

```
    begin                                                          (6)
        power:=1; for i:= 1 to x do power:=power*x;
        sum:= sum + power
    end;
    writeln(sum)
end.
```

As a second example of the nesting of loops, consider (7), which reads the contents of the input stream and outputs them with the line structure of the input preserved.

```
program copy (input, output) ;
var c : char ;
begin
    while not eof (input) do
    begin {copy a line}
        while not eoln (input) do                                  (7)
        begin
            read (c) ; write (c)
        end ;
        readln ; writeln
    end
end.
```

PROGRAM 2   (Tabulating examination marks)

A class consists of 50 students, each of whom studies 5 subjects. The grades obtained by each student in each subject are input to a computer, as one line of input per student. Each line consists of the student's name, which is not more than 30 characters long and terminated by a period, followed by five grade numbers in the range 0 to 10, separated by spaces; e.g.

MARY SMITH. 7 7 10 6 4
HOWARD BLACKBURN. 4 7 5 4 5

A program is required to read this input and tabulate the students' overall performance in a table which shows each student's name, his overall total grade in a vertically aligned column, and a horizontal bar measure of this overall performance. For example, the above inputs might produce outputs:

MARY SMITH.   34   **************
HOWARD BLACKBURN.   25   **********

The program clearly has an overall structure of a loop which is executed once for each student:

for *student* := 1 **to** 50 **do**
        read and print data on one student

The process *read and print data on one student* can be broken down into a sequence of simpler steps, as in (8).

begin
    read and print name ;
    read and print grades ;   (8)
    align input, output for next student
end

The action *read and print name* is apparently a simple character-by-character read and print loop which terminates on a period, as in (9).

repeat
    read (*nextchar*) ;
    write (*nextchar*)   (9)
until *nextchar* = '.'

The action *read and print grades* can be broken into the sequence (10).

read and total grades ;
print total grade ;   (10)
print bar measure

Then *read and total grades* can be written as in (11).

total := 0 ;
for *subject* := 1 **to** 5 **do**
begin
    read (*grade*) ;   (11)
    total := *total* + *grade*
end

However, to print the grade total at an aligned column position we must know how many print positions have been used by the student's name. We therefore amend the *read and print name* loop to print sufficient spaces to bring the total number of characters output up to 30, as shown in (12).

```
    namelength := 0 ;
    repeat
        read (nextchar) ;
        write (nextchar) ;                                          (12)
        namelength := namelength + 1
    until nextchar = '.' ;
    while namelength<30 do
    begin write (' ') ; namelength := namelength+1 end
```

Thus, to print the total with its final digit in the 40th print position we write

write (total : 10)

To print a bar measure of the student's performance simply involves printing a sequence of identical characters, '*', say, where the length of the sequence is proportional to the grade total achieved. Since the raw grade total may vary from 0 to 50 we scale this down by a factor of 2/5 to give a more convenient printed line length. For visual clarity the first '*' of the bar is separated from the preceding grade total by two blank characters. Printing the bar measure can therefore be programmed as

```
write ('    ') ;
for star := 1 to round (0.4*total) do write ('*')
```

Finally, re-aligning the input and output position for the next student involves:

readln ; writeln

We can now assemble the various program fragments into a final program, with suitable declarations of the variables introduced. The resultant program, and a sample of the output it produces, is shown in Listing 2.

LISTING 2

PROGRAM GRADES (INPUT,OUTPUT) ;

```
VAR  STUDENT : 1..50 ;
     NAMELENGTH : 0..30 ;
     NEXTCHAR : CHAR ;
     TOTAL : 0..50 ;
     SUBJECT : 1..5 ;
     GRADE : 0..10 ;
     STAR : 0..20 ;
```

```
BEGIN
   FOR STUDENT := 1 TO 50 DO
   BEGIN
     (* READ AND PRINT NAME *)
     NAMELENGTH:=0;
     REPEAT
        READ (NEXTCHAR) ;
        WRITE (NEXTCHAR) ;
        NAMELENGTH := NAMELENGTH+1
     UNTIL NEXTCHAR = '.' ;
     WHILE NAMELENGTH<30 DO
     BEGIN WRITE (' ') ; NAMELENGTH := NAMELENGTH + 1 END ;
     (* READ AND PRINT GRADES *)
        (* READ AND TOTAL GRADES *)
     TOTAL := 0;
     FOR SUBJECT := 1 TO 5 DO
     BEGIN
        READ (GRADE) ;
        TOTAL := TOTAL+GRADE
     END;
        (* PRINT TOTAL IN ALIGNED POSITION *)
     WRITE (TOTAL:10) ;
     '  (* PRINT BAR MEASURE *)
     WRITE (' ') ;
     FOR STAR := 1 TO ROUND (0.4*TOTAL) DO WRITE ('*') ;
     (* ALIGN INPUT AND OUTPUT *)
     READLN ; WRITELN
   END
END.
```

```
ALAN LEWIN.                          22  *********
BETTY CALLAGHAN.                     19  ********
CHRIS FARMER.                        17  *******
DEBORAH HIBBETT.                     20  ********
ERNEST ATKINS.                       28  ***********
FRANCES WEST.                        30  ************
GRAHAM BARTLETT.                     17  *******
DAVID ANDERSON.                      29  ************
BRIAN REITH.                         31  ************
JACQUELINE HARRISON.                 27  ***********
KENNETH LAMB.                        17  *******
CRAIG RICHARDS.                      19  ********
JOHN BANKS.                          18  *******
STEPHEN STEWART.                     25  **********
WILLIAM JONES.                       27  ***********
ANNE SMITH.                          29  ************
ELAINE PASCOE.                       18  *******
STEPHANIE OLD.                       22  *********
```

CONDITIONAL STATEMENTS

It is often necessary to make the execution of a statement dependent upon some condition, or else at some point to choose to execute one of a number of possible statements depending upon some condition. PAS-CAL provides two statement forms for this purpose

  conditional-statement = *if-statement* | *case-statement* .

If-statements

The *if-statement* allows the conditional execution of one statement, or the choice between execution of two statements. It takes one of two corresponding forms

  if-statement = "**if**" *expression* "**then**" *statement* ["**else**" *statement*] .

In either form the expression must produce a boolean result.

The action of the shorter form is to evaluate the *expression* and, if and only if its value is *true*, to execute the *statement*. In either case execution then continues at the statement following the *if-statement*.

In the longer form the boolean *expression* is evaluated and if its value is *true* then the first *statement* (i.e., the statement following **then**) is executed, otherwise the second *statement* (i.e., the statement following **else**) is executed. Once again, in either case execution continues at the statement following the *if-statement*. These control structures are illustrated in Fig. 6.4.

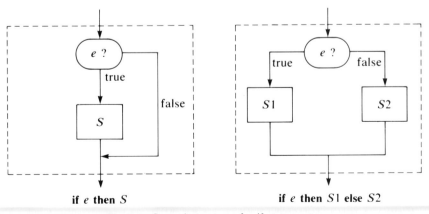

if *e* then *S*   if *e* then *S*1 else *S*2

Fig. 6.4 Control structures for if-statements.

With the **else** form care must be taken to ensure that a semi-colon is not placed before the **else** as this would imply that the *if-statement* as a whole terminated there, i.e.,

> **if** *e* **then** *S*1 ; **else** *S*2

which is an error since "**else** *S*2" is not a legal PASCAL statement.
Some examples of *if-statements* are shown in (13)–(16).

> **if** *ch* = '?' **then** *query*: = *true*   (13)

> **if** *eof(input)* **then** *writeln('data all read')* **else** *read(ch)*   (14)

> **if** *thismonth* = *Dec*
> **then begin** *thismonth*: = *Jan*; *thisyear*: = *thisyear* + 1 **end**   (15)
> **else** *thismonth*: = *succ(thismonth)*

> **if** *sqr(b)* < 4 ∗ *a* ∗ *c* **then** *write('quadratic has complex roots')*
>   **else begin**
>   *d*: = *sqrt(sqr(b)−4∗a∗c)*;   (16)
>   *writeln* ((−*b*+*d*)/(2∗*a*) , (−*b*−*d*)/(2∗*a*))
>   **end**

Note that a sequence of statements to be brought under the control of an *if-statement* must be grouped into a single statement by using **begin** and **end** brackets to form a *compound-statement*.

The program shown in (17) reads in two positive integers and calculates their greatest common divisor.

> **program** *greatestcommondivisor* (*input,output*);
> **var** *a,b* : 1..*maxint* ;
> **begin**
>   *read(a,b)*;
>   **while** *a* < > *b* **do**   (17)
>   **if** *a* > *b* **then** *a*: = *a* − *b*
>   **else** *b*: = *b*−*a* ;
>   *writeln(a)*
> **end**.

The statement(s) whose execution is controlled by an *if-statement* may include further *if-statements* to form more complex conditional statements. In this case the statements are said to be *nested*, e.g.,

> **if** *x* < 0 **then** *sign*: = *true* **else**
> **if** *x* > 0 **then** *sign*: = *false* **else** *write('value is zero')*

A nested *if-statement* of the form

    if $e1$ **then if** $e2$ **then** $S1$ **else** $S2$

may appear ambiguous in that it is not clear whether execution of $S2$ is controlled by the value of $e1$ or by the value of $e2$. To resolve this ambiguity this construction is considered to be equivalent to

    if $e1$ **then**
    begin *if* $e2$ **then** $S1$ **else** $S2$ **end**

Thus, execution of $S2$ is dependent upon the value of $e2$. If it is required to make execution of $S2$ dependent instead upon the value of $e1$ then it is necessary to write

    if $e1$ **then begin if** $e2$ **then** $S1$ **end**
        else $S2$

The program of (18) reads an integer value (assumed to be positive and less than 100) and outputs one of the following messages:

(a)   the word *'buzz'* if the value contains the digit 7, otherwise
(b)   the word *'buzz-buzz'* if the value is a multiple of 7, otherwise
(c)   the value itself.

```
program buzzbuzz (input,output);
var i : 1..100;
begin
    read(i);                                                    (18)
    if (i div 10 = 7) or (i mod 10 = 7)
    then writeln ('buzz')
    else if i mod 7 = 0 then writeln('buzz-buzz') else writeln(i)
end.
```

PROGRAM 3   (Analyzing a triangle)

A program is required which reads in three positive integers, in ascending order, which are assumed to represent the lengths of the sides of a triangle, and prints out these input data, one of the following descriptions of the nature of the triangle defined:

    not a triangle
    an equilateral triangle
    an isosceles triangle
    a scalene triangle,

together with the area of the triangle (when appropriate).

In outline the required program can be broken into two steps:

> **begin**
>   *read in and print out the lengths of the sides* ;
>   *determine and print the details of the triangle*
> **end**

The step *read in and print out the lengths of the sides* is immediately expressible as *read* and *write* statements using three integer variables *a*,*b*,*c* to represent the lengths of the three sides in ascending order.

The step *determine and print details of the triangle* can first be broken down as

> **if** *it is a triangle*
> **then** *determine and print its nature and area*
> **else** *write('not a triangle')*

Three lines can form a triangle if and only if the length of the longest line is less than the sum of the lengths of the two shorter lines. Since *a*,*b*,*c* represent the sides in ascending order of length the condition *it is a triangle* is immediately expressible as

$$a+b>c$$

Determining the nature of the triangle is also readily expressible in terms of these ordered lengths, thus:

> **if** $a = c$ **then** *triangle is equilateral* **else**
> **if** $(a = b)$ **or** $(b = c)$ **then** *triangle is isosceles* **else** *triangle is scalene*

The area of a triangle of sides *a*,*b*,*c* is given by the formula

$$area = \sqrt{s(s-a)(s-b)(s-c)}$$

where s is half the sum of the sides *a*,*b*,*c* and so this too is easily programmed using real values for s and the area to allow for the possible fractional parts.

We can thus construct the final program, which is shown in Listing 3, together with a sample of the output produced.

The *case-statement*

One complex selection pattern which occurs frequently in programming, and so deserves special consideration, is the *selection* of one of a set of actions according to the value of some expression. This could be

```
                    LISTING 3

PROGRAM TRIANGLES (INPUT,OUTPUT);

VAR    A, B, C : 1..MAXINT ;
       S,AREA : REAL;

BEGIN

    (* READ AND PRINT SIDES IN ASCENDING ORDER *)

    READ (A,B,C) ;
    WRITE (A,B,C,'....') ;
    IF A+B>C
    THEN BEGIN

          (* DETERMINE NATURE OF TRIANGLE *)

          IF A=C
          THEN WRITE ('AN EQUILATERAL TRIANGLE')
          ELSE IF (A=B) OR (B=C) THEN WRITE ('AN ISOSCELES TRIANGLE')
                                 ELSE WRITE ('A SCALENE TRIANGLE') ;

          (* DETERMINE AREA *)

          S := 0.5*(A+B+C) ;
          AREA := SQRT (S*(S-A)*(S-B)*(S-C)) ;
          WRITELN (' OF AREA', AREA:8:2)
       END
    ELSE WRITELN ('NOT A TRIANGLE')
END.
```

```
    7       7       9....AN ISOSCELES TRIANGLE OF AREA   24.13
```

expressed as a nested *if-statement*, e.g.,

if $ch = 'I'$ **then** $n := 1$ **else**
if $ch = 'V'$ **then** $n := 5$ **else**
if $ch = 'X'$ **then** $n := 10$ **else**
if $ch = 'L'$ **then** $n := 50$

A more elegant way of expressing such an action in PASCAL is to use the *case-statement*, which has the following syntax:

case-statement = "**case**" *expression* "**of**" *caselimb* { ";" *caselimb* }
[";"] "**end**".
caselimb = *case-label-list* ":" *statement*.
case-label-list = *constant* { "," *constant* } .

The *expression* following *case* is known as the *selector*, and must yield a value of an ordinal type. The constants which prefix the *statement* in each *caselimb* are known as *case labels,* and must be of the same unstructured type as the selector.

The action of a *case-statement* is to evaluate the selector *expression* and then execute the *statement* labeled by the resulting value. After this, execution proceeds to the statement which follows the *case-statement.* If there is no *case-label* corresponding to the selector value an error occurs.

Figure 6.5 shows the general form of a *case-statement* and the resultant control structure.

case *e* **of**
c 1   : *S*1;
c 2,*c* 3 : *S*2;
c 7   :   ;
c 5   : *S*3
end

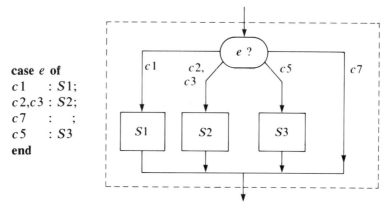

Fig. 6.5 Case-statement structures.

The statement at the start of this sub-section can now be re-written as in (19).

case *ch* **of**
'*I*' : *n* := 1 ;
'*V*': *n* := 5 ;
'*X*': *n* := 10 ;   (19)
'*L*' : *n* := 50
end

Note that two or more case labels may be associated with the same statement, in which case they are separated by commas (and need not be written in any particular order), e.g.,

4,7,2,1,15 : *x*:=*y*+2

The order of the labeled statements within a case-statement is also irrelevant. Each value which may be taken by the selector expression must appear once and once only as a label in the *case-statement.* If no action is to be taken with certain values then they should be associated with an empty statement.

The program in (20) simulates the action of a pocket calculator. It reads in a sequence of numeric values separated by arithmetic operators $(+,-,/,*)$ and calculates the value of the expression defined by this sequence. The result of the calculation is output when the operator $'='$ is read. Thus, input of $7+5*3/8=$ produces output of 4.5000.

```
program pocketcalculator (input,output);
var  result,value : real;
     operator : char;
begin
     read(result) ;
     read(operator) ;
     while operator <> '=' do
     begin
          read(value) ;
          case operator of                                    (20)
          '+' : result:=result+value ;
          '-' : result:=result-value ;
          '*' : result:=result*value ;
          '/' : result:=result/value
          end;
          read(operator)
     end ;
     writeln(result:12:4)
end.
```

PROGRAM 4   (Calculating tomorrow's date)

Construct a program which, given three integers whose values represent a day between 1 January, 1900 and 31 December, 1999, will output the values representing the day following.

The input data consist of three integers representing the month, day of month, and year of a date, e.g., 12 2 1978 represents the 2nd of December, 1978. The outline structure of the program is given in (21).

```
begin
     read date ; output date ;
     update date to following day ;                           (21)
     output date
end.
```

The date can be represented by three variables

month ,   a variable of the subrange type   1..12 ;
day ,   a variable of the subrange type   1..31 ;
year ,   a variable of the subrange type   1900..2000.

The *read date* operation is simply programmed as

read (month,day,year)

The output of this date might be in the form

write ('the day following', month:3, '/', day:2, '/', year:4)

Expressing the updating operation abstractly as

if *lastdayofmonth*
then *firstdayofnextmonth*
else *nextdayofthismonth*

we need, first of all, to find the number of days in the month denoted by the value of *month*. Introducing a variable *daysinmonth* this can be computed using a case-statement.

case *month* **of**
1,3,5,7,8,10,12 : *daysinmonth*:=31 ;
4,6,9,11 : *daysinmonth*:=30 ;
2 : **if** (*year* **mod** 4 = 0) **and** (*year*<>1900)
    then *daysinmonth*:=29
    else *daysinmonth*:=28
end

The updating operation then becomes

if *day*=*daysinmonth* **then**
begin
    day:=1 ;
    if *month*=12 **then begin** *month*:=1; *year*:=*year*+1 **end**
                    else *month*:=*month*+1
end else *day*:=*day*+1

The output of the new date is by

writeln ('is', month:3, '/', day:2, '/', year:4)

The resultant program and a sample of the output which it produces is shown as Listing 4.

LISTING 4

```
PROGRAM NEXTDAY (INPUT,OUTPUT) ;

VAR  DAY : 1..31 ;
     MONTH : 1..12 ;
     YEAR : 1900..2000 ;
     DAYSINMONTH : 28..31 ;

BEGIN
   READ (MONTH,DAY,YEAR) ;
   WRITE ('THE DAY FOLLOWING', MONTH:3, '/', DAY:2, '/', YEAR:4) ;

   (* FIND NUMBER OF DAYS IN MONTH *)

   CASE MONTH OF
      1,3,5,7,8,10,12 : DAYSINMONTH:=31;
      4,6,9,11 : DAYSINMONTH:=30;
      2 : IF (YEAR MOD 4 = 0) AND (YEAR<>1900)
          THEN DAYSINMONTH:=29
          ELSE DAYSINMONTH:=28
   END ;

   (* UPDATE *)

   IF DAY=DAYSINMONTH THEN
   BEGIN
      DAY:=1 ;
      IF MONTH=12 THEN BEGIN MONTH:=1; YEAR:=YEAR+1 END
                  ELSE MONTH:=MONTH+1
   END ELSE DAY:=DAY+1 ;
   WRITELN (' IS', MONTH:3, '/', DAY:2, '/', YEAR:4)
END.
```

```
THE DAY FOLLOWING 12/31/1978 IS  1/ 1/1979
```

EXERCISES

6.1 Write a program which reads a positive integer N and tabulates the factorials of the numbers from 1 to N in the form

I		1	2	3	4	$\cdots$	N
FACTORIAL (I)	1	2	6	24		$\cdots$	

{ *factorial* $(i) = 1*2*3*\cdots*(i-1)*i$ }

Rewrite your program to tabulate all the factorials less than the maximum integer value allowed by your implementation of PASCAL (i.e., *maxint*).

6.2   A building society lends money to house purchasers subject to a monthly payment of one per cent of the amount borrowed. This payment covers both capital repayment and interest due, interest being charged at a rate of eight per cent per annum, calculated monthly. Write a program which reads in the amount of a loan, and tabulates the series of payments required, as a four column table showing the payment number, the interest due that month, the capital repayment that month, and the outstanding capital balance. The table should also show the final non-standard payment required to complete the repayment.

6.3   Write a program to print out the digit pyramid in Fig. 6.6.

1
121
12321
1234321
123454321
12345654321
1234567654321
123456787654321
12345678987654321

Fig. 6.6

6.4   (a)   Modify Program 1 so that, if the expected time of arrival is not on the same day as the take-off, the output takes the following form :

> *EXPECTED TIME OF ARRIVAL = hh/mm/ss ON DAY PLUS d*

If the arrival is on the same day as take-off the output should be as before.

  (b)   Make a further modification such that, if the arrival is on the day following take-off, the output has the form

> *EXPECTED TIME OF ARRIVAL = hh/mm/ss NEXT DAY*

6.5   Some letters are drawn with straight lines only, e.g., A,E,F,H, ... while others require curves, e.g., B,C,D,G, ... Write a program which reads and prints a line of text, replacing all letters requiring curves with an asterisk. Write the program using

  (a)   an if-statement;
  (b)   a case-statement.

6.6   Write a program to read and print an input text, and determine the number of lines, sentences, and words involved. You may assume

  (a)   that each sentence ends with a period, and that the period character is not used for any other purpose;
  (b)   words consist solely of letters.

7

Procedures and Functions

THE PROCEDURE CONCEPT

The method used in the construction of case-study programs in this book is to take the initial problem and break it down into a series of simpler problems. This break-down of the problem is expressed using a combination of PASCAL structured statements and natural English. For instance, at an early stage of its development Program 2 was expressed as:

for *student* := 1 **to** 50 **do**
    read and print data on one student

with the process *read and print data on one student* subsequently being refined as a compound-statement involving a sequence of simpler steps, as in (1).

for *student* := 1 **to** 50 **do**
begin
    read and print name ;
    read and print grades ;   (1)
    align input, output for next student
end.

Each of the three sub-problems in the compound-statement (1) was then refined in terms of further sub-problems or, if possible, expressed directly in PASCAL itself. Eventually this stepwise refinement process led to a situation in which all parts of the program design were expressed fully in PASCAL.

When we design larger and more complex programs this approach becomes of even greater value. However, the actions isolated in the early levels of the refinement process may themselves go through many further levels of refinement before developing into large and complicated sequences of PASCAL, each of which covers many lines, or even pages, of the program. When one comes to read the program the sheer length of the text makes the structure of the program difficult to appreciate—using the PASCAL facilities described so far the only method of incorporating the levels of refinement explicitly within the final program is by the use of comments. What we need is a means of textually dividing the program into units corresponding to the significant sub-problems identified during the construction, and expressing the program's overall action by a short sequence of text which refers to these units. This would assist the reader in observing more clearly the design of the program and thus make it easier for him not only to understand the program but also to make any changes that are required.

PASCAL, in common with most programming languages, provides a facility for the description of programs in this way. The programmer may define an action or group of actions in the form of a *procedure*, to which he gives a name, known as the *procedure-identifier*. This procedure may then be invoked from another point in his program by means of a *procedure-statement* naming the *procedure-identifier*.

The syntax of a *procedure-statement* is

> *procedure-statement = procedure-identifier*
> > [*actual-parameter-list*] .
> *procedure-identifier = identifier* .

For the moment we shall deal only with the simplest form of *procedure-statement*, i.e., an identifier. A *procedure-statement* is said to *call* the procedure named by the identifier. Its effect is to execute the actions defined by that procedure (and then to continue to execute the statement immediately following the *procedure-statement*).

A *procedure-statement* is one of the allowed forms of a *simple-statement* defined in Chap. 4 and therefore can be used anywhere that it is legal to use a statement. We can thus retain the above refinement of Program 2 as an active part of the final program itself by writing it as in (2). In (2), *readandprintname*, *readandprintgrades* and *aligninputand-output* are now *procedure statements* and the procedures defining the required actions are declared elsewhere in the program.

```
begin
    forstudent := 1 to 50 do
    begin
        readandprintname ;
        readandprintgrades ;                           (2)
        aligninputandoutput
    end
end.
```

The declaration of a *procedure* takes the form shown in (3). That is, a *procedure-declaration* consists of a *procedure-heading* and a *procedure-body* separated by a semi-colon. The essential role of the *procedure-heading* is to associate a name or identifier with the *procedure* being declared. The purpose and use of a *formal-parameter-list* are discussed later in this chapter.

procedure-declaration = *procedure-heading* ";" *procedure-body* .
procedure-heading = "**procedure**" *identifier*
$$[formal\text{-}parameter\text{-}list] . \qquad (3)$$
procedure-body = *block* .

The action of the *procedure* is defined by the *procedure-body*, which takes the form of a *block*. As we saw in Chap. 2 a block may begin with a non-empty declaration part but its essential component is a statement part, thus

block = *declaration-part statement-part* .

Just as the *statement-part* of the program block defines the action of the program, the *statement-part* of a procedure block defines the action of that procedure, i.e., the action to be carried out each time the procedure is called. Thus we may declare the procedure *readandprintname* as in (4). Note that the *while-statement* in Program 2 which printed the spaces following the name may now be replaced by an *if-statement*. The other two procedures required by Program 2 can be declared in a similar manner.

```
procedure readandprintname ;
var nextchar : char ;
    namelength : 0 . . 30 ;
begin
    namelength := 0 ;
    repeat                                          (4)
        read (nextchar) ;
        write (nextchar) ;
        namelength := namelength + 1
    until nextchar = '.' ;
    if namelength<30 then write (' ':30−namelength)
end ;
```

Procedure declarations in PASCAL are grouped to form a *procedure-and-function-declaration-part* which, as we saw in Chap. 2, is the final component of the *declaration-part*. Its form is defined as in (5). That is, the *procedure-and-function-declaration-part* consists of zero or more *procedure* or *function-declarations* terminated by semi-colons (the declaration and use of functions are discussed later in this chapter).

procedure-and-function-declaration-part =
  { (procedure-declaration | function-declaration) ";" } .   (5)

Thus, in Program 2 re-written with procedures, the three procedures are declared between the remaining variable declaration and the revised statement part, as in (6). The repositioning of the other variable declarations is discussed in the next section.

```
program grades (input, output) ;
var student : 1 .. 50 ;
      procedure readandprintname ;
      var nextchar : char ;
          namelength : 0 .. 30 ;
      begin
          namelength := 0 ;
          repeat
              read (nextchar) ;
              write (nextchar) ;
              namelength := namelength + 1
          until nextchar = '.' ;
          if namelength <30 then write (' ':30−namelength)
      end ;

      procedure readandprintgrades ;                    (6)
      var subject : 1 .. 5 ;
          grade : 0 .. 10 ;
          total : 0 .. 50 ;
          star : 1 .. 20 ;
      begin
          { read and total grades }
          total := 0 ;
          for subject := 1 to 5 do
          begin
              read (grade) ;
              total := total + grade
          end ;
          { print total grade }
          write (total : 10) ;
          { print bar measure }
          write (' ') ;
          for star := 1 to round (0.4*total) do write ('*')
      end ;
```

```
    procedure aligninputandoutput ;
    begin
        readln ; writeln
    end ;

    begin
        for student := 1 to 50 do                          (6 cont.)
        begin
            readandprintname ;
            readandprintgrades ;
            aligninputandoutput
        end
    end.
```

In this revised program the statement-part shows explicitly the overall structure conceived for the program—that of a loop whose body involves a sequence of three subsidiary actions—while the procedure declarations give the details of how each of these actions is to be carried out. In this example some of these actions are trivial and their expression as procedures may seem extravagant. However, the example shows clearly how, in a larger and more complex program, the significant levels of refinement of the program's actions may be expressed as short sequences of statements including procedure calls. The further refinements of the actions which these statements invoke are textually separated from the statements themselves, and from each other, as an appropriate set of procedure declarations.

The declaration of a procedure does not cause its body or statement part to be executed—this is only caused by the execution of a corresponding *procedure-statement*, or *call*. In our example above, each procedure had exactly one calling statement but this is not necessarily so—two or more independent statements calling the same procedure may be used in a program. To illustrate this let us reconsider the program *buzzbuzz* given in Chap. 6. Let us amend the program so that it will read in an integer n $(0 < n < 100)$ and produce as output the sequence of integers n, $n+1$, $n+2$, ... interspersed with the words *buzz* and *buzz-buzz*, as before. On reaching 100 the sequence should continue cyclically at 1 and on reaching $n-1$ the program should stop. This can be achieved quite simply by the use of a procedure, as in (7).

In this case the use of two **for**-loops expresses, simply and clearly, the control required to generate the appropriate sequences of values for i. Each loop body applies the same action to the current value of i and is therefore expressed as a call to the common procedure *writebuzz*.

To use the same control structure without a procedure in this case would involve writing two copies of the procedure body—one for each

```
program buzzbuzz (input, output) ;
var i, n : 1 .. 99 ;
    procedure writebuzz ;
    begin
        if (i div 10 = 7) or (i mod 10 = 7)
        then writeln ('buzz')
        else if i mod 7 = 0 then writeln('buzz-buzz')
        else writeln(i)                                        (7)
    end ;

begin
    read (n) ;
    for i:= n to 99 do writebuzz ;
    for i:= 1 to n-1 do writebuzz
end .
```

for-loop. Using a procedure thus reduces the overall length of the final program text. In general when a procedure is called from two or more distinct points within a program there is a net reduction in the length of the program text compared with the same program written without procedures. This reduction in the textual length of the program is normally reflected by a corresponding reduction in the size of the executable program held within the computer. Use of a procedure which is called from two or more points in the program has a threefold economic advantage in that it reduces

(a)   the programming task as measured by the textual length of the program,
(b)   the area for potential programming error,
(c)   the size of the resultant executable program.

These savings have been the primary motivation for the inclusion of procedures in many languages.

Conversely it may be argued that the use of a procedure which is only called at one point in a program increases the length of the program text—by the overhead of the extra symbols involved in the procedure declaration and procedure statement. It is also true that a corresponding overhead is normally introduced into the resultant executable program—both in its size and in the time which it takes to execute its task. These overheads must be balanced against the increased clarity, and the consequent decreased probability of programming errors, which the introduction of a procedure brings about. In most programming situations the latter advantages far outweigh the overheads involved. In the remainder of this book procedures are used freely, both to emphasize the perceived program structure, and to share a common action between two or more program points, where appropriate.

BLOCK STRUCTURE AND SCOPE

In rewriting Program 2 as in (6), the declarations of variables used in each procedure have been located in that procedure – in general the syntactic definition of a *procedure-body* as a *block* allows us to declare data inside a procedure. Indeed, not only can we declare constants, types and variables, but also procedures.

Any identifiers introduced within the declaration part of a block to represent constants, types, variables and procedures are said to be *local* to the block. The block is the only part of the program in which these identifiers may be referenced and is known as the *scope* of the identifiers. For instance, suppose we declare a variable a within a procedure P, as in (8). Then the variable a may only be referenced in the body of procedure $P—a$ is said to be a *local variable* of the procedure P, and is unknown outside the procedure.

> **procedure** P ;
> **var** a : *integer* ;
> **begin**   (8)
> ⋮
> **end**

However, identifiers declared outside a block, i.e., in the declaration part of the enclosing block, are known and may be referenced inside the enclosed block. Such identifiers are said to be *non-local*, or *global*, to the enclosed block. For example, in (9) the variable b may be referenced inside the procedure P, and is said to be a *non-local* or *global variable* of the procedure P.

> **var** b : *integer* ;
> **procedure** P ;
> **begin**   (9)
> ⋮
> **end**

Consider again the revision of Program 2 given on pages 84 and 85. The variables *nextchar* and *namelength* are used only within the procedure *readandprintname* and may be declared local to that procedure. Likewise the variables *total, subject, grade* and *star* may be declared local to procedure *readandprintgrades.* The variable *student* is used by the statement part of the program itself and must therefore be declared in the program block. This means that *student* could be referenced as a global variable by any of the procedures, though none in fact does so.

This use of local declarations has three significant advantages:

(a)   it makes explicitly clear that the variables *nextchar, namelength, total, subject, grade* and *star* are significant only within the procedures in which they are declared, a considerable simplification for a reader of the program;
(b)   it ensures that certain errors involving inadvertent use of these variables by other parts of the program are immediately detected by the compiler;
(c)   as we shall see, it helps the implementation to minimize the storage used by variable data.

In the examples which we have used so far we have only used procedures declared in the declaration part of the program block itself. In principle, however, each procedure body is itself a block, whose declaration part may contain further procedure declarations and hence further blocks. A procedure declared within another procedure is said to be *nested.* For example, in refining the procedure *readandprintgrades* in Program 2 we might have introduced further procedures as in (11).

```
procedure readandprintgrades ;
var total : 0 . . 50 ;
    procedure readandtotalgrades;
    var subject : 1 . . 5 ;
        grade : 0 . . 10 ;
    begin
        total := 0 ;
        for subject := 1 to 5 do
        begin                                              (11)
            read (grade) ;
            total := total + grade
        end

    end ;
    procedure printtotalgrade ;
    begin
        write (total : 10)
    end ;
```

```
        procedure printbarmeasure ;
        var star : 1 . . 20 ;
        begin
            write ('      ') ;
            for star := 1 to round (0.4*total) do write ('*')     (11 cont.)
        end ;
    begin
        readandtotalgrades ;
        printtotalgrade ;
        printbarmeasure
    end
```

The overall structure of a PASCAL program is thus a set of blocks, some of which are nested within others to an arbitrary level of nesting. Any of these blocks may introduce new identifiers in its declaration part, and the *rules of scope* must determine the accessibility of all these identifiers throughout the nested block structure.

In the examples used so far the identifiers used have all been unique throughout the program. In Chap. 3 we said that the association of each identifier must be unique within its range of use—this range of use, or scope, has now been defined as the block in which the identifier is declared. Clearly an identifier must not be declared for two distinct purposes in the same block. However, there is no reason why the same identifier may not be declared for distinct purposes in different blocks provided the rules of scope make clear which declaration, if any, applies at all points in the resultant program.

The rules of identifier scope in PASCAL are now formally stated, as follows:

(i)   The scope of an identifier declaration is the block in which the declaration occurs, and all blocks enclosed by that block, subject to rule (ii).

(ii) When an identifier declared in a block *A* is re-declared in some block *B* enclosed by *A*, then block *B* and all blocks enclosed by it are excluded from the scope of the identifier's declaration in *A*.

The standard identifiers of PASCAL are considered to be declared in an imaginary block enclosing the entire program.

The general rule introduced in Chap. 3, that an identifier must be declared before it is used, still applies. However, note that scope rule (ii) means that if an identifier *I* is redeclared in a block *B* it cannot be used in the part of *B* preceding its redeclaration with some non-local meaning from an enclosing block *A*, since *all* of block *B* is excluded from the scope of *I*'s declaration in *A*.

The skeleton program (12) illustrates the application of the scope rules to define the identifiers that can be referred to in the statement parts of the various procedures and the main program. The reader should ensure, before continuing, that he understands how the scope rules lead to the accessible identifiers listed by the comments in each statement part.

```
program P ;
var i, j : integer ;
    procedure Q ;
    const i = 16 ;
    var k : char ;
        procedure R ;
        var j : real ;
        begin
            { this statement part may use
              local variable j : real ;
              non-local constant i = 16 ;
              non-local variable k : char ;
              non-local procedures R , Q ;
              and all standard identifiers }
        end ;
    begin                                                    (12)
        { this statement part may use
          local constant i = 16 ;
          local variable k : char ;
          local procedure R ;
          non-local variable j : integer ;
          non-local procedure Q ;
          and all standard identifiers }
    end ;
begin
    { this statement part may use
      local variables i , j : integer ;
      local procedure Q ;
      and all standard identifiers }
end .
```

Note that procedure identifiers are subject to the same rules of scope as other identifiers, and hence a procedure can only be used within the block in which its declaration appears (and any blocks enclosed by that block). The ability of a procedure to refer to, and hence call, itself (known as *recursion*) is discussed later in this chapter.

Note also the use of indentation to indicate the nesting of procedure blocks within the program text. This is good programming practice which enables a reader of the program to appreciate the procedural structure of the program.

The scope rules determine the textual limits on the use of identifiers within a particular program. The same rules are used to determine the lifetime, or *existence*, of variables. PASCAL decrees that variables declared local to a procedure exist only during execution of the procedure, being created upon entry to the procedure and destroyed upon exit. It follows that

(a)   a variable declared local to a procedure cannot be referenced by the program sequence which called the procedure since the variable is created only on entry to the procedure and ceases to exist before control returns to the calling sequence; and

(b)   there is no necessary relationship between the values of variables created by successive executions of the same procedure. The value of a local variable is always undefined upon entry to a procedure (and so the first action of a procedure will generally be to initialize its local variables) since, each time a procedure is called, a new set of variables is created with undefined values.

This limit on the existence or lifetime of variables enables implementations to control the storage used in representing them within the computer. The storage used to represent the local variables of a procedure is acquired only when the procedure is entered, and becomes available for re-use when execution of the procedure is complete. Thus two procedures called in sequence may use the same storage for their local variables. By localizing variables wherever possible, the programmer helps the implementation to minimize the variable data storage required.

Initially the rules of identifier scope and lifetime may seem complex to a user who is unfamiliar with any block-structured programming language. However he will quickly find these rules a positive aid to the construction of programs which are clear, free from error, and economical in data storage. The proper positioning of declarations to obtain these benefits usually follows quite naturally from a stepwise refinement in which procedures are freely used to express the program structure developed. Within this structural framework the following guiding principles should be observed:

(a)   Declare an identifier in the block in which it is used, wherever possible. Doing so increases program clarity, minimizes the likelihood of errors through inadvertent use of the identifier elsewhere, and minimizes the storage requirements produced by variable data.

(b)   When an identifier must be used in two or more blocks to denote the same object, declare it in the block which immediately encloses all the uses of the identifier.

(c)   When a variable used by a procedure must hold its value from one call of the procedure to the next, declare it in the first enclosing block which ensures that its lifetime embraces all of the dependent procedure calls.

Localizing identifiers wherever possible also increases the programmer's freedom in choosing the identifiers to be used. The identifiers local to two procedures which are completely separate from each other (i.e., one does not enclose the other) may be chosen quite independently. Thus, (13) is a valid PASCAL representation of two procedures occurring in the same program. The items denoted by the identifiers used in one procedure bear absolutely no relation to those of the same name used in the other.

```
procedure P ;
const c = '?' ;
var d , e : char ;
begin
 ⋮
end ;
procedure Q ;                                           (13)
type e = 1 .. 100 ;
var c : boolean ;
    d : char ;
begin
 ⋮
end ;
```

PARAMETERS

As we have seen, a procedure may be used to define an action, or sequence of actions, which is required at two or more distinct points in a program. For example if, at various points in a program, we wish to order the values of two global integer variables x and y so that the value of x is not greater than the value of y, by exchanging their values if necessary, instead of writing the statement (14) at each point where the ordering operation is required, we might declare a procedure (15) and call the procedure by means of the procedure statement

   order

at the relevant points in the program.

```
if x>y then
begin                                                    (14)
     t:=x ; x:=y ; y:=t
end

procedure order ;
var t : integer ;
begin
     if x>y then                                         (15)
     begin
          t:=x ; x:=y ; y:=t
     end
end
```

This procedure orders the values of the two integer variables x and y. In practice it is often more convenient to declare a procedure which orders the values of any two integer variables, not just x and y. Then, if at some point in the program we wish to order the values of x and y, we may write

   $order\ (x, y)$

whereas if, at another point, we wish to order the values of y and another integer variable z, we may write

   $order\ (y, z)$

This is possible in PASCAL by the declaration of a procedure which includes a *formal-parameter-list* in its heading, thus:

   procedure *identifier formal-parameter-list* ;
          . . .
          . . .

The *formal-parameter-list* defines a set of dummy quantities, called *formal-parameters*, in terms of which the procedure body is expressed. When the procedure is called these *formal-parameters* are replaced by corresponding *actual-parameters* specified in the *procedure-statement*, thus

   procedure-identifier actual-parameter-list

For the procedure *order* an appropriate declaration would be as shown in (16). In (16), a and b are the *formal-parameters* in terms of which procedure *order* is defined. To order the values of variables x and y the procedure statement required is

   $order\ (x, y)$

where *x* and *y* are the *actual* parameters which replace *a* and *b* in this particular execution of the procedure.

procedure *order* (**var** *a* , *b* : *integer*) ;
var *t* : *integer* ;
begin
   if *a*>*b* **then**
   begin   (16)
      t:=*a* ; *a*:=*b* ; *b*:=*t*
   end
end

In detail, a *formal-parameter-list* consists of one or more sections, separated by semi-colons and enclosed by parentheses, thus

formal-parameter-list = "(" *formal-parameter-section*
                     { ";" *formal-parameter-section* } ")" .

Each *section* introduces one or more formal parameters of the same *class*. There are four *classes* of formal parameter in PASCAL, viz.,

(a)   *value* parameters;
(b)   *variable* parameters;
(c)   *procedure* parameters;
(d)   *function* parameters.

The class of each formal-parameter is determined by the form of the *formal-parameter-section* in which it occurs, as indicated by (17).

formal-parameter-section = *value-parameter-section* |
                       variable-parameter-section |
                       procedure-parameter-section |
                       function-parameter-section.
value-parameter-section = *identifier-list* ":" *parameter-type.*
variable-parameter-section = "**var**" *identifier-list* ":" *parameter-type*
procedure-parameter-section = *procedure-heading* .   (17)
function-parameter-section = *function-heading.*
parameter-type = *type-identifier* | *conformant-array-schema.*

Within each section one or more identifiers are declared to denote the formal parameters required and, except for those of class procedure, the corresponding type is specified. Note that a parameter-type (other than a conformant-array-schema) can only be specified by a type-identifier which has already been defined in some enclosing block.

Each *actual-parameter-list* used in a procedure statement takes a form corresponding to the procedure's *formal-parameter-list*. It consists of an appropriate number of *actual-parameters* separated by commas, thus

$$actual\text{-}parameter\text{-}list = "(" \ actual\text{-}parameter$$
$$\{"," \ actual\text{-}parameter \} \ ")" .$$

The form of each *actual-parameter* is determined by the class of the corresponding *formal-parameter*. There are four possible forms as in (18).

$$actual\text{-}parameter = actual\text{-}value \mid actual\text{-}variable \mid$$
$$actual\text{-}procedure \mid actual\text{-}function .$$
$$actual\text{-}value = expression .$$
$$actual\text{-}variable = variable .$$
$$actual\text{-}procedure = procedure\text{-}identifier .$$
$$actual\text{-}function = function\text{-}identifier .$$

(18)

The correspondence between the actual- and formal-parameter-lists of a procedure statement and the procedure declaration must be as follows:

(i)   the number of parameters in the two lists must be the same;
(ii) each actual-parameter corresponds to the formal-parameter occupying the same position in the formal-parameter-list;
(iii) corresponding actual- and formal-parameters must agree as detailed for each class in following sections of this book.

The most commonly used parameter classes are variable and value parameters whose parameter-type is denoted by a type-identifier. These we now consider. Parameters of class procedure and function are discussed later in this chapter, and conformant array parameters are discussed in Chap. 9.

Variable Parameters

A variable formal-parameter is used to denote an actual-parameter whose value may be altered by execution of the procedure. Each corresponding actual parameter must therefore be a variable of the same type. Execution of a particular procedure statement determines the actual parameter involved and, throughout the resultant execution of the procedure body, each operation involving the formal-parameter is applied directly to this actual variable.

In some cases the procedure may use the existing value of an actual variable parameter before changing it. For example, the procedure *order* which we define as in (19), examines and, if necessary, exchanges the values of its two parameters.

```
procedure order ( var a , b : integer ) ;
var t : integer ;
begin
    if a>b then
    begin                                              (19)
        t:=a ; a:=b ; b:=t
    end
end
```

The formal parameters *a* and *b* must be declared as variable parameters—hence the prefix **var** on their declaration. In a corresponding procedure statement

order (x, y)

the actual parameters *x* and *y* must be integer variables. Furthermore, they must have already been assigned values since the procedure first examines these values to determine its subsequent action.

In other cases the existing values of variable parameters may be irrelevant. For example, the procedure (20) reads a real number representing a distance in metres and converts it to feet and inches (to the nearest inch). In a corresponding calling statement, e.g.,

readasmetres (ft, ins)

the actual parameters *ft* and *ins* must be integer variables, but their existing values are irrelevant since the procedure makes no attempt to use them before assigning new values to them.

```
procedure readasmetres (var feet, inches : integer) ;
var metres : real ; lengthininches : integer ;
begin
    read (metres) ;
    lengthininches := round (metres*39.39) ;           (20)
    inches := lengthininches mod 12 ;
    feet := lengthininches div 12
end
```

Parameters, such as those of *readasmetres*, which are used to carry values out of a procedure are sometimes known as *output* parameters. Parameters, such as those of *order*, which are used to carry values into and out of a procedure, are known as *transput* parameters. In either case they must be declared as variable parameters in PASCAL.

Value Parameters

A value parameter is used when the parameter's only role is to carry a value into a procedure—a so-called *input* parameter. The formal parameter simply denotes a value which is supplied by the calling statement, and the corresponding actual parameter may therefore be any expression which produces a value that is assignment compatible with the formal parameter type.

> **procedure** *writeasmetres* (*feet, inches* : *integer*) ;
> **var** *metres* : *real* ; *lengthininches* : *integer* ;
> **begin**
>   *lengthininches* := 12*feet* + *inches* ;   (21)
>   *metres* := *lengthininches*/39.39 ;
>   *write* (*metres* : 6 : 2)
> **end**

For example, the procedure (21) accepts two integer values representing a distance in feet and inches and writes it out in metres. In this case *feet* and *inches* are value parameters, which is indicated by the absence of the prefix **var** in their declaration. The corresponding actual parameters in statements calling the procedure may be any expressions producing integer values. For example

> *writeasmetres* (6, 4)
> *writeasmetres* (*ft, ins*)
> *writeasmetres* (*ft*+1, 0)

are all acceptable calling statements for this procedure, assuming *ft* and *ins* are integer variables as before.

In PASCAL the expression forming an actual value parameter is evaluated when the procedure statement is executed and assigned to the corresponding formal parameter as if the latter were a local variable of the procedure. During its execution the procedure body may examine this formal parameter *and* may assign further values to it, again as if it were a local variable. However, such assignments have no effect on the actual parameter in the procedure statement.

> **procedure** *writeasmetres* (*feet, inches* : *integer*) ;
> **var** *metres* : *real* ;
> **begin**
>   *inches* := 12*feet* + *inches* ;   (22)
>   *metres* := *inches*/39.39 ;
>   *write* (*metres* : 6 : 2)
> **end**

For example, we might have programmed the procedure *writeasmetres* without the local variable *lengthininches*, as in (22). The outward effect of this procedure is exactly as before. In particular, a call of the form

writeasmetres (ft, ins)

will not make any change to the variable *ins* which supplied the input value for *inches*. { In practice of course the procedure body could be written without any local variables—simply as a single write statement

write ((12*feet+inches)/39.39 : 6 : 2) } .

The ability to re-use value parameters as local variables is a convenient one in some cases. However, in consequence, a programmer must be very careful to ensure that all intended variable parameters are declared as such. Omission of the **var** symbol in the formal parameter list simply means that the formal parameters are taken as value parameters. Assignments to them within the procedure body remain valid but produce no effect on the corresponding actual variables supplied by calling statements. The result is a program which seems correct but does not produce the desired effect. The actual mistake—the omission of one **var** symbol—is often difficult to discern.

Many procedures involve a mixture of variable and value parameters. Their declarations require formal parameter lists with two or more sections to distinguish the classes of the formal parameters involved. For example, we might define procedures for internal conversion between metres and feet and inches as in (23).

```
procedure converttometres (feet , inches : integer ;
                           var metres : real) ;
begin
    metres := (12*feet + inches)/39.39
end


procedure convertfrommetres (metres : real ;
                             var feet , inches : integer) ;     (23)
var lengthininches : integer ;
begin
    lengthininches := round (metres*39.39) ;
    feet := lengthininches div 12 ;
    inches := lengthininches mod 12
end
```

The procedure (24) accepts the coefficients of a quadratic equation

$$ax^2 + bx + c = 0$$

and computes its real roots if they exist, setting a boolean flag to indicate whether or not they do.

```
procedure solvequadratic (a, b, c : real ;
                          var root1, root2 : real ;
                          var rootsexist : boolean) ;
var d : real ;
begin
    d := b*b−4*a*c ;
    if d<0
    then rootsexist := false                              (24)
    else begin
            rootsexist := true ;
            d := sqrt (d) ;
            root1 :=−(b−d)/(2*a) ;
            root2 :=−(b+d)/(2*a)
         end
end
```

Note that

(a) although the first five parameters are all of type *real*, two formal parameter sections are required to distinguish the value and variable parameters;

(b) the symbol **var** must be repeated for each section of variable parameters of distinct type.

PROGRAM 5 (Alphabetic output of a sum of money)

A program is to accept as input a number of sums of money less than \$1000 represented as two integers separated by a space, and should output both the numeric form and its alphabetic equivalent for each sum. For example, input of

542 99

should produce the output

542 99 *FIVE HUNDRED AND FORTY TWO DOLLARS AND NINETY NINE CENTS*

The input sequence is terminated by a sum whose dollars amount is negative. An actual application of a program of this kind would be the printing of computerized bank cheques.

The overall structure of the program might be seen, after one or more refinement steps, as in (25).

```
begin
     read (dollars) ;
     while dollars >=0 do
     begin
          read (cents) ;
          write (dollars, cents) ;
          if both dollars and cents are zero
          then write ('nil')
          else begin
                    if dollars>0 then begin                          (25)
                                        convert dollars into words ;
                                        write (' dollars') ;
                                        if cents >0 then write (' and')
                                      end ;
                    if cents >0 then begin
                                        convert cents into words ;
                                        write (' cents')
                                      end
               end ;
          writeln;
          read (dollars)
     end
end
```

The steps *convert dollars into words* and *convert cents into words* will involve similar actions and are suitable for expression as calls of a procedure *convertintowords* which takes suitable parameters, e.g.,

convertintowords (dollars)
convertintowords (cents)

The procedure *convertintowords* has the heading

procedure *convertintowords* $(x : range)$;

where the type *range* is defined in the main program as the subrange $0..999$. The action of the procedure is to write out the alphabetic form of its value parameter x. The outline of this procedure is as in (26). Note that, in the treatment of the last two digits of x, values between 11 and 19 take a different alphabetic form from other values and thus have to be considered separately.

```
begin
      split x into its hundreds, tens and units digits ;
      if the hundreds digit >0 then
      begin
            convert the hundreds digit ; write (' hundred') ;
            if the sum of the tens and units digits >0 then write (' and')
      end ;
      if the tens digit = 1 then convert a number between 10 and 19
                        else begin
                              convert the tens digit ;              (26)
                              convert the units digit
                        end
end
```

The actions *convert the hundreds digit* and *convert the units digit* can both be expressed as calls of a procedure, say,

procedure *units* (*i* : *digit*)

where the type *digit* of the value parameter *i* is declared non-locally as the subrange $0 . . 9$. This procedure will be a local procedure of *convertintowords* and the type *digit* will be declared within *convertintowords*.

Writing the procedure *units* and expanding the abstract actions within *convertintowords* and the main program we arrive at the final program which is shown, together with sample output, as Listing 5.

```
                    LISTING 5

PROGRAM NUMBERSTOWORDS (INPUT, OUTPUT) ;

(*  THIS PROGRAM ACCEPTS AS INPUT A SEQUENCE OF NUMBERS
    REPRESENTING SUMS OF MONEY LESS THAN $1000 AND PRINTS
    THEIR ALPHABETIC EQUIVALENT.
    THE SEQUENCE IS TERMINATED BY A NEGATIVE NUMBER.      *)

TYPE  RANGE = 0..999;

VAR   DOLLARS : INTEGER ;
      CENTS : 0..99 ;

PROCEDURE CONVERTINTOWORDS (X:RANGE) ;
    TYPE  DIGIT = 0..9 ;
    VAR   H, T, U : DIGIT;

    PROCEDURE UNITS (I:DIGIT) ;
      BEGIN
        CASE I OF
          0 : ;
          1 : WRITE (' ONE ') ;
          2 : WRITE (' TWO') ;
          3 : WRITE (' THREE') ;
```

```
                4 : WRITE (' FOUR') ;
                5 : WRITE (' FIVE') ;
                6 : WRITE (' SIX') ;
                7 : WRITE (' SEVEN') ;
                8 : WRITE (' EIGHT') ;
                9 : WRITE (' NINE') ;
            END
        END ; (* UNITS *)

    BEGIN
        H := X DIV 100  ;  T := X MOD 100 DIV 10  ;  U := X MOD 10 ;
        IF H>0 THEN BEGIN
                        UNITS (H) ;
                        WRITE (' HUNDRED') ;
                        IF T+U>0 THEN WRITE (' AND')
                    END;
        IF T=1 THEN CASE U OF
                        0 : WRITE (' TEN') ;
                        1 : WRITE (' ELEVEN') ;
                        2 : WRITE (' TWELVE') ;
                        3 : WRITE (' THIRTEEN') ;
                        4 : WRITE (' FOURTEEN') ;
                        5 : WRITE (' FIFTEEN') ;
                        6 : WRITE (' SIXTEEN') ;
                        7 : WRITE (' SEVENTEEN') ;
                        8 : WRITE (' EIGHTEEN') ;
                        9 : WRITE (' NINETEEN')
                    END
               ELSE BEGIN
                        CASE T OF
                          0 : ;
                          2 : WRITE (' TWENTY') ;
                          3 : WRITE (' THIRTY') ;
                          4 : WRITE (' FORTY') ;
                          5 : WRITE (' FIFTY') ;
                          6 : WRITE (' SIXTY') ;
                          7 : WRITE (' SEVENTY') ;
                          8 : WRITE (' EIGHTY') ;
                          9 : WRITE (' NINETY')
                        END ;
                        UNITS (U)
                    END
    END ; (* CONVERTINTOWORDS *)

BEGIN
    READ (DOLLARS) ;
    WHILE DOLLARS>=0 DO
    BEGIN
        READ (CENTS) ;
        WRITE (DOLLARS:4, CENTS:3, ' ':5) ;
        IF (DOLLARS=0) AND (CENTS=0)
        THEN WRITE (' NIL')
        ELSE BEGIN
                IF DOLLARS>0 THEN BEGIN
                                    CONVERTINTOWORDS (DOLLARS) ;
                                    WRITE (' DOLLARS') ;
                                    IF CENTS>0 THEN WRITE (' AND')
                                END;
```

```
            IF CENTS>0 THEN BEGIN
                           CONVERTINTOWORDS (CENTS) ;
                           WRITE (' CENTS')
                         END
        END;
      WRITELN ;
      READ (DOLLARS)
   END
END.
```

```
653 37    SIX HUNDRED AND FIFTY THREE DOLLARS AND THIRTY SEVEN CENTS
  0  0    NIL
250  0    TWO HUNDRED AND FIFTY DOLLARS
116 27    ONE HUNDRED AND SIXTEEN DOLLARS AND TWENTY SEVEN CENTS
  0 83    EIGHTY THREE CENTS
100 16    ONE HUNDRED DOLLARS AND SIXTEEN CENTS
 17 90    SEVENTEEN DOLLARS AND NINETY CENTS
```

FUNCTIONS

In previous chapters we have described the *standard functions* of PASCAL (e.g., *sqrt, succ, trunc, eof*) and discussed how they may be used in the construction of expressions. For example, in the expression

$y/sqrt(x) + 3$

$sqrt(x)$ is a *function call* which has the effect of performing a computation to produce a result whose value is the square root of x, where x is an actual parameter of the function call. The value produced by the computation is substituted into the above expression and the expression then evaluated.

PASCAL not only provides these standard functions (which do not require any declaration in the program) but also a means whereby the programmer can declare his own *functions* and have them evaluated, with appropriate parameters, as components of expressions. A function is a special form of procedure which describes a computation that produces a single value as its result. However, whereas a procedure is activated by a procedure statement, a function is activated from within an expression to whose value the result of the function contributes.

The declaration of a function is similar to that of a procedure and takes the following form.

function-declaration = function-heading ";" function-body .
function-heading = "function" identifier [formal-parameter-list]
                                       ":" result-type .

result type = type identifier .
function-body = block .

A *function-declaration* appears, with any other procedure and function declarations, in the *procedure-and-function-declaration-part* of a block, i.e., a *function-declaration* may appear anywhere *that a procedure-declaration* may appear.

A *function-heading* is similar to a procedure-heading except that it begins with the symbol **function** and contains an indication of the type of the result computed by the function—the *result-type*. The type identified must be a previously defined unstructured type or pointer type (see Chap. 13).

The *identifier* and *formal-parameter-list*, if any, in the *function-heading* play the same role as those in a *procedure-heading*—determining how the function may be called. However, the *function-identifier* plays an additional role within the *function-body* in denoting the result to be produced by execution of the function.

The syntax category

function-identifier = *identifier* .

is used hereafter to denote the class of identifiers introduced by *function-declarations*.

The *function-body* is a block, and may therefore include declarations of further local constants, types, variables, procedures and functions. The same rules of identifier scope apply to blocks arising from function declarations as to those from procedures. However, within the *function-body* there must appear at least one assignment statement which assigns a value of the result type to the *function-identifier*. In each execution of the function the last value so assigned determines the result of the function evaluation. If no assignment to the function identifier takes place during an execution the result of that function evaluation is an error.

The following is an example of a function-declaration defining a function *max* which yields as its result the larger of the values of its two real value parameters x and y.

```
function max (x, y : real) : real ;
begin
    if x > y then max := x else max := y
end
```

The heading of the function specifies the identifier *max* by which the function is known, its formal parameters, and the type *real* of the result of the computation performed by the function. The function-body defines this computation such that the result returned will be the larger of its two value parameters.

A function is called (invoked, or *designated*) simply by the occurrence of its identifier and *actual-parameter-list* within an expression, as we have already seen in the case of standard function calls. Recalling the syntactic definition of an expression given in Chap. 4:

factor = *variable* | *unsigned-constant* | *function-designator* |
   bound | *set* | *"(" expression ")"* | **"not"** *factor*.

we define a *function-designator* as

function-designator = *function-identifier* [*actual-parameter-list*] .

The *actual-parameter-list* of a function call must obey the same rules of correspondence with the *formal-parameter-list* of the function-declaration as have already been stated for procedure calls.

The effect of a function call is to execute the statement-part of the corresponding function-declaration with actual parameters being substituted for formal-parameters (according to their class). Provided that a value is assigned to the function-identifier during this execution, the function then returns a single value of its result type and this value is then used in the evaluation of the expression containing the function call. If x, y and z are variables of type *real*, then

$x := max\ (y, z)$

will assign to x the larger of the values of the variables y and z;

$x := 2 * max(y, 1.5)$

will assign to x twice the value of the larger of y and 1.5;

$x := max\ (x, max(y, z))$

will assign to x the largest of the values of x, y and z. Since the expressions in the actual parameter list of the function call must be evaluated before the function itself is evaluated, this last example is equivalent to

$t := max\ (y, z)$;
$x := max\ (x, t)$

where t is an auxiliary variable not used for any other purpose.

(27)–(29) are further simple examples of function-declarations which assume the existence of type definitions

nonnegativeinteger = 0 .. *maxint* ,
positiveinteger   = 1 .. *maxint* ;

```
function power (x :real ; n : nonnegativeinteger) : real ;
{this function computes x raised to the power n, where n>=0}
var i : nonnegativeinteger ; answer : real ;
begin
    answer := 1 ;                                              (27)
    for i := 1 to n do answer := answer*x ;
    power := answer
end
```

```
function sumofsquares (n : nonnegativeinteger) : nonnegativeinteger ;
{this function computes the sum of the squares of the first n whole
numbers}
var i, sum : nonnegativeinteger ;
begin
    sum := 0 ;                                                 (28)
    for i := 1 to n do sum := sum + sqr(i) ;
    sumofsquares := sum
end
```

```
function multiple (i, j : positiveinteger) : boolean ;
{this function determines whether i and j are multiples of each other}
begin                                                          (29)
    multiple := (i mod j = 0) or (j mod i = 0)
end
```

Note that, although the function-identifier may be assigned more than one value during execution of the function-body, a previously assigned value cannot be re-accessed by use of the function-identifier, as a local variable might. Where the function result is obtained by some cumulative calculation an auxiliary local variable, such as *answer* in the function *power*, or *sum* in the function *sumofsquares*, must be used. As we see later in this chapter any occurrence of the function identifier in an expression within the function body is considered to be a further (recursive) call on the function.

The following are examples of statements which call the above functions:

```
y := power (6.3, 5)
x := sumofsquares(3) + sumofsquares(n)
while not multiple(y, x) do begin y:=y+1 ; x:=x+1 end
```

The program (30) reads in two integers n and m (n assumed to be less than m) and produces as output a list of all the perfect numbers between n and m, inclusive. A perfect number is one for which the sum of its factors equals the number itself, e.g., $6 = 1+2+3$. The function *perfect* determines whether or not its integer-value parameter is a perfect number.

```
program perfectnumbers (input, output) ;
type nonnegativeinteger = 0 .. maxint ;
var i, n, m : nonnegativeinteger ;
        function perfect (j : nonnegativeinteger) : boolean ;
        var i, sum : nonnegativeinteger ;
        begin
            sum := 1 ;
            for i := 2 to j div 2 do
                if j mod i = 0 then sum := sum+i ;                    (30)
            perfect := (sum=j)
        end ;
begin
        read (n, m) ;
        writeln ('list of all perfect numbers between',n,' and',m) ;
        for i := n to m do
            if perfect (i) then writeln (i)
end.
```

Side Effects of Functions

When a statement executed during evaluation of a function alters the value of a variable which is known outside the function this is called a *side effect* of the function. Side effects represent a potential data interaction between the function and the program which calls it which is always dangerous, since it makes the program difficult to understand (the value of a variable may change during evaluation of an expression containing a function call), and can make the meaning of a program ambiguous.

```
function f (x : integer) : real ;
begin
    v := v*x ;                                                        (31)
    f := sqrt(x)+1
end
```

Suppose we have a function f which, during its execution, alters the value of some non-local variable v, as, for example, in (31). Now consider the evaluation of the expression

$$f(x) + v$$

The value of this expression depends upon the order of evaluation of its operands, i.e., on whether the value of v is taken before or after the value of $f(x)$ is determined. If $f(x)$ is evaluated first, then the value of v produced by the assignment in f is added to the result of $f(x)$, otherwise the original value of v is added to the result. In PASCAL the order of evaluation of the operands of a dyadic operator such as $+$ is implementation dependent, and so the expression value is implementation dependent. Even when the order of evaluation is known, the expression $f(x) + v$ may produce a different result from $v + f(x)$!

In the interests of avoiding such ambiguous situations, functions with side effects should be avoided where possible. It follows that formal parameter lists of functions should not include variable parameters, and functions should refrain from assigning values to non-local variables and from calling procedures which perform such assignments.

The evaluation of a function may require the execution of a substantial piece of program and so one should take care to avoid unnecessary function calls in a program. For instance, if f is a function with a real-value parameter, the statement

$$x := f(y/2) + f(y/2)*sqrt(f(y/2))$$

calls the function f three times with the same actual parameter value and thus all three calls produce the same result (assuming that f has no side effects). It is more efficient to evaluate the function once and store its result in a variable, thus:

$$t := f(y/2) ;$$
$$x := t + t*sqrt(t)$$

However, if the function f has side effects, then these two approaches will produce different effects since f is called three times in the first form but only once in the second.

PROGRAM 6   (Finding prime numbers)

We wish to write a program which reads a positive integer n and then reads a further n integers, each greater than 1, and outputs the nearest prime number to each. In the case of two prime numbers being equidistant from an input integer both should be output.

The required program has an overall action which may be expressed as in (32). The action *output nearest prime to j* might first be refined as in (33). The step *locate and output nearest prime(s)* involves looking at the odd numbers starting with the closest odd number to the input value and working away from the input value until a prime number is found. If the input value is an even number then the nearest odd numbers are one

```
begin
    read (n) ;
    for i := 1 to n do
    begin
        read (j) ;                                              (32)
        write ('nearest prime to', j, ' is') ;
        output nearest prime to j
    end
end
```

```
if j is prime
then output j                                                   (33)
else locate and output nearest prime(s)
```

greater and one less than it, otherwise they are two greater and two less. It can thus be expressed as a loop which tests the odd numbers working away from the input value and terminates when it finds a prime number. Remembering that if two primes are found equidistant from the input value they are both to be output, this may be written as in (34).

```
if odd(j) then k:=2 else k:=1 ;
repeat
    if j+k is prime then output j+k ;
    if j−k is prime then output j−k ;                           (34)
    k := k+2
until prime found
```

Since the loop must terminate if either of the output actions is executed, the terminating condition is best expressed as a boolean variable *found*, initially false, which is set true when either value is output.

We thus have three points at which we must test whether a particular value, j, $j+k$ and $j-k$ respectively, is prime. The appropriate step is to introduce a function *prime*, which takes a positive integer value as parameter, and returns a boolean result, true or false, according to whether the integer is prime or not, thus:

```
function prime (p : positiveinteger) : boolean ;
    . . .
```

where the type *positiveinteger* is globally defined as

```
positiveinteger = 1 .. maxint
```

Assuming such a function, the action *locate and output nearest prime(s)* may be expressed as in (35).

```
found := false ;
if odd(j) then k:=2 else k:=1 ;
repeat
    if prime(j+k) then begin found:=true ; write (j+k) end ;
    if prime(j−k) then begin found:=true ; write (j−k) end ;      (35)
    k:=k+2
until found ;
writeln
```

We must now program the required function *prime*. We may assume 2 and 3 to be prime numbers and take advantage of the fact that an even number greater than 2 is never prime because it is always divisible by 2. Therefore only odd numbers greater than 3 are further tested to determine if they are prime. Thus the outline of the function is

if $p < 4$ **then** *prime* := $p > 1$ **else**
if not *odd*(p) **then** *prime* := *false* **else**
test if p is prime

Since factors of a number occur in pairs such that one factor is greater than or equal to the square root of the number and the other factor is less than or equal to the square root, it follows that no number has any factors greater than its square root if it does not have factors less than its square roct. In the step *test if p is prime* we are guaranteed that p is an odd number and so, in order to test for the primeness of p, we need only test if any of the odd numbers from 3 up to the square root of p are factors of p. Then p is a prime number if, and only if, this process is unable to find a factor of p. We thus write *test if p is prime* as a loop which divides p by the odd numbers starting from 3 until either a factor of p is found or all the odd numbers up to, and including if necessary, the square root of p, have been tested. If the square root of p is not a whole number then we test the odd numbers up to the whole number part of the square root. To compute this limit we might, at first, write

trunc ($sqrt(p)$)

However, if p is a square of the form $(q+1)^2$, say, inaccuracies in the *sqrt* function might give a square root of the form $q.999\ldots.$ and truncation would then give a limiting value q rather than $q+1$. To guard against such inaccuracies we instead write

round ($sqrt(p)$)

though this will sometimes give a limit one greater than necessary.

The action *test if p is prime* is thus programmed as in (36). The complete program with sample output is shown as Listing 6.

```
begin
    root := round (sqrt(p)) ;
    divisor := 3 ;
    while (divisor <= root) and (p mod divisor<>0)              (36)
    do divisor := divisor+2 ;
    prime := divisor>root
end
```

LISTING 6

```
PROGRAM FINDNEARESTPRIMES (INPUT, OUTPUT) ;

(* THIS PROGRAM READS A POSITIVE INTEGER N  AND THEN
   READS A FURTHER N POSITIVE INTEGERS (EACH > 1) AND OUTPUTS
   THE NEAREST PRIME NUMBER TO EACH.  IN THE CASE OF
   TWO PRIME NUMBERS BEING EQUIDISTANT FROM AN INPUT
   INTEGER BOTH ARE OUTPUT.                                    *)

TYPE  POSITIVEINTEGER = 1..MAXINT ;

VAR   N, I, K : POSITIVEINTEGER ;
      J : 2..MAXINT ;
      FOUND : BOOLEAN ;

FUNCTION PRIME (P : POSITIVEINTEGER) : BOOLEAN ;
   (* DETERMINES WHETHER P IS PRIME OR NOT *)
   VAR  ROOT, DIVISOR : POSITIVEINTEGER ;
   BEGIN
      IF P<4 THEN PRIME := P>1 ELSE
      IF NOT ODD(P) THEN PRIME := FALSE ELSE
      BEGIN
         ROOT := ROUND (SQRT(P)) ;
         DIVISOR := 3 ;
         WHILE (DIVISOR<=ROOT) AND (P MOD DIVISOR <> 0)
         DO DIVISOR := DIVISOR + 2 ;
         PRIME := DIVISOR>ROOT
      END
   END ;  (* PRIME *)

BEGIN
   READ (N) ;
   FOR I := 1 TO N DO
   BEGIN
      READ (J) ;
      WRITE ('NEAREST PRIME TO', J, ' IS') ;
      IF PRIME (J)
      THEN WRITELN (J)
      ELSE BEGIN
              FOUND := FALSE ;
              IF ODD(J) THEN K:=2 ELSE K:=1;
              REPEAT
                 IF PRIME (J+K) THEN BEGIN
                                        FOUND := TRUE ;
                                        WRITE (J+K)
                                     END ;
```

```
                    IF PRIME (J-K) THEN BEGIN
                                         FOUND := TRUE ;
                                         WRITE (J-K)
                                       END ;
                 K := K+2
                 UNTIL FOUND ;
                 WRITELN
            END
      END
   END.
```

```
      NEAREST PRIME TO      100 IS     101
      NEAREST PRIME TO      246 IS     251       241
      NEAREST PRIME TO        2 IS       2
      NEAREST PRIME TO      333 IS     331
      NEAREST PRIME TO     2007 IS    2011      2003
      NEAREST PRIME TO      761 IS     761
```

PROCEDURES AND FUNCTIONS AS PARAMETERS

In discussing parameters earlier in this chapter we explained two classes of parameters in detail, variable and value parameters. PASCAL allows other classes of parameter to be specified, such as procedure and function parameters which we now consider.

A formal procedure parameter is specified by a formal-parameter section which itself has the form of a procedure heading. Such a formal-parameter section thus specifies the name of the procedure parameter involved, and its own parameter requirements, if any. For example, the heading

procedure P (**procedure** A)

introduces a procedure P with one formal procedure parameter A which itself takes no parameters. Within the body of P the identifier A is used like any other parameterless procedure identifier, e.g. in a procedure statement.

A formal function parameter is similarly specified by a formal-parameter section in the form of a function heading. For example, the heading

procedure Q (**function** F (x : $integer$) : $integer$)

introduces a procedure Q with one formal function parameter F which takes one integer value parameter and produces an integer result. Within the body of Q the identifier F is used like any other function identifier of this kind, e.g. in a function designator.

When a procedure (or function) which has a parameter of class procedure or function is called, the corresponding actual parameter must be the identifier of a procedure or of a function with the same parameter requirements and the same result type. As the called procedure (or function) body is executed, each occurrence of the formal parameter implies a corresponding use of the actual procedure or function supplied as parameter.

```
procedure tabulate (function f (x : real) : real ;
                             lower, upper, step : real) ;
var x : real ;
    j : integer ;
begin
    x := lower ;
    for j := 0 to trunc ((upper−lower)/step) do                 (37)
    begin
        writeln (x:13, f(x):20) ;
        x := x+step
    end
end
```

Consider the procedure (37). The procedure *tabulate* takes a function parameter *f* which returns a real result, and three value parameters of type real. Its effect is to generate a succession of values for *x*, as determined by the value parameters *lower, upper* and *step*, and to evaluate and print $f(x)$ for each. Thus a procedure statement

tabulate (f1, 0.0, 1.0, 0.01)

would cause the values of *x* and $f1(x)$ to be tabulated for values of *x* in the range 0 to 1 at intervals of 0.01, while the procedure statement

tabulate (f2, 0.0, 1.0, 0.01)

would produce a similar tabulation for the values of a function $f2$ where $f1$ and $f2$ are both functions that take one real parameter and produce a real result, declared elsewhere in the program.

As an example of a function taking a function as parameter we might declare a function *sigma* (38) which computes the sum

$$\sum_{i=lower}^{upper} f(i)$$

where f is an integer-valued function of one integer argument.

```
function sigma (function f (i : integer) : integer ;
                lower, upper : integer) : integer ;
var i, sum : integer ;
begin
    sum := 0 ;                                                    (38)
    for i := lower to upper do sum := sum + f(i) ;
    sigma := sum
end
```

If the program also contains a function such as (39), then the function call

$$s := sigma \, (fourthpower, 1, 10)$$

would evaluate the sum

$$\sum_{i=1}^{10} i^4$$

and assign the result to s.

```
function fourthpower (x : integer) : integer ;
begin
    fourthpower := sqr (sqr(x))                                   (39)
end
```

The formal function f in (38) and the actual function *fourthpower* are *congruous*, in that they take the same number and type of parameters and produce results of the same type. Note however that different identifiers are used to denote their respective formal parameters, i in one case, x in the other. In fact the identifier i in the function heading that defines f serves no real purpose, since no corresponding function body using i exists. PASCAL retains the identifiers in formal procedure and function headings simply to avoid different notations for formal and actual specifications. In general the formal-parameter lists of corresponding formal and actual procedures or functions may differ only in the identifiers that denote their formal parameters, or bound identifiers when conformant array parameters are involved. Otherwise the parameter lists must be identical in the number of formal-parameter sections they contain, in the number and class of parameters defined by corresponding sections, and in any types used in their definition. Where the parameter lists of corresponding formal and actual procedures or functions themselves include formal procedures or functions these too must be congruous in the same way.

The ability to pass procedures and functions to other procedures and functions is a useful one in some situations and may be used to construct very general-purpose procedures or functions, such as *tabulate* and *sigma* above. However, the facility should be used with caution, as the effect of executing a procedure which receives another procedure as parameter is not always obvious. Interaction through the non-local data which each procedure manipulates can produce complex and sometimes unexpected effects. Programs using procedures as parameters are often both difficult to understand and debug for this reason.

An additional problem is that PASCAL does not allow standard procedures or functions to be passed as parameters. Thus calls such as

   tabulate (*sin*, 0.0, 1.0, 0.01)

and

   $s := sigma$ (*sqr*, 1, 100)

are invalid. This restriction is easily overcome by declaring an equivalent function whose sole action is simply to call the standard function, and then calling the procedure (or function) with this equivalent function as actual parameter. This is shown in (40).

   function *sine* (*x* : *real*) : *real* ;
   begin
   $\qquad sine := sin(x)$ (40)
   end

With this declaration a valid call of *tabulate* becomes

   tabulate (*sine*, 0.0, 1.0, 0.01)

RECURSION

In defining the structure of statements in PASCAL we have seen various examples of a *recursive* description, i.e., one expressed in terms of the structure being described. For example, the syntactic definition of a PASCAL *statement* can be expressed as

   statement = "**if**" *expression* "**then**" *statement* | ...

where the syntactic entity *statement* is defined in terms of itself. Such recursive definitions occur throughout the syntax of PASCAL and permit the construction of nested statements, expressions, procedures, etc.

This same technique can be used in describing a process. Consider for example the process which accepts a non-negative integer value and outputs the sequence of decimal digits representing the number in *reverse* order. This process might be described abstractly as in (41).

> **begin**
>> *output last digit of N* ;
>> **if** *digits remain*   (41)
>> **then** *reverse remaining digits*
> **end**

In PASCAL a procedure or function is permitted not only to call another procedure or function but also to call itself. Such a call is said to be *recursive*. Thus the above process may be written in PASCAL as a recursive procedure, as in (42), where the number to be reversed at each

> **procedure** *reverse* (*N* : *nonnegativeinteger*) ;
> **begin**
>> *write* (*N* **mod** 10) ;
>> **if** *N* **div** 10<>0   (42)
>> **then** *reverse* (*N* **div** 10)
> **end**

stage is passed as a value parameter in a call to the recursive procedure *reverse*. An integer value *i* may be output with its digits reversed by the procedure statement

> *reverse* (*i*)

Consider what happens when *reverse* is called with a particular parameter value, say 327. The effect of the call *reverse* (327) is

> **begin**
>> *write* (7) ;
>> **if** *true* **then** *reverse* (32)
> **end**

since 327 **mod** 10 = 7 and 327 **div** 10 = 32. The effect of the embedded recursive call *reverse* (32) is

> **begin**
>> *write* (2) ;
>> **if** *true* **then** *reverse* (3)
> **end**

The effect of the embedded recursive call *reverse* (3) is

```
begin
    write (3) ;
    if false then reverse (0)
end
```

and because 3 **div** 10 = 0 no further recursive call arises. The call *reverse* (3) is complete and so the call *reverse* (32) continues. This too is complete so the call *reverse* (327) continues, and is in turn complete. Thus the net effect of the original call is to output the digits 7, 2, 3 in that order, with one call being made for each digit output. The succession of recursive calls terminates because of the conditional statement which controls the recursive call within the body of *reverse*, a necessary property of all useful recursive procedures.

The duration, or *lifetime*, of each recursive call of procedure *reverse* is strictly nested within the lifetime of its parent call. This nesting brings additional advantages when data are declared local to the recursive procedure. As we have already seen, the call of a procedure creates a set of local variables which is entirely unrelated to the set used in the previous execution of the procedure. This is also true when a procedure calls itself but, as the previous execution of the procedure has not been completed before it is called again recursively, the previous local variables still exist. (They can not, however, be accessed until the recursive call has been completed.) Thus, for each variable v declared local to a recursive procedure R, a call of R which results in the generation of k recursive procedure calls will produce $k+1$ distinct instances of the variable v, the lifetime of each being strictly nested in that of its predecessor.

This property of the local variables of a recursive procedure can be used to advantage in many applications of recursion. Consider a variation of our first recursive process—one which reads a sequence of characters of arbitrary length terminated by some special character such as '.' say, and prints out the sequence in reverse. This process can be programmed recursively as shown in (43).

```
procedure reverseinput ;
var c : char ;
begin
    read (c) ;                                                    (43)
    if c<>'.' then reverseinput ;
    write (c)
end
```

When called to reverse an input sequence of length n, *reverseinput* generates a total of n recursive procedure calls with n instances of the variable c. At the ith level of recursion the variable instance c holds the ith character input, and as the recursion unwinds (i.e., the recursive calls are completed) these instances of c have their values output in the order c_n, c_{n-1}, ..., c_1. Thus, *reverseinput* automatically generates the exact number of variable instances required to reverse the particular input sequence, and each instance exists only as long as it is required to do so.

Many simple processes can be expressed recursively, but can also be expressed as equally simple non-recursive processes involving repetition. For instance, the procedure *reverse* for reversing the digits of an integer value may be expressed non-recursively as in (44).

```
procedure reverse (N : nonnegativeinteger) ;
begin
    repeat
        write (N mod 10) ;                              (44)
        N := N div 10
    until N = 0
end
```

Many mathematical functions are defined recursively and it thus appears natural to write recursive functions to compute their values. The factorial function is a familiar example which may be defined as

$$fac\ (0) = 1$$
$$fac\ (n) = n * fac\ (n-1)\ ,\qquad \text{for } n > 0$$

and so a PASCAL function may be declared to evaluate the factorial of a given value n, as in (45).

```
function fac (n : nonnegativeinteger) : positiveinteger ;
begin
    if n = 0 then fac := 1                              (45)
             else fac := n*fac(n-1)
end
```

However, the function *fac* could also be written in a simple non-recursive form, as in (46).

```
function fac (n : nonnegativeinteger) : positiveinteger ;
var x, i : integer ;
begin
    x := 1 ;                                            (46)
    for i := 1 to n do x := x*i ;
    fac := x
end
```

For many implementations these non-recursive forms of *reverse* or *fac* are more efficient in data storage and execution time then their recursive equivalents. Replacement of recursive formulations by equivalent repetitive forms may therefore be appropriate for reasons of both simplicity and efficiency.

In general it is possible to re-express any recursive procedure as a non-recursive procedure using a suitable form of repetition, but the re-expression is often far from trivial. Therefore, there are significant advantages in using recursive procedures in many situations:

(a) In many cases they are the most natural and most transparent means of describing a process, as is illustrated by some of the case-study programs later in this book. In particular, they are the primary tool used in describing the processing of data which are themselves recursive in nature (see Chap. 13).

(b) They permit the generation of certain repetitive processes, and of the data items necessary to control and support them, without the introduction of an explicit data "structure" to contain the data items. Unlike the procedure *reverse*, the effect of the recursive procedure *reverseinput* cannot be generated non-recursively without the introduction of some means of holding the entire input sequence of characters simultaneously. The procedure *reverseinput* generates exactly the required number of character variables to hold the input characters, by means of its local variable c.

PROGRAM 7   (The Towers of Hanoi)

This is a legendary problem (now marketed as a children's toy) which, although appearing at first to be very difficult to solve, can be solved quite simply by the use of a recursive procedure.

You are given three wooden poles (call them the left pole, middle pole, and right pole). A stack of n disks of decreasing size (such that the disk of largest diameter is at the bottom) is held on the left pole which passes through a hole in the center of each disk. The initial layout of the poles and disks is illustrated in Fig. 7.1 for the case $n=5$.

The problem is to move all the disks from the left pole to the right pole according to the following rules:

(a) only one disk may be moved at a time;
(b) a disk must never be placed on top of a smaller one;
(c) at any time each of the disks must be on one of the three poles.

We wish to construct a program which reads in an integer n and outputs the sequence of moves required to solve the problem for n disks.

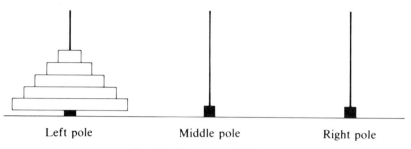

Left pole   Middle pole   Right pole

Fig. 7.1   The towers of Hanoi.

The problem of moving n (>1) disks can be reduced to a problem of moving $n-1$ disks by considering the solution as involving three steps:

(a)   move the topmost $n-1$ disks from the left pole to the middle pole, using the right pole as an "auxiliary" pole;
(b)   move the remaining disk from the left pole to the right pole;
(c)   move the $n-1$ disks on the middle pole to the right pole, using the left pole as an "auxiliary" pole.

This method can be seen to obey the rules of the game.

Thus the problem of moving n disks has been reduced to a problem of moving $n-1$ disks. Expressed another way, the problem of moving n disks has been described recursively in terms of the same problem involving one disk fewer.

When $n=1$ the problem is solved simply by moving the disc from the left pole to the right pole.

We can thus attempt a recursive formulation of the problem of moving n discs from any pole to another. This procedure will require four parameters—the number of disks to be moved, the "source" pole from which the disks are to be moved, the "destination" pole to which the disks are to be moved, and the "auxiliary" pole which is to be used to hold disks during the intermediate moves.

By analogy with the previous recursive description of moving n disks

```
procedure move (n : positiveinteger ;
                source, auxiliary, destination : pole) ;
begin
    if n = 1 then move one disk from source to destination
        else begin
                                                                    (48)
                move (n-1, source, destination, auxiliary) ;
                move one disk from source to destination ;
                move (n-1, auxiliary, source, destination)
        end
end
```

from the left pole to the right pole we can write the procedure *move* as in (48). The type *pole* is defined in the main program as an enumerated type

$pole = (left, middle, right)$

and the statement part of the main program requires only to read the number of disks *numberofdisks* from the input stream and then call

move (numberofdisks, left, middle, right)

Since the output required is the sequence of moves which solve the problem, the action *move one disk from source to destination* is programmed as a procedure, each call of which prints out the corresponding move. It uses a local procedure to output the identities of the poles involved in each move.

LISTING 7

```
PROGRAM TOWERSOFHANOI (INPUT, OUTPUT) ;

TYPE    POLE = (LEFT, MIDDLE, RIGHT) ;
        POSITIVEINTEGER = 1..MAXINT ;

VAR     NUMBEROFDISKS : POSITIVEINTEGER ;

PROCEDURE MOVE (N : POSITIVEINTEGER ;
                SOURCE, AUXILIARY, DESTINATION : POLE) ;

   PROCEDURE MOVEADISKFROMSOURCETODESTINATION ;

      PROCEDURE PRINTPOLE (P : POLE) ;
         BEGIN
            CASE P OF
              LEFT :   WRITE ('LEFT') ;
              MIDDLE : WRITE ('MIDDLE') ;
              RIGHT :  WRITE ('RIGHT')
            END
         END ; (* PRINTPOLE *)

      BEGIN
         WRITE ('MOVE A DISK FROM ') ;  PRINTPOLE (SOURCE) ;
         WRITE (' TO ') ;  PRINTPOLE (DESTINATION) ;
         WRITELN
      END ; (* MOVEADISKFROMSOURCETODESTINATION *)

   BEGIN
      IF N=1 THEN MOVEADISKFROMSOURCETODESTINATION
            ELSE BEGIN
                    MOVE (N-1, SOURCE, DESTINATION, AUXILIARY) ;
                    MOVEADISKFROMSOURCETODESTINATION ;
                    MOVE (N-1, AUXILIARY, SOURCE, DESTINATION)
                 END
   END ; (* MOVE *)
```

```
BEGIN
  READ (NUMBEROFDISKS) ;
  WRITELN ('FOR', NUMBEROFDISKS:3, ' DISKS ',
           'THE REQUIRED MOVES ARE :') ;  WRITELN ;
  MOVE (NUMBEROFDISKS, LEFT, MIDDLE, RIGHT)
END.
```

```
FOR  4 DISKS THE REQUIRED MOVES ARE :

MOVE A DISK FROM LEFT TO MIDDLE
MOVE A DISK FROM LEFT TO RIGHT
MOVE A DISK FROM MIDDLE TO RIGHT
MOVE A DISK FROM LEFT TO MIDDLE
MOVE A DISK FROM RIGHT TO LEFT
MOVE A DISK FROM RIGHT TO MIDDLE
MOVE A DISK FROM LEFT TO MIDDLE
MOVE A DISK FROM LEFT TO RIGHT
MOVE A DISK FROM MIDDLE TO RIGHT
MOVE A DISK FROM MIDDLE TO LEFT
MOVE A DISK FROM RIGHT TO LEFT
MOVE A DISK FROM MIDDLE TO RIGHT
MOVE A DISK FROM LEFT TO MIDDLE
MOVE A DISK FROM LEFT TO RIGHT
MOVE A DISK FROM MIDDLE TO RIGHT
```

The complete program, and the output which it produces for $n=4$, is shown in Listing 7.

Mutual recursion

Recursive procedures and functions usually take one of two forms:

(a)   *self-recursion*, in which the recursive procedure or function explicitly calls itself, as in the examples already presented;

(b)   *mutual recursion*, in which a procedure or function A calls some other procedure or function B which in turn (directly or indirectly) calls A.

In the case of mutual recursion a problem arises since the scope rules of PASCAL require that a procedure or function must be declared at a point in the text of the program preceding any call of it. Obviously, if two procedures *A* and *B* declared in the same block call each other, then it is impossible for each procedure to be declared before its first call. The PASCAL definition overcomes this problem by allowing a procedure or function to have a dummy declaration preceding its declaration proper. This dummy declaration announces the procedure's existence, and calls of the procedure may then appear before the procedure declaration itself. The dummy declaration has the form

> *procedure-heading* ; *"forward"* ;

or

> *function-heading* ; *"forward"* ;

and appears within the same *procedure-and-function-declaration-part* as the declaration proper. The formal parameter list (if there is one) and the result type (in the case of a function) are only included in the dummy declaration and are omitted in the full declaration.

For example, the functions *A* and *B* in (47) may be mutually recursive and *B* called from within *A*, even though its declaration proper follows that of *A*.

```
function B (x : integer) : char ; forward ;
function A (y : integer) : char ;
begin
    ... B(i) ...
end ;                                                              (47)
function B ; {parameters and result type omitted}
begin
    ... A(j) ...
end ;
```

To enable mutual recursion the *forward* mechanism in effect splits the procedure heading that defines the name and calling requirements of a procedure from the body that defines the corresponding action involved. This enables calls to the procedure to be recognized and checked for correctness before the procedure body itself has been seen. There are several contexts in which this separation of a procedure heading from the corresponding procedure body may be useful. For example, it may be useful to hold the text of the procedure separately from the text of the program that calls it, or to compile the procedure separately from the program that calls it. Indeed it may be necessary to write the procedure in a different programming language.

In practice the definition of PASCAL provides a general framework within which implementations may provide such facilities as appropriate by allowing a range of so-called *directives* of which *forward* is one example.

The full syntax of a procedure declaration is as follows:

> *procedure-declaration* =
> > *procedure-heading* ";" *procedure-body* |
> > *procedure-heading* ";" *directive* |
> > *procedure-identification* ";" *procedure body*.
> *procedure-heading* = "**procedure**" *identifier* [*formal-parameter-list*].
> *procedure-identification* = "**procedure**" *procedure-identifier*.
> *procedure-body* = *block*.

In the normal case a procedure heading and the corresponding procedure block are directly juxtaposed as a procedure declaration. However, any such declaration may take the form of a procedure heading and a *directive* chosen from the range provided by the implementation. The effect of such a declaration depends on the directive chosen. In the case of the directive *forward* its effect is to defer the definition of the procedure body itself to a later point in the program. At that point a corresponding procedure identification is used to indicate that the following procedure body is that for the identified procedure whose heading was given earlier.

A similar syntax allows the use of directives in function declarations.

> *function-declaration* =
> > *function-heading* ";" *function-body* |
> > *function-heading* ";" *directive* |
> > *function identification* ";" *function-body*.
> *function-heading* =
> > "**function**" *identifier* [*formal-parameter-list*] ":" *result-type*.
> *function-identification* = "**function**" *function-identifier*.
> *function-body* = *block*.
> *result-type* = *type-identifier*

The directive *forward* is the only one required by the definition of PASCAL, but implementations may provide additional directives for other purposes. Details of the directives available should be found in the documentation of each implementation. Their use will not be considered further in this book.

EXERCISES

7.1 Write a procedure *order3* which interchanges the values of its three integer parameters *a*, *b*, *c* if necessary, such that $a \leqslant b \leqslant c$. (Make use of the procedure *order* given on p. 96).

Use your procedure in rewriting Program 3 so that the lengths of the sides of the triangle to be analyzed need not be input in ascending order.

7.2 Extend the procedure *convertintowords* in Program 5 to convert any number in the range 1 to 999999. Modify the program to accept sums of money less than one million dollars, and re-test it with suitable data.

7.3 Write
   (a) a procedure *readoctal* which reads a sequence of octal digits and assigns the equivalent positive integer value to a parameter;
   (b) a procedure *writeoctal* which prints the sequence of octal digits denoting the value of its positive integer parameter.

Use these procedures in a program which reads a sequence of octal numbers, one per line, and prints out the numbers, followed by their octal sum.

7.4 The exponential e^x of a number *x* may be defined as

$$\exp(x) = \sum_{i=0}^{\infty} \frac{x^i}{i!} \quad \left(= 1 + x + \frac{x^2}{2!} + \frac{x^3}{3!} + \cdots \right).$$

Write a function with heading

   function *exponential* (*x* : *real*) : *real*

to compute this formula to an accuracy of four significant decimal digits.

   Hint: stop adding new terms when the size of the new term is less than one ten-thousandth of the size of the sum so far.

   Incorporate this function in a program which tabulates the values of e^x for *x* = 0.0, 0.1, 0.2, . . . ,1.0. Compare these values with those given by the standard function *exp*.

7.5 Write a function which accepts a positive integer and a decimal digit as parameters and determines whether the decimal representation of the integer contains the digit.

   Write a program which reads a digit *d* and tabulates all integer numbers from 1 to 100 such that the decimal representation of the number, its square, and its cube all contain the digit *d*. For example, if *d* = 1, 13 is such a number, since 13, 169 and 2197 all contain the digit 1.

7.6 Rewrite the program to print a digit pyramid (Exercise 6.3) using one loop and a recursive procedure.

8

The Goto-statement

All of the programs that have been presented in the previous chapters have been constructed using the simple PASCAL statement forms (assignment, input, output) combined into more powerful structures using the structured statements introduced in Chap. 6, and procedure and function declarations as described in Chap. 7. The statements of the resulting PASCAL programs are executed in the sequence in which they appear in the program text, subject to the control patterns imposed by the various structured statements. These control patterns are almost always sufficient to express the actions required within a program.

However, situations occasionally arise in the design of a program which make it either clumsy or inefficient to describe the action of part of the program in terms of PASCAL's structured statements. In such circumstances it may be desirable, for reasons of program efficiency and clarity, to deviate from the implicit order of execution associated with these statements. This is made possible by the use of *labels* and *goto-statements*.

In Chap. 4 the syntax of a *statement* was given as

> *statement* = [*label* ":"] (*simple-statement* | *structured-statement*) .
> *simple-statement* = [(*assignment-statement* | *procedure-statement* | *goto-statement*)] .

A statement may be *labeled* by prefixing it with a *label*, i.e., an unsigned integer in the range 0 to 9999, followed by a colon.

> *label* = *unsigned-integer* .

Some examples of labeled statements:

> 99 : *writeln* ('*error detected*')
> 777 : *a* := *b*
>   1 : **repeat** *P* (*i*) ; *i* := *i*+1 **until** *i*=*j*

The labeling of a statement makes it possible to refer to that statement from other parts of the program, by means of a *goto-statement*, which has the form:

goto-statement = "**goto**" *label* .

This has the effect, when executed, of causing the statement prefixed by the given *label* to be executed as the next statement of the program, rather than the statement following the *goto-statement*. Examples of goto-statements:

goto 777
if $x > maxvalue$ **then goto** 99
if $i < j$ **then goto** 1

All labels must be declared in the *label-declaration-part* of the block in whose statement part they are used to label statements. The *label-declaration-part* appears as the first component of a *block* (see definition of *block* on p. 17, and its syntactic definition is

label-declaration-part = "**label**" *label* { "," *label* } ";" .

That is, it consists of the symbol **label** followed by a sequence of unsigned integers separated by commas. For example, the program skeleton (1) declares and uses three labels in its program block.

```
program example (input, output) ;
label 1, 99, 777 ;
const maxvalue = 1000 ;
var i, j, x : integer ;
begin
    ⋮
    777 : a := b ;
        ⋮
        if i<j then goto 1 ;
        ⋮                                    (1)
    1 : repeat P(i) ; i:=i+1 until i=j ;
        ⋮
        if x>maxvalue then goto 99 ;
        ⋮
    99 : writeln ('error detected') ;
        ⋮
        goto 777
        ⋮
end.
```

The scope of a label declaration is the entire text of the block in which it appears, subject to its possible re-declaration in an enclosed block, i.e., the scope rules for labels are the same as those for identifiers. A label declared in a block must be used to label a statement in the statement part of that block. However, the statement so labeled may be referenced by a goto-statement within the statement part of any enclosed block—provided that the label has not been re-declared at an intervening level.

Obviously two statements in any block must not be prefixed by the same label value, otherwise there will be an ambiguity in deciding the destination of any goto-statement referencing that label.

A goto-statement is sometimes used to exit from a control structure when an error or exceptional circumstance arises. Suppose that a program is required to read the names of clients from the first 30 characters of each line of input and output them in the same format, stopping when the input is exhausted. The program might be written as in (2).

```
program list (input, output) ;
    procedure oneclient ;
        var i : 1 .. 30 ; c : char ;
        begin
            for i := 1 to 30 do
            begin
                read (c) ;
                write (c)
            end ;
            readln ; writeln
        end ;
    begin
        repeat
            oneclient
        until eof (input)
    end.
```

(2)

Now suppose the program is to check that each name read consists only of alphabetic characters and blanks. When an error is found the partially printed name is to be followed by a distinctive error marker, and printing continued with the next name. This could be achieved by modifying the procedure *oneclient* as in (3). Here the goto-statement is used to override the normal for-loop control, so ending the processing of this client prematurely.

```
procedure oneclient ;
    label 99 ;
    var i : 1 .. 30 ; c : char ;
    begin
        for i := 1 to 30 do
        begin
            read (c) ;
            if ((c<'A') or (c>'Z')) and (c<>' ')            (3)
            then begin
                    write ('*****ERROR') ;
                    goto 99
                end ;
            write (c)
        end ;
    99:readln ; writeln
    end ;
```

Note that, in the above procedure *oneclient*, we have assumed that all the characters between $'A'$ and $'Z'$ in the available character set are letters.

When it is necessary to transfer control, by a goto-statement, to the end of a compound-statement, a labeled empty statement must be placed before the **end** symbol, viz.,

```
begin
    ⋮
    if x<0 then begin error:=true ; goto 1 end ;
    ⋮
    ... ;
1 : end
```

Note that, in order to introduce the empty statement, the label must be preceded by a semicolon.

Within compound-statements a goto-statement may only transfer control to a labeled statement occurring within the same compound-statement or within an enclosing compound-statement, i.e., it is not possible to transfer control into a compound-statement. In this respect the sequence of statements enclosed in a repeat-statement by the symbols **repeat** and **until** is also regarded as a compound-statement. The program fragment (4a) illustrates a legal goto-statement, but the fragment (4b) contains an illegal use of a goto-statement.

```
9 :                                    repeat
  ⋮                                       ⋮
begin                                   77 : ...
  ⋮            (4a)                        ⋮            (4b)
    goto 9 ;                            until a < b ;
  ⋮                                       ⋮
end                                     goto 77
```

The statements controlled by if-, while- and for-statements should not be labeled. Although the definition of PASCAL allows such a label to be referenced from within the labeled statement, the effect of such a goto-statement is confusing and it is recommended that such practice be avoided.

Integers used as case labels in case-statements and those used for labeling statements referenced by gotos are textually similar but quite independent. Thus, one may use labels as in (5), where the label 1 and the case label 1 are quite distinct, if somewhat confusing!

```
1 : case p div q of
        1 :   S ;
        2,3 : T ;
        4 :   W                                        (5)
    end ;
  ⋮
  goto 1
```

A non-local label may be used in a goto-statement to transfer control out of a procedure or function to a statement in some enclosing block, but only if the labeled statement occurs at the outermost level of statement nesting in that block. In the above example, suppose that it is required to abort the processing of the entire sequence of client names when the first error is found. To achieve this we can introduce a label at the end of the program block itself and use this label within the procedure *oneclient*, as in (6).

```
program list (input, output) ;
label 99 ;
     procedure oneclient ;
          var i : 1 .. 30 ; c : char ;
          begin
               for i := 1 to 30 do
               begin
                    read (c) ;
                    if ((c<'A') or (c>'Z')) and (c<>' ')
                    then begin
                              writeln ('*****ERROR') ;
                              writeln ('RUN ABANDONED') ;        (6)
                              goto 99
                         end ;
                    write (c)
               end ;
               readln ; writeln
          end ;
begin
     repeat
          oneclient
     until eof (input) ;
99 :
end.
```

In this case the goto-statement is used to override the for-loop control within the procedure *oneclient*, the procedure call itself, and the program loop within which the call occurred.

The effect of a non-local goto-statement is very powerful in some situations. Consider the program outline (7). The procedure Q is not called directly from the statement part of P but, instead, is called from R which has been called from P. Therefore, the effect of the **goto** 99 statement in Q is to exit not only from the execution of Q but also from the execution of R (which called Q) and thence transfer control to the statement of P labeled 99. If Q or R is a recursive procedure which has called itself several times, then execution of **goto** 99 within Q causes exit from *all* the recursive activations of Q and R back to the statement 99 in P.

If *P* itself is recursive, then execution of the **goto** 99 statement within *Q* always returns control to the most recent activation of *P*.

```
procedure P;
label 99 ;
    procedure Q ;
    begin
        ⋮
        Q ;
        ⋮
        goto 99 ;
        ⋮
    end ;
    procedure R ;
    begin                                              (7)
        ⋮
        Q ;
        ⋮
    end ;
begin
    ⋮
    R ;
    ⋮
99 : ...
    ⋮
end ;
```

We have illustrated the use of goto-statements to handle exceptional situations not otherwise catered for by facilities of PASCAL. In principle the goto-statement, used with a simple conditional clause such as **if** ... **then goto** ..., can also be used to realize the effect of all of the PASCAL repetition and selection structures described in Chap. 6. The disadvantage of doing so is that the intended structure is no longer apparent, and an error in realizing that structure may go undetected. The structural consistency of a program expressed in terms of the constructs **if** ... **then** ... **else** ..., **case** ... **of** ..., **while** ... **do** ..., **repeat** ... **until** ..., etc. is guaranteed by the language rules themselves. The consistency of the same program expressed with goto-statements is the programmer's responsibility. It is this freedom to destroy useful structure which makes the goto-statement a dangerous programming tool. It is good programming practice to regard the goto-statement as a last resort, to be used only when the control structure required cannot reasonably be expressed in terms of PASCAL's other control constructs.

9

Arrays

THE ARRAY CONCEPT

In Chaps. 6 and 7 we saw how a composite program action could be constructed out of elementary actions such as assignments, input, and output, by means of the compound-statement, selection and repetition statements, and procedural abstraction. The data manipulated by such composite actions are themselves often composite, or structured, where the elementary components are values of the simple types introduced in Chap. 3. Describing the data in a structured way may both clarify the nature of the data and simplify their manipulation by the program.

Consider the following example. A firm employs a group of twenty salesmen (with reference numbers 1–20) who are paid commission on that portion of their sales which exceeds two-thirds of the average sales of the group. A program is required to read in the sales of each of the twenty salesmen and print out the reference number of those salesmen who qualify for commission, together with their sales.

There are two features of this problem which make it difficult to program using the PASCAL facilities described so far. It appears that the program must carry out similar processing with each salesman's figures—read in each of the twenty sales figures; compute the average sales amount; compare each salesman's sales with two-thirds of the average to decide whether or not he has qualified for any commission. This similarity of processing suggests some form of repetition. Secondly, it is necessary to store the salesmen's amounts throughout the program—they are read in at the start and used to determine the commission level, but must also be available for the final part of the program when it is determined which salesmen will be receiving commission. Thus we require twenty variables to hold the twenty sales amounts.

Twenty variables could be declared, of appropriate type, say
*sales*1,*sales*2,....,*sales*20. However, programming the problem now
becomes extremely cumbersome—resulting in a program such as (1).

> **begin**
>   *read(sales*1,*sales*2, . . .,*sales*20) ;
>   *calculate commission level* ;
>   **if** *sales*1 > *commission level* **then** *writeln*(1,*sales*1) ;
>   **if** *sales*2 > *commission level* **then** *writeln*(2,*sales*2) ;   (1)
> $\vdots$
>   **if** *sales*20 >*commission level* **then** *writeln*(20,*sales*20)
> **end**

Because the variables *sales*1,*sales*2,... are distinct we are forced to
write the printout as a sequence of if-statements rather than the repetition of a single if-statement. Likewise, the potential repetition in reading
the sales values, and in computing their sum, is precluded by the
independence of these variables. Clearly this is a rather tedious program
to write. Consider how much more tedious it would be if the firm had
not 20, but 200, salesmen working for it!

A preferable solution is to consider these variables as components of
a single data item *sales*, and to denote the *i*th component by the
mathematical convention of subscripting, thus $sales_i$. The problem solution for any number *N* of salesmen can then be expressed as in (2).

> **begin**
>   *sum* := 0.0 ;
>   **for** *i* := 1 **to** *N* **do**
>   **begin** *read(sales$_i$)* ; *sum* := *sum*+*sales$_i$* **end** ;   (2)
>   *commissionlevel* := 2/3*(*sum/N*) ;
>   **for** *i* := 1 **to** *N* **do**
>   **if** *sales$_i$* > *commision level* **then** *writeln* (*i*,*sales$_i$*)
> **end**

This solution assumes two language features not so far available:

(a)   the ability to denote a group of variables, or composite variable, by
     a single identifier *sales*, and
(b)   the ability to distinguish a particular variable of the group, or
     component, by subscripting this identifier with a suitable value *i*.

In PASCAL an *array-type* is defined as follows:

array-type = **"array"** "[" *index-type* {"," *index-type*} "]" **"of"** *type* .
index-type = *type* .

That is, an *array-type* consists of the symbol **array** followed by one or more *index-types* separated by commas and enclosed in square brackets, followed by the symbol **of** and an indication of the type of the individual variables of the array (the *element type*). An index-type may be any ordinal type, and the element type may be any type. A variable of an array type consists of one element for each value of the index type, or one element for each combination of values of the index types where two or more index types are specified.

For example,

   sales : **array** [1 . . 20] **of** *real*

is an array-variable declaration which creates an array of 20 elements. In this case the index type is the integer subrange 1 . . 20 and the element type is *real*.

The index type of an array type is often an integer subrange but need not necessarily be so. For example, an enumerated type

   color = (*red,blue,yellow*)

might be used in an array type, thus

   flowercount : **array** [*color*] **of** *integer*

to create an array of three integer elements, one for each of the index values *red*, *blue*, and *yellow*.

An individual element of an array variable is denoted, as an *indexed-variable*, by writing the name of the array followed by the corresponding value (or values) of the index type(s) enclosed in square brackets:

   indexed-variable = *array-variable* "[" *expression* { "," *expression* } "]" .
   array-variable = *variable* .

The expression(s) enclosed in square brackets must yield value(s) that are assignment-compatible with the corresponding index type(s).

For example

   sales [14]

denotes the element of the array *sales* corresponding to the index value 14, while

   flowercount [*red*]

denotes the element of array *flowercount* corresponding to index value *red*.

This indexing operation is sometimes known as *subscripting* and the index value is referred to as the *subscript*, since it corresponds to the conventional mathematical notation $sales_{14}$. However, in PASCAL the 'subscript' can only be written in square brackets immediately following the array name.

As the above definition shows, the index value within an indexed-variable need not be a constant—it may be any expression which produces a value belonging to the declared index type of the array. Thus we may refer to any of the following:

> *sales* [*i*]
> *sales* [*i*+*j*]
> *sales* [*trunc*(*x*∗4.2)+*j*]

provided that the expressions *i*, *i*+*j*, and *trunc*(*x*∗4.2)+*j* all produce integer values which lie in the range 1 .. 20. In general,

> *sales* [*n*]

is an acceptable indexed variable provided *n* yields an integer value in the range 1 .. 20. If the value of *n* lies outside this range then reference is being made to an array element which does not exist. This is known as an *array subscript error*. Most implementations provide means of detecting such errors during the execution of a program.

An array type enables a (possibly large) number of variables of identical type to be declared and manipulated as (components of) a single array variable. When combined with the for-statement described in Chap. 6, arrays provide an extremely powerful and compact means of processing large numbers of variable data. For example, if a group of 500 real variables is represented as an array

> *x* : **array** [1 .. 500] **of** *real*

then only one statement is required in order to set all 500 variables to zero, namely

> **for** *j* := 1 **to** 500 **do** *x*[*j*] := 0

We are now in a position to present a complete program (3) to solve the sales commission problem considered earlier. Should the number of salesmen in the group subsequently change, then the only modification required to this program is the alteration of the value of the constant *numberofsalesmen*.

> **program** *salescommission* (*input,output*) ;
> **const** *numberofsalesmen* = 20 ;
> **var** *sales*: **array** [1 .. *numberofsalesmen*] **of** *real* ;   (3)
>   *i*: 1 .. *numberofsalesmen* ;
>   *sum,commissionlevel* : *real* ;

```
begin
    sum := 0 ;
    for i := 1 to numberofsalesmen do
    begin read(sales[i]); sum := sum+sales[i] end ;
    commissionlevel := sum*2/3 / numberofsalesmen ;        (3 cont.)
    for i := 1 to numberofsalesmen do
        if sales[i] > commissionlevel then
            writeln (i:6, sales[i]:11:2)
end.
```

A palindrome is a sentence which (considering only the letters and ignoring all spaces and punctuation marks) reads the same both backwards and forwards. For example

MADAM I'M ADAM

The program (4) will read a sentence of up to 100 letters ending with a full stop and determine whether it is a palindrome or not.

```
program palindrome (input,output) ;
var     letter : array [1 .. 100] of char ;
        i : 0 .. 100 ; j : 1 .. 100 ;
        ch : char ;
begin
    {read and write sentence storing
     all letters in the array letter}
    i := 0 ; read (ch) ;
    repeat
        if (ch >= 'A') and (ch <= 'Z') then              (4)
        begin i := i+1 ; letter[i] := ch end ;
        write (ch) ; read (ch)
    until ch = '.' ;
    {test if array contents form a palindrome}
    j := 1 ;
    while (j<i) and (letter[j] = letter[i]) do
    begin j := j+1 ; i := i-1 end ;
    if j >= i then write (' is') else write (' isn"t') ;
    write (' a palindrome')
end.
```

TWO-DIMENSIONAL ARRAYS

In our examples so far we have used only arrays with one index type in their declared type, and which therefore require only one appropriately valued index to select a corresponding element. Such arrays are known as *one-dimensional* arrays. However, PASCAL permits array types with more than one index type. For example, a printed page consisting of 66 lines each providing 120 character positions may be declared as an array variable

   page : **array** [1 .. 66, 1 .. 120] **of** *char*

The *j*th character of line *i* of *page* would then be the element denoted by

   page [*i,j*]

where *i* has a value in the range 1 to 66, and *j* a value in the range 1 to 120.

The following statement would set each of the 7920 character elements of the array *page* to the blank character

   for *i* := 1 **to** 66 **do**
       for *j* := 1 **to** 120 **do** *page* [*i,j*] := ' '

The array *page* is said to be a *two-dimensional* array. Arrays may be specified with any number of indices—if an array has *n* indices it is said to be an *n-dimensional* array and its elements are referenced using the array identifier followed by *n* indexing expressions.

A two-dimensional array is often used to represent the mathematical concept of a *matrix* (in the same way a one-dimensional array may be used to represent a *vector*). The program (5) reads a 6 × 8 matrix from the input stream into a two-dimensional array *A*, forms the row sums in a vector *B* and the column sums as a vector *C*, and outputs the three arrays in the form shown in Fig. 9.1.

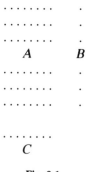

Fig. 9.1

```
program   matrices (input,output) ;
const     rowmax = 6 ; columnmax = 8 ;
type      row = 1 .. rowmax ;
          column = 1 .. columnmax ;
var       A : array [row, column] of integer;
          B : array [row] of integer ;
          C : array [column] of integer ;
          i : row ;
          j : column ;
          sum : integer ;
begin
    {read matrix values into A}
    for i := 1 to rowmax do
        for j := 1 to columnmax do read (A[i,j]) ;
    {form row sums in B}
    for i := 1 to rowmax do
    begin
        sum := 0 ;
        for j := 1 to columnmax do sum := sum + A[i,j] ;      (5)
        B[i] := sum
    end ;
    {form column sums in C}
    for j := 1 to columnmax do
    begin
        sum := 0 ;
        for i := 1 to rowmax do sum := sum + A[i,j] ;
        C[j] := sum
    end ;
    {output A,B,C in form required}
    for i := 1 to rowmax do
    begin
        for j := 1 to columnmax do write (A[i,j]) ;
        writeln (B[i] : 15)
    end ;
    writeln ; writeln ;
    for j := 1 to columnmax do write (C[j])
end.
```

In fact a very much shorter program with an equivalent effect could be written using only the vector C. This is left as an exercise for the reader.

The elements of a PASCAL array may be of any other type, in particular they may be of another array type. This possibility enables the effect of a two-dimensional array to be created by a one-dimensional array whose elements are of another one-dimensional array type. For example the array *page* illustrated earlier could also be declared as

page : **array** [1 .. 66] **of array** [1 .. 120] **of** *char* ;

The array again has a total of 7920 character elements, the *j*th character of the *i*th line being denoted by

page[*i*][*j*]

In addition the identifier *page* followed by only one subscript *i* thus

page[*i*]

denotes an element of type **array**[1 .. 120] **of** *char*, in fact the *i*th line of the page represented. In fact the definition of PASCAL states that this and the previous declaration of *page* are completely equivalent, so that any of the indexed variable forms

page [*i*, *j*]
page [*i*] [*j*]
page [*i*]

may be used with either declaration.

WHOLE ARRAY OPERATIONS

An array type may be defined at the point of declaration of an array variable, as in the examples so far in this chapter, or it may be given a name in a type definition, e.g.,

type *punchcard* = **array** [1 .. 80] **of** *char* ;
    line = **array** [1 .. 120] **of** *char* ;
    printedpage = **array** [1 .. 66] **of** *line* ;
    monthlytotals = **array** [1970 .. 1979,*month*] **of** *real* ;

These type names may then be used in variable declarations such as

var *card*1,*card*2 : *punchcard* ;
    *page*1 : *printedpage* ;
    l : *line* ;
    rainfall,sunshine : *monthlytotals* ;

Where arrays of the same type have to be declared at different points in the program such a type name must always be introduced, but even when used at one point only such a name often improves the clarity of a program.

If two array variables are of the same type, then it is possible to assign the values of each of the elements of one array to the corresponding elements of the other array in a single assignment statement. For example, the assignment

$card1 := card2$

is equivalent to the for-loop

for $i := 1$ **to** 80 **do** $card1[i] := card2[i]$

but is more efficient than the latter on most implementations.

Like other variables, a complete array may be passed as an actual parameter to a procedure or function. In this case the array type must have been defined previously in a type definition in a block enclosing the procedure, since the type of the parameter in the formal parameter list can only be specified as an identifier. For instance, if we define an array type

$sometype =$ **array** $[1 .. 10]$ **of** $integer$

and require a function to return as its result the sum of the values of the elements of an array of this type, the function could be declared as in (6).

```
function sum (a:sometype) : integer ;
var i : 1 .. 10 ; total : integer ;
begin
    total := 0 ;                                                    (6)
    for i := 1 to 10 do total := total + a[i];
    sum := total
end
```

If $array1$ and $array2$ are declared as variables of type $sometype$, then the function may be called with them as parameters, e.g.,

if $sum (array1) > sum (array2)$ **then** $array2 := array1$

The procedure (7) will multiply two square matrices A and B and leave the result in a matrix C, where A, B and C are arrays of a type

$squarematrix =$ **array** $[1 .. N, 1 .. N]$ **of** $real$

and N is a constant. Since the array C is altered by the procedure it must be declared as a variable parameter, as in (7).

```
procedure matrixmultiply (A,B:squarematrix;var C:squarematrix) ;
var i,j,k : 1 .. N ; sum : real ;
begin                                                               (7)
    for j := 1 to N do
    begin
```

```
        for k := 1 to N do
        begin
            sum := 0 ;
            for i := 1 to N do sum := sum+A[j,i]*B[i,k] ;
            C[j,k] := sum
        end
    end
end
```

Each array assignment and each passing of an array as a value parameter involves the copying of the entire array, i.e., copying each of its element values. For large arrays this is a time-consuming operation, and the storage required by the value parameters is also large. A programmer should be mindful of this expense in manipulating whole arrays. It may be necessary in designing a program to minimize the array-copying operations which it involves.

PROGRAM 8   (Calculating notes and coins)

Each week the wages department of a firm must establish the number of notes and coins of the available denominations required from the bank in order to make up the staff pay packets. This is to be calculated by a program whose input is a sequence of lines detailing the take-home pay of the staff. Each line contains the name of an employee (in character positions 1–20) followed by his pay for the week.

The program is to calculate the way in which each pay packet can be made up using the least number of notes and coins. The available denominations are $10, $5 and $1 notes, and 25 cents, 10 cents, 5 cents, and 1 cent coins ($1 = 100 cents). In order to assist the staff in the preparation of the pay packets the program must output, for each employee, his name and how his pay packet is to be made up. This should be followed by the total withdrawal required from the bank in terms of the required number of each denomination of note and coin. It is assumed that no employee takes home more than $100 per week.

```
    for each employee do
    begin
        read and write name and pay ;
        calculate notes and coins required ;                    (8)
        output notes and coins required ;
        update totals for pay, notes and coins
    end ;
    output totals
```

The basic structure of the program is a loop which processes the data on each employee and accumulates the required totals, as shown in (8). At this stage the only significant problem arises in the expression of *calculate notes and coins required*. We shall express this as a procedure statement

change (wageincents,numberrequired)

where the first parameter is a value parameter giving the employee's wage in cents (in the range $0 .. 10000$) and the second parameter is a variable parameter of type

moneyarray = **array** [*denominations*] **of** *integer*

The array *numberrequired* will have its value set by the procedure *change* to indicate the number of notes and coins of the various denominations required to make up *wageincents* in the most efficient manner. The type *denominations* is an enumeration of the available kinds of notes and coins, i.e.,

denominations = (*tendollars, fivedollars, onedollar,*
                              twentyfivecents, tencents, fivecents, onecent) ;

We postpone further refinement of the procedure *change* for the moment.

The main program keeps totals of the payroll and the number of notes and coins of each denomination required. Thus we introduce a variable

totalpay : *real*

(since we shall read in each employee's pay as a real number) and an array

total : *moneyarray*

which is initialized to zero and then used to keep running totals for the notes and coins.

The processing of the data for each employee involves reading a line of input and the overall processing terminates when the input data have all been read. Thus, the previous main program can now be extended as in (9).

```
begin
      totalpay := 0 ;
      initialize array total to zero ;                          (9)
      write heading ;
      while not eof(input) do
```

```
    begin
        read line containing employee's name and wage ;
        write name and wage ;
        totalpay := totalpay + wage ;
        change (wageincents,numberrequired) ;                    (9 cont.)
        update totals by numberrequired ;
        write out number of notes and coins required
    end ;
    print totals
end
```

The statement *initialize array total to zero* is expressed as a for-loop

> **for** *d* := *tendollars* **to** *onecent* **do** *total* [*d*] := 0

and *update totals by numberrequired* and **write out number of notes and coins required** can be amalgamated into a single loop as in (10). The remainder of the main program can now be readily expressed in PASCAL. It should print appropriate headings to make the output more readable.

```
    for d := tendollars to onecent do
    begin
        write (numberrequired [d]) ;                             (10)
        total [d] := total [d] + numberrequired [d]
    end
```

The procedure *change* is now examined in detail. Its heading is

> **procedure** *change* (*amount:payrange*;
>   **var** *numberofeach:moneyarray*)

The strategy of expressing an amount in terms of the least number of notes and coins is clearly to use as many $10 notes as possible, then to make up the remainder with as many $5 notes as possible, then as many $1 notes, twentyfive cent pieces, etc., i.e., the body of *change* might be expressed informally as in (11).

```
    for each of the denominations taken in descending order of value do
    begin
        calculate maximum number of that denomination that
            can be used ;                                        (11)
        adjust the amount still to be considered
    end
```

In fact we cannot express this, at present, as a for-loop, since the value associated with each denomination has to be introduced separately, e.g., we might write it as in (12).

$numberrequired$ [$tendollars$] := $amount$ **div** 1000 ;
$amount$:= $amount$ **mod** 1000 ;
$numberrequired$ [$fivedollars$] := $amount$ **div** 500 ;
$amount$:= $amount$ **mod** 500 ;   (12)
⋮
$numberrequired$ [$fivecents$] := $amount$ **div** 5 ;
$amount$:= $amount$ **mod** 5 ;
$numberrequired$ [$onecent$] := $amount$ **div** 1

However, we can express this sequence of statements as a simple for-loop by introducing an array, say,

$values$: **array** [$denominations$] **of** 1 . . 1000

to store the values associated with each denomination. Provided that this array is initialized properly, i.e.,

$values$[$tendollars$] := 1000; $values$[$fivedollars$] := 500; . . .;
$values$[$onecent$] := 1

then the for-loop is as shown in (13).

for d := $tendollars$ **to** $onecent$ **do**
begin
    $numberrequired$[d] := $amount$ **div** $values$[d] ;   (13)
    $amount$:= $amount$ **mod** $values$[d]
end

Listing 8 shows the complete program together with sample output.

LISTING 8

```
PROGRAM PAYPACKETS (INPUT, OUTPUT) ;

TYPE  PAYRANGE = 0..10000 ;
      DENOMINATIONS = (TENDOLLARS, FIVEDOLLARS, ONEDOLLAR,
                       TWENTYFIVECENTS, TENCENTS, FIVECENTS, ONECENT );
      MONEYARRAY = ARRAY [DENOMINATIONS] OF INTEGER ;

VAR   VALUES : ARRAY [DENOMINATIONS] OF 1..1000 ;
      TOTAL, NUMBERREQUIRED : MONEYARRAY ;
      D : DENOMINATIONS ;
      WAGEINCENTS : PAYRANGE ;
      X, TOTALPAY : REAL ;
      CH : CHAR ;
      I : 1..20 ;
```

```
PROCEDURE CHANGE (AMOUNT : PAYRANGE ; VAR NUMBEROFEACH : MONEYARRAY) :
VAR    D : DENOMINATIONS ;
BEGIN
   FOR D:=TENDOLLARS TO ONECENT DO
   BEGIN
      NUMBEROFEACH[D] := AMOUNT DIV VALUES[D] ;
      AMOUNT := AMOUNT MOD VALUES[D]
   END
END ; (*  CHANGE  *)



BEGIN
   FOR D:=TENDOLLARS TO ONECENT DO TOTAL[D]:=0 ;
   VALUES[TENDOLLARS]:=1000 ;  VALUES[FIVEDOLLARS]:=500 ;
   VALUES[ONEDOLLAR]:=100 ;      VALUES[TWENTYFIVECENTS]:=25 ;
   VALUES[TENCENTS]:=10 ;        VALUES[FIVECENTS]:=5 ;
   VALUES[ONECENT]:=1 ;
   WRITELN ('     EMPLOYEE          WAGE   $10   $5   $1   25C   10C',
            '   5C   1C') ;
   WRITELN ;
   WHILE NOT EOF (INPUT) DO
   BEGIN
      FOR I:=1 TO 20 DO BEGIN READ (CH) ; WRITE (CH) END ;
      READLN (X) ; WRITE (X:7:2) :
      WAGEINCENTS := ROUND (X*100) ;
      TOTALPAY := TOTALPAY+X ;
      CHANGE (WAGEINCENTS, NUMBERREQUIRED) ;
      FOR D:=TENDOLLARS TO ONECENT DO
      BEGIN
         WRITE (NUMBERREQUIRED[D] :5) ;
         TOTAL[D] := TOTAL[D]+NUMBERREQUIRED[D]
      END ;
      WRITELN
   END ;
   WRITELN ('*** TOTAL WITHDRAWAL ***') ; WRITELN ;
   WRITE (TOTALPAY:27:2) :
   FOR D:=TENDOLLARS TO ONECENT DO WRITE (TOTAL[D] :5)
END.
```

EMPLOYEE	WAGE	$10	$5	$1	25C	10C	5C	1C
ALEC SLOAN	9.00	0	1	4	0	0	0	0
GORDON QUIRK	58.03	5	1	3	0	0	0	3
MARTIN MACDONALD	9.74	0	1	4	2	2	0	4
JIMMY THOMPSON	86.76	8	1	1	3	0	0	1
VIRGINIA WELLS	97.58	9	1	2	2	0	1	3
CHRISTINE GREEN	4.06	0	0	4	0	0	1	1
SAMUEL JENKINS	32.51	3	0	2	2	0	0	1
BETTY COHEN	42.00	4	0	2	0	0	0	0
DAVID BERNARD	33.10	3	0	3	0	1	0	0
MURIEL HOYTE	42.50	4	0	2	2	0	0	0
DENIS OAKES	16.17	1	1	1	0	1	1	2

*** TOTAL WITHDRAWAL ***

	431.45	37	6	28	11	4	3	15

PACKED ARRAYS

As we have just noted arrays may be very large data items in terms of the computer storage required to hold their components, e.g., the array

A : **array** $[-1000 .. 1000]$ **of** *boolean*

consists of 2001 component data items. A program containing a number of such arrays may require so much storage for its arrays that it cannot be run on a given computer. In some circumstances it is possible to reduce the amount of storage required for an array—particularly if the element type is *boolean, char*, an enumerated type, or a subrange type.

The prefixing of an array-type definition by the special symbol **packed**, e.g.,

B : **packed array** $[-1000 .. 1000]$ **of** *boolean*

is an instruction to the PASCAL implementation that it should attempt to minimize the storage used by the array (by packing the individual array elements more closely within the computer store).

This packing may well increase the time taken to access the individual array elements and so the decision to define an array as packed represents a trade-off between the size of a program and its speed of execution. However, it should be noted that if the most frequently executed array operation is copying, i.e., array assignment or passing an array as a value parameter, then packing may decrease *both* the program storage requirement *and* its execution time.

The effect of packing an array depends on the nature of its elements, and on the particular implementation of PASCAL. In some cases it may result in neither the program size nor the program execution time being affected, as compared with the array not being packed.

In general, the meaning of a program is not affected by an array being packed, only (possibly) its speed and size. However, packing is considered to be an integral aspect of the array type, and so alters the contexts in which an array or its elements may be used, as following sections will show. In particular, an element of a packed array may not be passed as an actual variable parameter to a procedure or function. Thus, if we have a procedure with the following heading:

procedure P (**var** q:*boolean*)

and arrays A and B declared as above, then

P $(A[i])$

is a permissible procedure call, but

P $(B[i])$

is not.

If a particular part of a program makes frequent reference to the elements of a packed array, this may result in a severe decline in the speed of execution of that part of the program. If packing is desirable for other reasons a possible remedy might be to unpack the array elements from a packed array into a local non-packed array before entering the part of the program which will make frequent reference to the array elements, and then, later, to pack the non-packed array elements back into the packed array. PASCAL provides two standard procedures which permit the transfer between packed and non-packed arrays to be programmed as a single operation.

Assume the following declarations

U : **array** $[a .. b]$ **of** *sometype* ;
P : **packed array** $[c .. d]$ **of** *sometype* ;

The standard procedure call

pack (U,i,P)

where i is an acceptable index for the array U, has the effect of copying elements from the unpacked array U, starting at the element $U[i]$, to the packed array P, starting at its first element $P[c]$, until the packed array P is filled. The effect is equivalent to

$k := i$;
for $j := c$ **to** d **do begin** $P[j] := U[k]; k := succ(k)$ **end**

Note that the array U must contain sufficient elements from $U[i]$ onwards to fill P, otherwise an array subscript error is implied.

The standard procedure call

unpack (P,U,i)

has the inverse effect, i.e., it copies elements from the packed array P, starting at the first element $P[c]$, to the unpacked array U, starting at the element $U[i]$, until the packed array P is exhausted. The effect is thus equivalent to

$k := i$;
for $j := c$ **to** d **do begin** $U[k] := P[j]; k := succ(k)$ **end**

Again, the array U must have sufficient elements from $U[i]$ onwards to hold the elements of P.

STRINGS

Although a packed array has, in general, the same range of operations associated with it as a non-packed array, there is one class of packed array which has a special status in PASCAL and some special operations associated with it. In Chap. 2 strings were introduced and defined as a sequence of characters enclosed by quotes. A string of length n characters (excluding the quotes) is considered to be a constant of the type

packed array $[1 .. n]$ **of** *char*

For example,

'*TODAY IS THURSDAY*'

is a constant of the type

packed array $[1 .. 17]$ **of** *char*

Variables of a type **packed array** $[1..n]$ **of** *char* are called *string variables of length* n and may be used to hold strings of length n.

We have already seen that the value of an array may be assigned to another array variable of the same type. If we define a type

name = **packed array** $[1 .. 12]$ **of** *char*

and declare

*name*1,*name*2 : *name*

as variables of type *name*, then the assignment

*name*1 := *name*2

is permitted, as it is for any two arrays of the same type. In addition, however, any string of length 12 characters may be used as the value to be assigned, e.g:,

*name*1 := '*JOHN F JONES*'

A string value, either variable or constant, is assignment compatible with any string type of the same length.

As we saw in Chap. 5, the standard procedures *write* and *writeln* allow the output of strings of any length, as in

writeln ('*the answer is* ', $x+y$)

It is also permitted to output the value of a string variable in this way. For example the statement

writeln ('*NAME* : ', *name*1)

outputs two strings, one constant and one variable, to produce an output line of the form

NAME : JOHN F JONES

Note, however, that this facility applies only to string variables and not to any other packed or unpacked arrays. Note also that it is not possible to read in a value for a string variable in this way—it must be read in character by character, for example as follows:

for $i := 1$ **to** 12 **do** *read* (*name*1[i])

The relational operators $= <> < <= > >=$ may be used with two string operands of the same length. For example we might write

if *name*1 $=$ 'JOHN F JONES' **then** . . .

The meaning of the equality and inequality operators $=$, $<>$, is obvious, remembering that the two operands must be of the same length. The meaning of the ordering operators $< <- > >=$ is defined by the normal lexicographic convention used to order words in a dictionary, i.e., the order of two string operands is determined by the order of the first pair of corresponding character elements which differ. Thus

'AZZZZ' $<$ 'BCCCC' gives *true*, since 'A' $<$ 'B'
'AXCYE' $>$ 'AXCDZ' gives *true*, since 'Y' $>$ 'D'

Again ordering is defined only for two string operands of the same length, unlike a dictionary, where words of different lengths must also be ordered.

Note also that the relational operators are defined only for string values and not for any other packed or unpacked arrays.

PROGRAM 9 (Constructing a concordance)

A program is required to examine a piece of text and produce a list, in alphabetical order, of all the distinct words which appear in the text, e.g., examination of the input

the black dog chased the black cat

would produce the corresponding output

black
cat
chased
dog
the

It may be assumed that no words are more than 16 letters long, and that no words contain apostrophes or hyphens.

The program requires the construction of a list of all the distinct words which appear in the text. Defining the type *wordspelling* as a string type of length 16

wordspelling $=$ **packed array** [1 .. 16] **of** *char*

a suitable structure for the representation of this list is an array

   index : **array** [1 .. *indexsize*] **of** *wordspelling*

together with a variable

   size : 0 .. *indexsize*

defining the length of the list, i.e., the number of significant entries held in the array *index*.

The contents of the list, when the input has all been examined, are to be output in alphabetical order. We must therefore decide whether to construct the list in such a way that its contents are always in alphabetical order (i.e., by inserting new entries into the list so that the ordering is maintained), or else by constructing an unsorted list and then sorting it immediately before output of the list of occurring words. We shall choose the former method, since it is somewhat more efficient, i.e., we shall construct the list so that the contents of the array *index* always satisfy the relation

   for all i,j such that $i<j \le$ size, index[i]<index[j]

The basic structure of the program is a loop which determines the next word in the input stream and, if necessary, inserts its spelling into the list. The loop (14) terminates when the input stream has been completely scanned.

```
endoftext := false ;
getnextword ;
while not endoftext do
begin
    addtolist ;                                         (14)
    getnextword
end ;
printtable
```

The procedure *getnextword* scans through the text looking for the next word. If the input is exhausted then it sets the value of the global boolean variable *endoftext* to *true*, otherwise it stores the next word in a global variable

   spelling : *wordspelling*

so that the procedure *addtolist* can, if necessary, add this word to the list of words which have occurred in the text. The structure of the procedure *getnextword* is therefore

> *scan through text until letter or end of text is found* ;
> **if** *letter found* **then** *scan and record word spelling*
>   **else** *endoftext* := *true*

Each execution of this procedure reads any non-letter characters preceding the next word, the letters making up the word, and one character following. Assuming a line structured input stream the character read when *eof(input)* becomes true must be a blank corresponding to the final end of line. Thus *eof(input)* may become true during the non-letter scan, in which case *endoftext* must be set true, or on reading the character following the word, in which case *endoftext* must be set true by the *following* call of *getnextword*.

Introducing a character variable *ch* the above may therefore be rewritten as in (15).

> **if not** *eof(input)* **then**
>   **repeat** *read(ch)* **until** *ch is a letter* **or** *eof(input)* ;   (15)
>   **if not** *eof(input)* **then** *scan and record wordspelling*
>   **else** *endoftext* := *true*

If we assume that the letters form a coherent subrange of the values of type *char*, as they do in many implementations, the condition *ch is a letter* can be written as

$$(ch >= 'A') \text{ and } (ch <= 'Z')$$

If this is not so, a more complex test is required. An alternative means of writing conditions such as *ch is a letter*, using a constant of a set type, is explained in Chap. 11.

The step *scan and record wordspelling* must scan the input text up to the first non-letter, record the letters scanned in the array *spelling* and space fill this array if less than 16 letters have been scanned. Introducing a variable *length* to count the letters recorded, we may write the block shown in (16). Here we have assumed that the last character of the input stream cannot be a letter. Hence *eof(input)* can only become true as the end of a word is detected, and will be correctly dealt with by the next call of *getnextword*.

> **begin**
>   *length* := 0 ;
>   **repeat**
>   *length* := *length* + 1 ; *spelling* [*length*] := *ch* ;
>   *read(ch)*   (16)
>   **until** (*ch* < 'A') **or** (*ch* > 'Z') ;
>   **for** *length* := *length* + 1 **to** 16 **do** *spelling* [*length*] := ' '
> **end**

On some implementations it may be more efficient to collect the letters
of the word scanned in an unpacked array of characters, and then pack
them into the string variable *spelling* using the standard procedure *pack*.
   The procedure *addtolist* takes the word recorded in *spelling* and
searches *index* to determine whether or not that word has already
occurred in the text. If not, the new word must be inserted in the index
in such a way as to maintain the alphabetic ordering of the entries in
index. The outline of *addtolist* is thus

```
begin
      search list ;
      create a new entry in list if necessary
end
```

We shall perform a linear search of the list, i.e., noting that the entries
in *index* are in ascending alphabetic order, we begin the search at the
first element of *index* and inspect successive elements until either the
required word is found, or the whole list has been inspected, or an
alphabetically greater word is encountered.
   By introducing local variables

```
i : integer ;
positionfound : boolean ;
```

the action *search list* may be expressed as

```
i := 1 ; positionfound := false ;
while (i<=size) and not positionfound do
if index[i]<spelling then i:=i+1 else positionfound := true
```

The boolean variable *positionfound* is necessary because PASCAL
does not specify that the second operand *b* in a boolean expression *a*
and *b* is not evaluated if the first, *a*, is *false* (see p. 41). Thus, if we
write

```
while (i <= size) and (index[i] < spelling) do i := i + 1
```

then when *i* reaches *size* + 1 an attempt to evaluate *index*[i] may still
occur, resulting in an access of an unassigned element of the array, or
even an array subscript error (if *size* = *indexsize*).
   There are faster methods of searching an ordered list, such as that
held in the array *index*, than the above linear search. In a binary split
search, for example, the mid-point entry in the list is first examined to
determine in which half of the list the required word may be. The
mid-point entry of the appropriate half is then examined, and so on, until
either the required word is found or it is established that the word is not

in the list. If the list contains 2^n entries, then this technique requires at most n comparisons. The program given in this case study uses a linear search—it is left as an exercise for the reader to modify the program to perform the more efficient binary search.

The statement *create a new entry in list if necessary* is then expressible as in (17).

```
if positionfound
then begin
        if index[i] <> spelling
        then add a new entry (at position i)            (17)
     end
else add a new entry (at end of list)
```

In either case the position of the new entry is indicated by the value of i on exit from the search list loop, so each addition process is expressible as a call to a local procedure *insertword*.

To add a new word to index we increase *size* by 1 and move all the words alphabetically greater than the new word down the list by one place to make room for the new word, which may then be inserted. To avoid over-writing the entries in the list, this re-positioning must begin at the last entry currently in the list. Remembering that the position of the new word is given by the value of i on exit from the search loop, the procedure *insertword* becomes as shown in (18).

```
procedure insertword ;
var j : integer ;
begin
    if size < indexsize
    then begin
            size := size + 1 ;                           (18)
            for j := size downto i+1 do index[j] := index[j-1] ;
            index[i] := spelling
         end
end
```

Finally, the outputting of the index is performed by a simple loop which prints the significant elements of *index*. Since these are represented as strings, each may be output directly, i.e.,

```
for i := 1 to size do writeln (index[i])
```

Listing 9 shows the complete program and a sample index produced by execution of the program with the following input:

THE PROFILE

THE PROFILE IS AN EDITED, AUTOMATICALLY FORMATTED, LISTING OF THE SOURCE
PROGRAM WHICH DISPLAYS THE FREQUENCY OF EXECUTION OF EACH STATEMENT OF THE
PROGRAM .

TO READ OFF THE FREQUENCY OF EXECUTION OF ANY STATEMENT, WE LOCATE THE
BEGINNING OF THE STATEMENT IN THE PROFILE LISTING.   IF AN ASTERISK IS PRESENT
ON THE SAME LINE, TO THE LEFT OF THE LISTING, THEN THE DESIRED FREQUENCY WILL
BE FOUND TO THE LEFT OF THE ASTERISK.   OTHERWISE, THE LINE WILL CONTAIN ONE OR
MORE UPWARD ARROWS ; WE SELECT THE RIGHTMOST ARROW, AND FOLLOW THE LINE OF
ARROWS VERTICALLY UPWARDS UNTIL AN ASTERISK IS ENCOUNTERED ; AGAIN, THE
DESIRED FREQUENCY WILL BE FOUND TO THE LEFT OF THE ASTERISK.

LISTING 9

```
PROGRAM CONCORDANCE (INPUT, OUTPUT) ;

CONST WORDMAX = 16 ;
      INDEXSIZE = 200 ;

TYPE  WORDSIZE = 1..WORDMAX ;
      WORDSPELLING = PACKED ARRAY[WORDSIZE] OF CHAR ;

VAR   INDEX : ARRAY[1..INDEXSIZE] OF WORDSPELLING ;
      SIZE : 0..INDEXSIZE ;
      SPELLING : WORDSPELLING ;
      ENDOFTEXT : BOOLEAN ;

PROCEDURE GETNEXTWORD ;
VAR   CH : CHAR ;
      LENGTH : 0..WORDMAX ;
BEGIN
   IF NOT EOF(INPUT) THEN
   REPEAT READ (CH) UNTIL ((CH>='A')AND(CH<='Z')) OR EOF(INPUT) ;
   IF NOT EOF(INPUT) THEN
   BEGIN
      LENGTH := 0 ;
      REPEAT
         LENGTH := LENGTH+1 ; SPELLING[LENGTH] := CH ;
         READ (CH)
      UNTIL (CH<'A')OR(CH>'Z') ;
      FOR LENGTH := LENGTH+1 TO WORDMAX DO SPELLING[LENGTH]:=' '
   END ELSE ENDOFTEXT := TRUE
END ; (* GETNEXTWORD *)

PROCEDURE ADDTOLIST ;
VAR   POSITIONFOUND : BOOLEAN ;
      I : 1..INDEXSIZE ;

   PROCEDURE INSERTWORD ;
   VAR  J : 1..INDEXSIZE ;
```

```
   BEGIN
      IF SIZE < INDEXSIZE
      THEN BEGIN
              SIZE := SIZE+1 ;
              FOR J:=SIZE DOWNTO I+1 DO INDEX[J]:= INDEX[J-1];
              INDEX[I]:=SPELLING
           END
   END ;  (* INSERTWORD *)

BEGIN
   I:=1 ;  POSITIONFOUND:=FALSE ;
   WHILE (I<=SIZE) AND NOT POSITIONFOUND DO
      IF INDEX[I] < SPELLING THEN I:=I+1 ELSE POSITIONFOUND := TRUE ;
   IF POSITIONFOUND
   THEN BEGIN
           IF INDEX[I]<>SPELLING THEN INSERTWORD
        END
   ELSE INSERTWORD
END ;  (* ADDTOLIST *)


PROCEDURE PRINTTABLE ;
VAR   I : 1..INDEXSIZE ;
BEGIN
   WRITELN ('*** INDEX ***') ; WRITELN ;
   FOR I:=1 TO SIZE DO WRITELN (INDEX[I])
END ; (*  PRINTTABLE  *)


BEGIN
   ENDOFTEXT := FALSE ;
   SIZE := 0 ;
   GETNEXTWORD ;
   WHILE NOT ENDOFTEXT DO
   BEGIN
      ADDTOLIST ;
      GETNEXTWORD
   END ;
   PRINTTABLE
END.


*** INDEX ***

AGAIN
AN
AND
ANY
ARROW
ARROWS
ASTERISK
AUTOMATICALLY
BE
BEGINNING
CONTAIN
DESIRED
DISPLAYS
```

```
EACH
EDITED
ENCOUNTERED
EXECUTION
FOLLOW
FORMATTED
FOUND
FREQUENCY
IF
IN
IS
LEFT
LINE
LISTING
LOCATE
MORE
OF
OFF
ON
ONE
OR
OTHERWISE
PRESENT
PROFILE
PROGRAM
READ
RIGHTMOST
SAME
SELECT
SOURCE
STATEMENT
THE
THEN
TO
UNTIL
UPWARD
UPWARDS
VERTICALLY
WE
WHICH
WILL
```

CONFORMANT ARRAY PARAMETERS

The facility for passing arrays as parameters described in the section Whole Array Operations is effective when the actual parameters corresponding to a given formal parameter in different calls of the procedure or function concerned are identical in type. In some cases, however, it is convenient to define a procedure or function whose actual array parameters vary in the number of elements they contain from one call to another. For example, we might envisage a function *sum* similar to that defined on page 141 which might be used at one point to compute the sum of the ten elements of an array defined as follows:

   X : **array** [1 . . 10] **of** *integer*;

and at another point to compute the sum of 100 elements of an array declared as follows:

   Y : **array** [0 . . 99] **of** *integer*;

The essential form of the function required is similar to that given on page 141 and might be written as follows:

```
function sum( ... a: ... ?) : integer;
   var l, total : integer;
   begin
      total : = 0;
      for i := first to last do total := total + a[i];
      sum := total
   end
```

where *first* and *last* represent the initial and final index values for the actual array parameter. The problem is how these values are actually transmitted to the function, and how the array parameter itself is described in the formal parameter list of the function. To overcome this problem, the definition of PASCAL allows parameters to be defined as *conformant array parameters*, though this is an *optional* feature which implementations may, or may not, provide. Using the conformant array parameter mechanism, the above problem can be solved by a function or definition of the following form:

```
function sum(var a : array[first .. last : integer] of integer) : integer;
   var i, total : integer ;
   begin
      total := 0;
      for i := first to last do total := total + a[i];
      sum := total
   end
```

In this form, the formal parameter list indicates that a is a one-dimensional array of integers but does not indicate the exact range of index values involved, only that they are of type *integer* and that the initial and final values may be referred to as *first* and *last*.

   The parameter a is said to be a *conformant array parameter* and the corresponding actual parameter must conform to the pattern described for a, that is, it must be a one-dimensional array of integers with an index type that is a subrange of integers. For each actual parameter that is passed, the identifiers *first* and *last* denote the lower and upper bounds of this index range and may be used in the body of the function to obtain the values of these bounds.

A conformant array parameter is introduced in a formal parameter list by a variable or value parameter section in which the parameter-type is expressed as a *conformant-array-schema*, whose form in detail is defined as follows:

> *conformant-array-schema* =
>   *packed-conformant-array-schema* |
>   *unpacked-conformant-array-schema*.
> *packed-conformant-array-schema* =
>   *"packed"* **"array"** *"["* *bound-specification* *"]"*
>   **"of"** *type-identifier*.
> *unpacked-conformant-array-schema* =
>   **"array"** *"["* *bound-specification* {*";"* *bound-specification*} *"]"*
>   **"of"** (*type-identifier* | *conformant-array-schema*).
> *bound-specification* =
>   *identifier* *" .. "* *identifier* *":"* *ordinal-type-identifier*.

A conformant array schema defines the number of dimensions of each conformant array parameter declared in the section, the type of its elements and the host type within which the index range of each dimension must lie. It does not, however, define the lower and upper bounds for each index range; instead, auxiliary identifiers are introduced as bound identifiers to denote these. Within the procedure or function that manipulates the conformant array parameter, these bound identifiers may be used in expressions to obtain the lower and upper bounds of the corresponding index type of the actual array parameter, as illustrated by the function *sum* earlier.

The syntax category

> *bound-identifier* = *identifier*.

is introduced to denote the class of identifiers so defined. Their use as factors in expressions is enabled by the syntax definitions

> *factor* = *variable* | *unsigned-constant* | *function-designator* |
>   *bound* | *set* | *"("* *expression* *")"* | **"not"** *factor*.
> *bound* = *bound-identifier*.

As with array types, a multi-dimensional conformant array schema of the form:

> **array** $[a1 .. b1 : T1; a2 .. b2 : T2; ... ; an .. bn : Tn]$ **of** T

is strictly equivalent to

> **array** $[a1 .. b1 : T1]$ **of**
>   **array** $[a2 .. b2 : T2]$ **of**
>   . . .
>   **array** $[an .. bn : Tn]$ **of** T

Note that in a multi-dimensional conformant array, only the final dimension may be packed and the conformant array schema must be written in the form:

> **array** $[a1 .. b1 : T1 ...$
> $...]$ **of**
> **packed array** $[an .. bn : Tn]$ **of** T

The restriction of packing to a single dimension does limit the use of the conformant array mechanism for some packed arrays, but it is sufficient to allow procedures and functions that manipulate strings of varying lengths to be written. For example, the following procedure can be used to write in coded form a string of any length, using the character encoding function supplied as a second parameter:

> **procedure** *Encode* $(s$: **packed array** $[a .. b : integer]$ **of** *char*;
>   **function** *code* $(c : char) : char)$;
>   **var** $i : integer$;
>   **begin**
>   **for** $i := a$ **to** b **do** *write* $(code\ (s[i]))$
>   **end**

Although the actual parameters passed to this procedure *Encode* may all be of string type, that is of the form:

> **packed array** $[1 .. n]$ **of** *char*

the fact that the lower bound of their index type is always 1 cannot be represented in the formal parameter list. If either bound of the index type of an array parameter is to vary, then both must be described in variable form within a conformant array parameter specification. In the case of a string manipulation, this means that parameters such as s above are not considered to be string variables within the procedure and the special operations applicable to string variables, such as their direct use in write statements, the assignment of literal strings, or their comparison using relational operators, cannot be applied.

When two or more conformant array parameters are defined in the same parameter section, the corresponding actual array parameters in any call to the procedure or function must be of the same type; this ensures that the bound values made available by the bound identifiers hold for all of the actual array parameters involved and that the corresponding formal arrays can be considered to have the same type within the procedure or function itself. Thus, the operation of assigning the value of one such parameter to another is valid. The following procedure maximizes the contents of two array parameters by assigning to both whichever of the initial array values has the greater element sum:

```
procedure Maximize (var x, y : array [m .. n : integer] of integer) ;
    begin
        if sum (x) > sum (y)
        then y := x
        else x := y
    end
```

The assignments

$$y := x \ and \ x := y$$

are only valid if the conformant array parameters x and y are declared in the same parameter section. The corresponding actual array parameters must then have the same type.

Between them, these examples illustrate the range of operations that can be applied to conformant array parameters; these are as follows:

(a) The individual elements of a conformant array parameter may be accessed using the normal notation for indexed variables, as in *Encode.*

(b) A conformant array parameter may be passed as parameter to another procedure or function that expects a similar conformant array parameter, as x and y are passed to *sum* within *Maximize.*

(c) Where two conformant array parameters are declared in the same parameter section, they are necessarily of the same type and their values may, therefore, be assigned from one to another, as in *Maximize.*

A conformant array schema may be used to define either *variable* or *value* parameters, with the usual consequent differences in how such parameters are used. For a formal variable conformant array parameter the corresponding actual parameter must be an array variable (or another conformant array parameter), and operations on the formal parameter within the procedure or function are applied directly to this actual parameter. Thus in the procedure *Maximize*, which is intended to alter one or other of its actual parameters, the formals x and y are declared as *variable* conformant array parameters.

For a formal value conformant array parameter the corresponding actual parameter may be an expression that produces an array value. (In practice, the only expressions in PASCAL that produce array values are array variables themselves, or strings). This value is assumed by the formal parameter when the procedure or function is called, and subsequent operations on the formal parameter do not alter the actual parameter itself. The procedure *Encode* is not intended to alter its actual array parameter, and therefore the formal parameter *s* is declared as a *value* conformant array parameter. This means that *Encode* may be called with a string variable *v* as parameter, thus,

Encode (v, ...)

or with a string constant as parameter, thus

Encode (`Mata Hari`, ...)

However, if we look at our first example of a conformant array parameter, in the function *sum*, this pattern is not maintained. The function is not intended to alter its actual array parameter, yet the formal *a* is declared as a *variable* parameter. The reason for this apparent anomaly is as follows. Value parameters are implemented by creating copies of the actual parameters, normally within the procedure or function being called. However, making provision within the procedure or function for a conformant array parameter, whose size is not pre-determined, can create difficulties in some implementations. For this reason the definition of PASCAL specifically allows the copies of value conformant array parameters to be made at the point of call, where the size of the actual parameters is known. However, to ensure that all copying problems are avoided the additional restriction is imposed that a formal conformant array parameter itself, or any component of it that is conformant (i.e. not fixed in size), cannot be passed to another procedure or function as an actual *value* conformant array parameter. Thus, if the function *sum* was declared with a value conformant array parameter, it could not be used in the procedure *Maximize* as illustrated.

Unfortunately, this interdependence between the parameter lists of procedures or functions that call each other is not always apparent when they are written, particularly if they are intended as general-purpose utilities. In such cases the restriction described above discourages the use of value conformant array parameters, even when the purpose of the procedure or function is not to change the actual parameters involved. However, exclusive use of variable conformant array parameters is also unacceptable when writing procedures or functions to manipulate character strings, since this precludes them being called with constant string parameters.

As a final example of the use of the conformant array parameter mechanism, consider the generalization of the matrix manipulation procedure given on pages 141 and 142. This can now be written to multiply any two rectangular matrices of compatible sizes and produce a corresponding rectangular product matrix, as follows:

```
procedure matrixmultiply
    (A : array[m1A .. n1A : integer ; m2A .. n2A : integer] of real ;
    B : array[m1B .. n1B : integer ; m2B .. n2B : integer] of real ;
    var C : array[m1C .. n1C : integer ; m2C .. n2C : integer] of real);
    {assertion :
        m1A = m1C, m2B = m2C, m2A = m1B
        n1A = n1C, n2B = n2C, n2A = n1B}
    var i, j, k : integer ; sum : real ;
    begin
        for j := m1C to n1C do
            for k := m2C to n2C do
            begin
                sum := 0 ;
                for i := m2A to n2A do sum := sum + A[j, i] * B[i, k];
                C[j, k] := sum
            end
    end
```

As the initial comment shows, the procedure relies on the actual parameter matrices having matching upper and lower bounds on each dimension and the programmer must ensure that the actual parameters used conform in this way. Alternatively, an explicit test to check that these relations hold could be coded at the entry to the procedure.

All the examples show that the conformant array parameter mechanism enables flexible procedures and functions to be defined, but they also show that greater programming care may be required in writing and in using these procedures than is the case with "fixed" array parameters. In discussing fixed array parameters in an earlier section, we noted that the programmer must consider the overhead of copying large arrays that are passed by value. The same considerations apply in the case of conformant array parameters, but in this case, overheads may also arise from the use of the conformant array parameter mechanism itself. For many implementations, the time taken to access an element of a conformant array parameter may be greater than that taken to access the element of a corresponding array parameter of fixed type, and the time taken to check that the subscripts involved lie in the correct range may be much greater. For all of these reasons, the conformant array parameter mechanism is one to be used with caution. In general, it should be used only in those situations where a procedure or function must handle arrays of varying sizes during a single execution of the program involved. In all other cases, the use of the normal parameter mechanism for arrays is simpler to understand, less prone to error, and in many cases, more efficient.

OTHER STRUCTURED TYPES

Array types are just one of a number of ways in which composite, or structured, data items may be defined in PASCAL. In Chap. 3 we defined *type* as follows

type = simple-type | structured-type | pointer-type | type-identifier.

Simple-types were discussed in Chap. 3 and *pointer-types* are introduced in Chap. 13. For *structured-types* there are in fact four possible forms, as the following definition shows

structured-type = [*"***packed***"*] *unpacked-structured-type* .
unpacked-structured-type = *array-type | record-type | set-type |*
          file-type .

Array types have been the subject of this chapter; record, set and file types are discussed in Chaps. 10, 11 and 12 respectively.

Any structured-type may be prefixed by **packed** with similar effect, i.e., the implementation may then minimize the amount of storage used by variables of that type, possibly with a consequent increase in the execution time of the program.

Variables of a structured-type may be manipulated as a whole, or their individual components may be manipulated by appropriate selection constructions.

For arrays the indexed-variable notation enabled individual elements to be referenced and manipulated as individual variables. In Chap. 3 we defined *variable* as follows

variable = entire-variable | component-variable |
          referenced-variable .
entire-variable = variable-identifier .

An *entire-variable* is simply an identifier introduced to denote a variable by a variable declaration—it may thus denote a variable of a simple (or a pointer) type, or a variable of a structured type as a whole. A *component-variable* is used to denote a particular component of a variable of a structured type and takes one of three forms

$$component\text{-}variable = indexed\text{-}variable \mid$$
$$field\text{-}designator \mid$$
$$file\text{-}buffer .$$

As we have already seen, *indexed-variables* are used to denote the components of variables of array type.

Field-designators and *file-buffers* are used to denote the accessible components of variables of record and file types respectively. The components of a variable of set type are not individually accessible as variables, though they can be manipulated in other ways, as Chap. 11 describes.

EXERCISES

9.1 Extend the text analysis program specified by Exercise 6.6, to determine the number of occurrences of each of the letters A to Z in the input text.

9.2 Write a program which reads a sequence of 10 positive integers and then finds the maximum of the sequence, outputs its value, the number of times that it occurs, and the positions in which it appears. The process is then repeated to find the next largest value, and so on.

example input :   7 10 143 10 52 143 72 10 143 7
example output :   143 *OCCURS* 3 *TIMES, AT POSITIONS* 3 6 9
. . .
7 *OCCURS* 2 *TIMES, AT POSITIONS* 1 10

9.3 Write a program which reads an input text and prints out the number of occurrences of each adjacent letter pair which appears within the text.

9.4 Write a program which reads a sequence of word pairs and prints each pair in dictionary order. You may assume that each word pair is on a separate input line, the words of each pair are separated by at least one blank, and each word is not more than 16 letters long. Use a similar format for the output.

9.5 Write a procedure

procedure *plot* (**function** $f(x : real) : real$;
$xlower, xupper : real$)

which "plots" a graph of the function $f(x)$ over the range *xlower* to *xupper*, with the x axis horizontal. The plot should be scaled to use 100 horizontal and 50 vertical output positions, and both axes should be printed.

Use this procedure in a program which plots a graph of sin (x) over the range 0 to 2π.

10

Records

THE RECORD CONCEPT

An array consists of a number of components which are identical in nature, and hence in type. It is often the case that an item of data is made up of a number of components which are distinct in nature and, perhaps, also of different types. In Program 4 we introduced three variables to denote a calender date, as follows:

month : 1 .. 12 ;
day : 1 .. 31 ;
year : 1900 .. 2000 ;

with an implicit assumption that the three variables represented the different components of the same date.

A date may therefore be considered as the composition of exactly three values, one from each of the three types above. PASCAL provides a means of defining a data type whose values are a composition of values of other, differing, data types—as a *record-type*. For dates we may define a record type (1). This definition specifies that a value of type *date* consists of exactly three component values, of type 1 .. 12, 1 .. 31 and 1900 .. 2000, respectively. The identifiers *m*, *d* and *y* introduced in the record type definition are names given to the individual components, or *fields*, and they enable reference to be made to the component values of a variable of type *date*.

$$
date = \textbf{record}
$$

             m : 1 .. 12 ;
             d : 1 .. 31 ;   (1)
             y : 1900 .. 2000
       end

The general form of a PASCAL record type is defined syntactically as

record-type = "**record**" *field-list* "**end**" .
field-list = [(*fixed-part* [";" *variant-part*] | *variant-part*)[";"]]

For the time being we ignore record types containing a *variant-part*, which are discussed later in this chapter.

fixed-part = *record-section* { ";" *record-section* } .
record-section = *identifier-list* ":" *type* .

Thus, for the present, a *record-type* consists of the symbols **record** and **end** enclosing a *fixed-part*, which is a list of one or more *record-sections* (separated by semi-colons). Each *record-section* introduces a list of one or more identifiers (separated by commas) and a specification of their type, or it may be empty. These identifiers are known as *field-identifiers* and hereafter the syntax category

field-identifier = *identifier* .

is used to denote the class of identifiers introduced in this way. The examples in (2) further illustrate record-type definitions.

```
cartesian = record x,y : real end ;
suit = (clubs,diamonds,hearts,spades) ;
rank = (two,three,four,five,six,seven,eight,nine,
          ten,jack,queen,king,ace) ;
card = record
             s : suit ;                                        (2)
             r : rank
         end ;
time = record
             hours : 0..24 ;
             minutes,seconds : 0..59
         end ;
```

The scope of the field identifiers introduced in a record-type definition is the record-type itself, and so the field identifiers must be distinct from any other field identifier of the same record-type, but not necessarily distinct from any other identifiers declared outside the record-type.

Having defined and named a record-type in a type definition such as those above, variables of the named type may be declared in a variable-declaration-part in the usual way, for example:

```
takeoff,landing : time ;
focus1,focus2 : cartesian ;
cardled : card ;
```

A record type might of course be defined in a variable declaration itself, as in (3), but in this case variables of the same type cannot be declared elsewhere in the program. The introduction of type identifiers to denote shared types is often necessary, and is always good programming practice.

$day1, day2$: **record**
$\qquad m : 1..12 ;$
$\qquad d : 1..31 ;$ (3)
$\qquad y : 1900..2000$
end

Data held as record variables within a program must be manipulated in some way. The simplest operation which may be applied to a record variable is to assign it the value of another variable of the same record type, e.g.,

$takeoff := landing$

which has the effect of assigning the value of each field of the variable *landing* to the corresponding field of the variable *takeoff*.

To refer to one of the component fields of a record a *field-designator* is used, in which the record variable is qualified by the required field identifier.

field-designator = *record-variable* "." *field-identifier* .
record-variable = *variable* .

Thus, given a variable $day1$ of type *date* as above,

$day1.m$ denotes the month component, of type $1..12$;
$day1.d$ denotes the day component, of type $1..31$;
$day1.y$ denotes the year component, of type $1900..2000$.

The following are further examples of field designators assuming the variable declarations given earlier:

takeoff.hours
cardled.s
*focus*1.*x*

A component of a record variable may be used anywhere that a variable of that component's type may be used, e.g.,

$xx := (focus1.x + focus2.x)/2 ;$
if $cardled.s = hearts$ **then** ...
$write (day1.m, day1.d, day1.y)$

An individual component of a record may thus have its value changed, leaving the values of all other components unchanged, by naming the required component in an assignment statement, e.g.,

$focus1.x := 0$;
$day1.year := 1949$;
$takeoff.hours := takeoff.hours + 1$

This is known as *selective updating*. The record variable assignment

$day1 := day2$

where $day1$ and $day2$ are variables of type *date*, is thus equivalent to the three selective updating assignments

$day1.m := day2.m$;
$day1.d := day2.d$;
$day1.y := day2.y$

In such a case the record-variable assignment is to be preferred, since it is clearer, more succinct, and more efficient in many implementations.

The use of field designators is illustrated by the procedure (4), which determines the mid-point c of the line joining two points $p1,p2$, where all the points are represented as records of type *cartesian*.

```
procedure bisect (p1,p2 : cartesian ; var c : cartesian) ;
begin
      c.x := (p1.x + p2.x)/2 ;                                    (4)
      c.y := (p1.y + p2.y)/2
end
```

WITH-STATEMENTS

When processing a record variable it is quite usual to make several references to its components within a small region of the program. For instance, to initialize the variable $day1$ one might write

$day1.m := 1$; $day1.d := 1$; $day1.y := 1980$

In these circumstances repeated reference to fields of a record by writing the record variable name qualified by the required field identifier soon becomes tedious, particularly if long identifiers are being used. PASCAL provides a statement for use with record variables that enables reference to record components without having to repeat the record variable identifier at each reference. This is the *with-statement*, which is defined as follows:

with-statement = "**with**" *record-variable* {"," *record-variable* }
"**do**" *statement* .

Within the statement controlled by a with-statement a field of any of the indicated record variables may be denoted by use of the field identifier alone. The effect of a with-statement is to open a new scope which contains the corresponding field identifiers for each of the named record variables, thereby permitting the use of the field identifiers as variables. The initialization of the variable *day*1 may thus be written as

with *day*1 **do begin** $m := 1$; $d := 1$; $y := 1980$ **end**

The general form of the with-statement

with $v1,v2,\ldots,vn$ **do** S

is equivalent to (5), i.e., the scopes are opened, and therefore nested, in the order in which the record variables are listed in the with-statement.

> **with** $v1$ **do**
>   **with** $v2$ **do**
> $\vdots$ (5)
>   **with** vn **do** S

Thus, if the record variables $v1$ and $v2$ each have a field identified by F, then a simple occurrence of F within S denotes the corresponding field of $v2$, not that of $v1$, by the rules of nested scopes. The field F of $v1$ can be denoted within S only by writing $v1.F$ explicitly.

The use of a with-statement not only reduces the length of the text of a program, but also increases its readability, and in some cases may produce a more efficient program.

The use of records and with-statements is illustrated in the re-formulation of Program 4 shown in (6). Dates are now held as variables of the record type *date*, and a procedure *update* is used which updates its variable parameter of type *date* to the day following its original date value. The main program reads in a sequence of dates, and outputs, for each, the date of the next day.

```
program nextday (input,output) ;
type date = record
                month : 1 .. 12 ;
                day : 1 .. 31 ;
                year : 1900 .. 2000
            end ;
var day : date ;
    procedure writedate (d : date) ;
    begin
        with d do write (month : 3,'/',day : 2,'/',year : 4)
    end ;
```
(6)

```pascal
procedure update (var d : date) ;
var daysinmonth : 28 .. 31 ;
begin
    with d do
    begin
        case month of
        1,3,5,7,8,10,12 : daysinmonth := 31 ;
        4,6,9,11        : daysinmonth := 30 ;
        2 : if (year mod 4 = 0) and (year <> 1900)
            then daysinmonth := 29
            else daysinmonth := 28
        end ;
        if day = daysinmonth then
        begin
            day := 1 ;
            if month = 12 then begin
                                    month := 1;          (6 cont.)
                                    year := year+1
                                end
                          else month := month+1
        end else day := day+1
    end
end ;
begin
    while not eof(input) do
    begin
        with day do readln(month,day,year) ;
        write('the day following') ; writedate(day) ;
        update(day) ;
        write (' is') ; writedate(day) ; writeln
    end
end.
```

MIXED STRUCTURES

The definition of a *record-section* indicates that a field of a record may be of any type—not only a simple type, as in the examples so far, but also a structured type such as an array type or another record type. For example, we might define a record type to describe the details of a person as follows:

```pascal
person = record
            name : packed array [1 .. 20] of char ;
            dateofbirth : date
         end
```

A value of type *person* consists of two component values—a field *name* which is itself a string of 20 characters, and a field *dateofbirth* which is itself a record made up of three component values, *m*, *d* and *y*.

Likewise a record may occur as a component of other structured types. Thus an array type may be defined whose elements are records. For example, we may define a type

$$bridgehand = \textbf{array} \ [1 .. 13] \ \textbf{of} \ card$$

where the record type *card* has already been defined as before.

In this way we can describe data structures of arbitrary complexity in terms of previously defined simple and structured data types. These structures and their components can be manipulated at several levels using the notation for variables and variable components already introduced.

For example, if we have a declaration

$$p : person$$

then

p itself	denotes a variable of type *person* which might be assigned to other variables of the same type;
p.name	denotes a string of 20 characters which might be assigned, compared, or output, as any such string variable may be;
p.name[*i*]	denotes the *i*th character of *p.name*, which might be used in any way appropriate to a character variable;
p.dateofbirth	denotes a record variable of type *date* which might be assigned to or from other variables of type *date*;
p.dateofbirth.d	denotes a variable of type 1 .. 31

and so on.

Thus the statement

$$writeln(p.name, \ p.dateofbirth.y)$$

prints out the name and year of birth of the person described by variable *p*. The statement

with *p* **do** *writeln(name,dateofbirth.y)*

has exactly the same effect.

PACKED RECORDS

In the previous chapter the use of packed arrays was described. Record variables may also be declared as packed by preceding the symbol **record** by **packed** in the record-type definition. The advantages of packing records are the same as for arrays, namely that packing normally results in a reduction of the storage space required at the cost of increased access time in the selection of fields. Thus packing is usually worthwhile only if the principal operation associated with a record type is copying of entire record values rather than selection of individual fields.

It is not permissible to pass a component of a packed record as a variable parameter in the call of a procedure or function.

PROGRAM 10   (Updating a league table)

There are six teams in a soccer league, in which each team plays each other team twice. A program is required whose input is a league table consisting of one line for each team, where each line contains the following information:

    the team name, as 12 characters;
    the number of games played, won, lost and drawn so far,
        as four integer numbers each followed by at least one blank;
    the number of points gained, where each win gains two points,
        each draw one point and each defeat none.

The input league table is followed by the results of the latest round of matches, where each result is on a separate line consisting of

    the home team's name,
    the home team's score,
    the away team's name,
    the away team's score,

each separated by at least one blank. The program is required to read in the league table and results and output an updated league table in which the teams and their playing records are listed in the order of their new league position.

```
begin
    readintable ;
    updatetable ;                                               (7)
    printtable
end
```

The basic structure of the program may be expressed as in (7). All of these three processes manipulate the league table and so we must first define a suitable structure for the representation of this table within the program. Since there will be one set of details in the table for each of the teams in the league, a suitable structure might be an array

> *leaguetable* : **array** [*teamposition*] **of** *teamdetails*

where the type *teamposition* is defined as

> *teamposition* = 1 .. *numberofteams*

The details associated with the team at each position are its name, the number of games played, won, lost and drawn, and the points gained so far. Thus the type *teamdetails* may be defined as a record type with six fields, as in (8).

> *teamdetails* = **record**
>   *name* : *teamname* ;
>   *played,won,lost,drawn* : 0 .. *maximumgames* ;
>   *points* : 0 .. *maximumpoints*
>   **end**   (8)

where

> *teamname* = **packed array** [1 .. 12] **of** *char*

With this data structure we can now proceed to design each of the three main processes of the program.

The process *readintable* simply involves reading the first lines of the input containing the current table and storing the details for each team in a corresponding element of the array *leaguetable*, as in (9).

> **procedure** *readintable* ;
> **begin**
>   *for each team do*
>   **begin**
>   *read name and details into the*   (9)
>   *next element of leaguetable*
>   **end**
> **end**

The details of this process are easily programmed, but since team names also have to be read in from the results lines it is useful to introduce a shared procedure for this task, of the form

> **procedure** *readname* (**var** N : *teamname*) ;

The process *updatetable* consists of reading in the latest results and, for each match, updating the league records of the teams involved according to the result of the match. Remembering that a win is worth 2 points, a draw 1 point, and a defeat 0 points, the procedure *updatetable* may be expressed informally as in (10).

```
procedure updatetable ;
begin
    for each match do
    begin
        read the teams and scores ;
        add 1 to games played by both teams ;
        case result of
        home win : begin
                        for home team add 1 to wins and 2 to
                        points ;
                        for away team add 1 to losses
                    end ;                                          (10)
        away win : begin
                        for home team add 1 to losses ;
                        for away team add 1 to wins and 2 to
                        points
                    end ;
        draw     : begin
                        for both teams add 1 to draws ;
                        for both teams add 1 to points
                    end
        end
    end
end
```

For each team in the results lines it is necessary to locate the corresponding details record in the existing league table. This is a simple search process which may be abstracted as a function of the form

function *position* (*name* : *teamname*) : *teamposition* ;

Using this function the remaining details of the update process may be easily programmed.

The process *printtable* breaks naturally into two parts, as in (11).

```
begin
    sort league table into points order ;                         (11)
    print ordered table
end
```

Sorting the league table into points order can be accomplished as in (12).

```
for i := 1 to numberofteams −1 do
begin
    find team with maximum points from position i onwards ;    (12)
    swap details with position i if necessary
end
```

To find the team with maximum points we introduce working variables *maxpoints* and *maxposition* as in (13) to record the maximum points and position seen so far. Swapping the team details if necessary then

```
maxposition := i ; maxpoints := leaguetable[i].points ;
for j := i+1 to numberofteams do
    if leaguetable[j].points > maxpoints                               (13)
    then begin
            maxposition := j ;
            maxpoints := leaguetable[j].points
        end
```

involves the sequence (14).

```
if maxposition <> i then
begin
    detailssaved := leaguetable[i] ;
    leaguetable[i] := leaguetable[maxposition] ;                       (14)
    leaguetable[maxposition] := detailssaved
end
```

The output of the updated and ordered league table then involves printing out the details from each record in the sorted *leaguetable* array in turn.

Listing 10 shows the final program and the output produced by input corresponding to the initial league table shown in Table 10.1.

	P	W	D	L	Pts
Red Rovers	3	2	1	0	5
Silver City	3	1	2	0	4
Blue United	3	1	1	1	3
Black Forest	3	1	1	1	3
Green Villa	3	1	0	2	2
Brown Town	3	0	1	2	1

and results

Black Forest	3	Brown Town	4
Green Villa	2	Red Rovers	2
Blue United	1	Silver City	0

Table 10.1   League table and results

LISTING 10

```
PROGRAM UPDATELEAGUETABLE (INPUT, OUTPUT);

CONST NUMBEROFTEAMS = 6 ;
      MAXIMUMGAMES = 10 ;
      MAXIMUMPOINTS= 20 ;

TYPE  TEAMPOSITION = 1..NUMBEROFTEAMS ;
      TEAMNAME = PACKED ARRAY [1..12] OF CHAR ;
      TEAMDETAILS = RECORD
                      NAME : TEAMNAME ;
                      PLAYED, WON, DRAWN, LOST : 0..MAXIMUMGAMES ;
                      POINTS : 0..MAXIMUMPOINTS
                    END;

VAR   LEAGUETABLE : ARRAY [TEAMPOSITION] OF TEAMDETAILS ;

PROCEDURE READNAME (VAR NAME : TEAMNAME) ;
VAR   CH : CHAR ;
      I : 2..12 ;
BEGIN
   REPEAT READ (CH) UNTIL CH<>' ' ;
   NAME[1] := CH ;
   FOR I:= 2 TO 12 DO READ (NAME[I])
END ; (* READNAME *)

PROCEDURE READINTABLE ;
VAR   I : TEAMPOSITION ;
BEGIN
   FOR I:= 1 TO NUMBEROFTEAMS DO
   WITH LEAGUETABLE[I] DO
   BEGIN
      READNAME (NAME) ;
      READLN (PLAYED, WON, DRAWN, LOST, POINTS)
   END
END ; (* READINTABLE *)

PROCEDURE UPDATETABLE ;
VAR   NAME : TEAMNAME ;
      TEAM1, TEAM2 : TEAMPOSITION ;
      GOALS1, GOALS2 : 0..MAXINT ;

   FUNCTION POSITION (NAMESOUGHT : TEAMNAME): TEAMPOSITION ;
   VAR I : TEAMPOSITION ;
   BEGIN
      I:=1;
      WHILE LEAGUETABLE[I].NAME <> NAMESOUGHT DO I:=I+1 ;
      POSITION := I
   END; (* POSITION *)

BEGIN
   REPEAT
      READNAME (NAME) ;   TEAM1:= POSITION (NAME) ;
      READ (GOALS1) ;
      READNAME (NAME) ;   TEAM2:= POSITION (NAME) ;
      READLN (GOALS2) ;
```

```
         WITH LEAGUETABLE[TEAM1] DO PLAYED := PLAYED+1 ;
         WITH LEAGUETABLE[TEAM2] DO PLAYED := PLAYED+1 ;
         IF GOALS1>GOALS2
         THEN BEGIN  (* HOME WIN *)
                WITH LEAGUETABLE[TEAM1] DO
                BEGIN WON:=WON+1 ; POINTS:=POINTS+2 END ;
                WITH LEAGUETABLE[TEAM2] DO LOST:=LOST+1
              END
         ELSE IF GOALS2>GOALS1
         THEN BEGIN  (* AWAY WIN *)
                WITH LEAGUETABLE[TEAM1] DO LOST:=LOST+1 ;
                WITH LEAGUETABLE[TEAM2] DO
                BEGIN WON:=WON+1 ; POINTS:=POINTS+2 END
              END
         ELSE BEGIN  (* DRAW *)
                WITH LEAGUETABLE[TEAM1] DO
                BEGIN DRAWN:=DRAWN+1 ; POINTS:=POINTS+1 END ;
                WITH LEAGUETABLE[TEAM2] DO
                BEGIN DRAWN:=DRAWN+1 ; POINTS:=POINTS+1 END
              END
    UNTIL EOF(INPUT)
END ; (* UPDATETABLE *)




PROCEDURE PRINTTABLE ;
VAR   I, J, MAXPOSITION : TEAMPOSITION ;
      MAX : 0..MAXIMUMPOINTS ;
      DETAILSSAVED : TEAMDETAILS ;
BEGIN
   (* SORT LEAGUE TABLE INTO POINTS ORDER *)
   FOR I:= 1 TO NUMBEROFTEAMS-1 DO
   BEGIN
      (* FIND TEAM WITH MAXIMUM POINTS FROM POSITION I ONWARDS *)
      MAX := LEAGUETABLE[I].POINTS ;
      MAXPOSITION := I ;
      FOR J:= I+1 TO NUMBEROFTEAMS DO
      IF LEAGUETABLE[J].POINTS > MAX
      THEN BEGIN
             MAX := LEAGUETABLE[J].POINTS ;
             MAXPOSITION := J
           END ;
      (* IF NECESSARY SWAP WITH POSITION I *)
      IF MAXPOSITION <> I
      THEN BEGIN
             DETAILSSAVED := LEAGUETABLE[I] ;
             LEAGUETABLE[I] := LEAGUETABLE[MAXPOSITION] ;
             LEAGUETABLE[MAXPOSITION] := DETAILSSAVED
           END
   END ;
   (* PRINT SORTED TABLE *)
   WRITELN ('P':16, 'W':4, 'D':4, 'L':4, '   PTS') ;
   FOR I:= 1 TO NUMBEROFTEAMS DO
   WITH LEAGUETABLE[I] DO
   WRITELN (NAME, PLAYED:4, WON:4, DRAWN:4,
            LOST:4, POINTS:6)
END ; (* PRINTTABLE *)
```

```
BEGIN
    READINTABLE ;
    UPDATETABLE ;
    PRINTTABLE
END.
```

	P	W	D	L	PTS
RED ROVERS	4	2	2	0	6
BLUE UNITED	4	2	1	1	5
SILVER CITY	4	1	2	1	4
BLACK FOREST	4	1	1	2	3
GREEN VILLA	4	1	1	2	3
BROWN TOWN	4	1	1	2	3

VARIANT RECORDS

The nature and types of some components of a data item sometimes depend on the values of other components. For instance, consider the record type definition (15) describing information associated with a register of all persons in a country at a given time. The types *person-name* and *date* are assumed to be defined elsewhere. The field *origin* distinguishes between nationals of the country, and aliens temporarily visiting the country.

> **type** *person* = **record**
>   *name* : *personname* ;
>   *dateofbirth* : *date* ;   (15)
>   *origin* : (*national,alien*)
> **end**

Suppose that we wish to extend this type definition to provide extra information about each person. In the case of nationals we wish to record their place of birth while, for aliens, the country of origin and date and port of entry to the country are required.

The record type *person* now has two alternative structures, or *variants*, according as to whether the person's origin is national or alien. In both cases the name and date of birth are still required but we have a different number, and different types, of further components in the record depending on the value of the *origin* field.

Records with alternative structures are catered for in a PASCAL record type definition by introduction of a so-called *variant-part*. As we saw earlier, the *variant-part* of a record follows the *fixed-part* (if there is one), i.e., declaration of the fields common to all of the alternative structures precedes the declaration of these alternatives.

A variant-part consists of a *tag-field*, of a previously defined type whose values distinguish the possible alternative structures or variants, followed by further *field-lists* corresponding to each of these alternative structures. Each *field-list* is labeled with the tag-field values to which it corresponds.

> *variant-part* = *"case"* *tag-field* *type-identifier* *"of"* *variant*
> $\qquad\qquad\qquad\qquad\qquad\qquad\qquad$ { *";" variant* } .
> *tag-field* = [*identifier* *":"*] .
> *variant* = *case-label-list* *":" "(" field-list ")"*.

The tag-field type must be an ordinal type, each value of which must appear exactly once as a case label in the variants that follow. Thus our augmented type *person* might be defined as in (16). Note that the type *personkind* must be introduced first, as the tag-field type can only be specified as a type identifier.

> **type** *personkind* = (*national,alien*) ;
> $\quad$ *person* = **record**
> $\qquad\qquad\qquad$ *name* : *personname* ;
> $\qquad\qquad\qquad$ *dateofbirth* : *date* ;
> $\qquad\qquad\qquad$ **case** *origin* : *personkind* **of**
> $\qquad\qquad\qquad$ *national* : (*birthplace* : *placename*) ; $\qquad$ (16)
> $\qquad\qquad\qquad$ *alien* : (*countryoforigin* : *placename* ;
> $\qquad\qquad\qquad\qquad\qquad$ *dateofentry* : *date* ;
> $\qquad\qquad\qquad\qquad\qquad$ *portofentry* : *placename*)
> $\qquad$ **end**

In a variant record definition, such as the above, the tag-field is an explicit field of the record which may be selected and updated in the same way as other fields. Thus, if *thisperson* is a variable of type *person*, one may write statements such as

> *thisperson.origin* := *national*

or

> **if** *thisperson.origin* <> *alien* **then** *writeln* (*thisperson.name*)

Field names appearing within each variant must be unique throughout the entire record. Use of such a field name then implies the variant (and hence the tag-field value) assumed, and no explicit indication of this is necessary. Thus fields within variants may be selected in the same way as fields within the fixed part. For example we might write

> *thisperson.countryoforigin* := *'Italy '*

or

> **if** *thisperson.birthplace* = *'USA '* **then** *processnationalbybirth*

However, these field selections are valid only when the tag-field *origin* does indeed have the assumed value (*alien* in the first case, *national* in the second). For reasons of efficiency, few implementations of PASCAL actually check the tag-field value when a field of a variant is selected. It is the responsibility of the programmer to ensure that the variant fields are accessed correctly, and failure to do so will generally produce incorrect programs.

Unfortunately no explicit language facility is provided in PASCAL to aid the programmer in this respect. However, systematic use of the case-statement in conjunction with a with-statement can reduce the likelihood of error. For instance, if we write the sequence shown in (17), then it is apparent that the field *birthplace* should be accessed only within the case-statement limb labeled *national*, while the fields *countryoforigin*, *portofentry* and *dateofentry* should be accessed only in the limb labeled *alien*.

```
with thisperson do
begin
    name := ... ;
    dateofbirth := ... ;
    case origin of
    national : birthplace := ... ;
    alien     : begin                                    (17)
                    countryoforigin := ... ;
                    dateofentry := ... ;
                    portofentry := ...
                end
    end ;
    ⋮
end
```

In some cases no further variant fields may be required for a particular variant *v* of a record-type, in which case the variant is defined with an empty field list, thus

```
v : ( )
```

For example, if we wished to record no further information on aliens, the record type *person* might be defined as in (18).

```
person = record
            name : personname ;
            dateofbirth : date ;
            case origin : personkind of             (18)
            national : (birthplace : placename) ;
            alien : ( )
        end
```

A record structure may have no fixed-part (i.e., no fields common to all of its alternative structures) and consist solely of a variant-part. For example, when playing poker with the jokers wild, any card dealt may be either one of the 52 suit cards, or a joker. To describe a poker card we might define the types specified in (19).

$$
\begin{array}{ll}
suit = (clubs,diamonds,hearts,spades) \; ; & \\
rank = (two,three,four,five,six,seven,eight,nine, & \\
\quad\quad ten,jack,queen,king,ace) \; ; & \\
joker = (redjoker,blackjoker) \; ; & \\
cardtype = (normal,wild) \; ; & \text{(19)} \\
pokercard = \textbf{record} & \\
\quad\quad\quad \textbf{case } which \; : \; cardtype \textbf{ of} & \\
\quad\quad\quad normal \; : \; (s:suit; \; r:rank) \; ; & \\
\quad\quad\quad wild \quad\quad : \; (j:joker) & \\
\quad \textbf{end} & \\
\end{array}
$$

In our examples so far the tag-field is an assignable component of the variant record type, and record processing involves inspecting this tag-field to determine the variant involved. However, the syntax of tag-field allows omission of the tag-field identifier, in which case the programmer has no means of assigning or inspecting the tag-field—the variant in force for any record is implied by the fields accessed. Such a record-type might be useful in programs where the variant which any record takes is always implied by context. For example, we might consider the pages of a book as records defined as in (20).

$$
\begin{array}{ll}
pagekind = (first,following) \; ; & \\
page \quad\quad = \textbf{record} & \\
\quad\quad\quad \textbf{case } pagekind \textbf{ of} & \\
\quad\quad\quad first \; : \; (title \; : \; bookname \; ; & \\
\quad\quad\quad\quad\quad author \; : \; personname \; ; & \text{(20)} \\
\quad\quad\quad\quad\quad ISBN \; : \; \textbf{packed array } [1 \, .. \, 10] \textbf{ of } char) \; ; & \\
\quad\quad\quad following \; : \; (text \; : \; \textbf{array } [1 \, .. \, pagesize] \textbf{ of } line) & \\
\quad \textbf{end} & \\
\end{array}
$$

By implication only those records representing the first pages of books will take the first variant; all others will take the second. If the program is always aware of which records represent first pages (by the order in which they are processed, say) then inclusion of an assignable tag-field is unnecessary.

The syntax definition for *field-list* specifies that the *variant-part* must follow the *fixed-part* (if there is one). Since the syntax for *variant-part* contains a *field-list* it is thus possible for the variant parts of a record themselves to contain nested variant parts. This is illustrated by expanding the definition of the record type *person* as in (21) to distinguish between nationals who were actually born in the country and those whose nationality was obtained by naturalization.

```
type personkind = (national,alien) ;
     status = (bybirth,naturalization) ;
     person = record
                  name : personname ;
                  dateofbirth : date ;
                  case origin : personkind of
                  national : (birthplace : placename ;          (21)
                              case qualification : status of
                              bybirth : ( ) ;
                              naturalization : (number : integer ;
                                                dateofnaturalization :
                                                date)) ;
                  alien     : (countryoforigin : placename ;
                              dateofentry : date ;
                              portofentry : placename)
             end
```

The fields within the nested variant part are selected in the same way as any other fields of the record, e.g., one may write

```
if  thisperson.qualification  =  naturalization
then writeln (thisperson.number)
```
or
```
thisperson.dateofnaturalization.y := 1980
```

In the latter case the tag fields *origin* and *qualification* are assumed to have the values *national* and *naturalization*, respectively.

Variant records are a convenient means of describing the data that arise in many practical programming applications. However, as already indicated, considerable care is required in programming their manipulation, particularly where changes of variant of a given record occur. For a variant record that has a tag field identifier, a change of variant occurs when a new value is assigned to the tag field. For a variant record without a tag field identifier, a change of variant is implied when a field of a different variant is referenced. In either case, the variant fields of the old variant cease to exist at this point, and the variant fields of the new variant come into existence with undefined values. The manipulation of fields must be consistent with this destruction and creation that occurs at each change of variant. To preclude certain inconsistent situations that could arise through changes of variant, PASCAL imposes the following additional rules:

(a)   A change of variant must not occur when a variant field is in use as an actual variable parameter, or as the record variable of a with-statement.

(b)   A tag field must not be passed as an actual variable parameter to a procedure or function.

Unfortunately, like the basic rules on accessing variant fields and on undefined values, these rules are either difficult or expensive to implement and many implementations fail to do so. All too often, the result is an undetected error whose effect is baffling and whose origin is difficult to diagnose. To minimize the likelihood of such errors, great care is recommended in programming the manipulation of variant records.

PROGRAM 11   (Text formatting)

In printing text the textual information must be formatted to suit the available line length of the printing device involved.

A program is required to read a series of lines of text, each line containing not more than 80 characters, and output this text as a series of lines containing not more than 60 characters. The input text consists of words (of not more than 16 letters), commas, semicolons, full stops and "layout devices" such as blank lines and new paragraphs. Any non-blank line having three or more leading blanks is considered to be the start of a new paragraph.

The output is to retain the blank lines and paragraph layout of the input text. Normal conventions are to be observed in positioning punctuation symbols—a punctuation symbol must immediately follow the preceding word and both must appear on the same line, with the punctuation symbol being followed by a blank, unless it is the last character of a line.

```
    begin
        read item ;
    repeat
        write item ;                                              (22)
        read item
    until endoftext
    end
```

We might initially conceive the program as a loop (22) which identifies the next item in the input text and transfers it to the output text. It is convenient to think of the end of the text as a special "item" which is read but not written in this process. However, this scheme is inadequate when we realize that how a word item is written depends on whether the next item is a punctuation symbol. The program input must thus be one item ahead of its output and so we rewrite it as in (23).

```
begin
        read nextitem ;
        repeat
                thisitem := nextitem ;
                read nextitem ;                                    (23)
                write thisitem
        until nextitem is endoftext
end.
```

This process is expressible as two procedures *readnextitem* and *writethisitem*, where the latter now has access to the details of the next item to carry out its task.

How should we represent the items which appear in the text? They may be words of up to 16 letters, punctuation symbols (comma, semicolon, or full stop), layout "devices" (a blank line or new paragraph), or the end of text item. We may thus define a variant record-type as in (24) to describe these possibilities.

```
type  itemkind  = (word,punctuation,layout,endoftext) ;
      textitem  = record
                        case kind : itemkind of
                        word : (length : 1 . . 16 ;
                                        spelling : array [1 . . 16] of char) ;   (24)
                        punctuation : (symbol : char) ;
                        layout : (device : (blankline,paragraph)) ;
                        endoftext : ( )
                  end
```

Two variables of type *textitem* can now be used to hold the details of the items processed by *readnextitem* and *writethisitem*:

```
var thisitem,nextitem : textitem ;
```

The procedure *readnextitem* must read the characters which make up the next item from the input, and leave its description in the variable *nextitem*. For some items such as words and new paragraphs it is not apparent that the item is complete until the following character has been read—at this point the character-by-character input must be one character ahead of the item scanned so far. However, this creates a further problem at the end of a line—if the additional blank which the PASCAL system provides at the end of each line is read, the end-of-line condition itself is lost. Rather than define a procedure which is sometimes one character ahead and sometimes not, the following strategy is adopted:

At the beginning of each new input line the entire line of characters is read into an array

> *line* : **array** [1 .. *inputmax*] **of** *char*

Within the array *line* a special character which does not occur in the input text, ' ↑ ', say, is stored immediately following the last actual character read. The item-scanning process is now programmed to operate on the array *line*, and can always be one character ahead since the character ' ↑ ' will be encountered at the end of each line. When this character is met as the first non-blank character of an item the procedure *readnextitem* can read the next input line and act accordingly, as in (25).

```
    procedure readnextitem ;
        begin
            skip blanks if necessary ;
            if next character is ' ↑ '
            then
                if eof(input)
                then item is endoftext
                else begin
                        read next line ;
                        skip and count leading blanks ;
                        if next character is ' ↑ '                    (25)
                        then item is blank line
                        else if more than 2 blanks
                            then item is paragraph
                            else scan first non-blank item in line
                    end
            else scan next non-blank item in line
        end
```

Now, *scan next non-blank item in line* can be expressed as a procedure whose action depends on the character of line currently under consideration, as in (26)

```
    procedure scannonblankitem ;
        begin
            with nextitem do                                          (26)
            case line [inpointer] of
```

```
'A','B', ... ,'Z' : begin
                        item is a word ;
                        scan word and record its length
                                    and spelling
                    end ;
',',';','.' : begin                                        (26 cont.)
                        item is a punctuation symbol ;
                        scan and record symbol
                    end
            end
        end
```

Introducing a variable

inpointer : 1 .. *inputmax*

which records the position in the array *line* of the next character to be processed, these procedures may be easily expressed in PASCAL. Note that *line* and *inpointer* must also be global variables since their values must be retained between calls of *readnextitem* and *scannonblankitem*.

Initializing *line* and *inpointer* as follows ensures that the first line of input is read by the first call of *readnextitem*:

line [1] := ' ↑ ' ; *inpointer* := 1

The structure required for the procedure *writethisitem* is a case statement which discriminates between the various kinds of text item, as

```
with thisitem do
    case itemkind of
    word : begin
                if no room on line then take a new line else
                if not start of line then precede word by a blank ;
                write out the word
            end ;                                          (27)
    punctuation : write out the symbol ;
    layout : begin
                if line partially full then take a new line ;
                if device = blankline then take a new line
                                      else take a new paragraph
            end
    end
```

in (27). By introducing a global variable

spaceleftonline : 0 .. *outputmax*

which records the number of available character positions remaining on the current output line, this procedure can readily be expressed in PASCAL. Splitting a word and a punctuation symbol over two lines is avoided by inspecting the variable *nextitem* when *thisitem* is of kind *word*.

Listing 11 shows the full PASCAL program. Note the use of constants for defining the lengths of the input and output lines—this makes the program readily adaptable to other than 80 character per line input or 60 character per line output.

The sample output produced corresponds to the same input data as used in Program 9.

```
                    LISTING 11

   PROGRAM TEXTEDITOR (INPUT, OUTPUT) ;

   CONST INPUTMAX = 81 ;
         EOL = '^' ;
         OUTPUTMAX = 60 ;
   TYPE  ITEMKIND = (WORD, PUNCTUATION, LAYOUT, ENDOFTEXT);
         TEXTITEM = RECORD
                         CASE KIND : ITEMKIND OF
                         WORD : (LENGTH : 1..16;
                                 SPELLING : ARRAY[1..16] OF CHAR);
                         PUNCTUATION : (SYMBOL : CHAR);
                         LAYOUT : (DEVICE : (BLANKLINE, PARAGRAPH));
                         ENDOFTEXT : ( )
                         END ;
         LINERANGE = 1..INPUTMAX ;

   VAR   THISITEM, NEXTITEM : TEXTITEM ;
         LINE : ARRAY [LINERANGE] OF CHAR ;
         INPOINTER : LINERANGE ;
         SPACELEFTONLINE : 0..OUTPUTMAX ;


   PROCEDURE READNEXTITEM ;

      PROCEDURE READLINE ;
      VAR I : LINERANGE ;
      BEGIN
        I:=1 ;
        WHILE NOT EOLN(INPUT) DO
        BEGIN READ (LINE[I]); I:=I+1 END ;
        READLN ;
        LINE[I]:=EOL ;  INPOINTER:=1
      END ; (* READLINE *)

      PROCEDURE SCANNONBLANKITEM ;
      VAR L : 0..16 ;
```

```
            BEGIN
              WITH NEXTITEM DO
              CASE LINE[INPOINTER] OF
              'A','B','C','D','E','F','G',
              'H','I','J','K','L','M','N',
              'O','P','Q','R','S','T','U',
              'V','W','X','Y','Z' :
                    BEGIN
                        KIND:=WORD;  L:=0;
                        REPEAT
                           L:=L+1;   SPELLING[L]:=LINE[INPOINTER] ;
                            INPOINTER := INPOINTER+1
                           UNTIL (LINE[INPOINTER]<'A')OR(LINE[INPOINTER]>'Z') ;
                           LENGTH:=L
                      END ;
                ',',',',',',';' :
                    BEGIN
                        KIND:=PUNCTUATION ;
                        SYMBOL:= LINE[INPOINTER] ;
                        INPOINTER := INPOINTER+1
                    END
                END
          END ; (* SCANNONBLANKITEM *)

      BEGIN (* READNEXTITEM *)
         WHILE LINE[INPOINTER] = ' ' DO INPOINTER:=INPOINTER+1 ;
      IF LINE[INPOINTER] = EOL
      THEN IF EOF(INPUT)
           THEN NEXTITEM.KIND := ENDOFTEXT
           ELSE BEGIN
                      READLINE ;
                      WHILE LINE[INPOINTER]=' ' DO INPOINTER:=INPOINTER+1;
                      WITH NEXTITEM DO
                      IF LINE[INPOINTER]=EOL
                      THEN BEGIN KIND:=LAYOUT; DEVICE:=BLANKLINE END
                      ELSE IF INPOINTER>2
                             THEN BEGIN KIND:=LAYOUT ; DEVICE:=PARAGRAPH END
                             ELSE SCANNONBLANKITEM
                  END
      ELSE SCANNONBLANKITEM
  END ; (* READNEXTITEM *)




PROCEDURE WRITETHISITEM ;
VAR   SPACENEEDED : 1..18 ;
      I : 1..16 ;

   PROCEDURE TAKENEWLINE ;
   BEGIN
      WRITELN ;
      SPACELEFTONLINE := OUTPUTMAX
   END ;  (* TAKENEWLINE *)

BEGIN
   WITH THISITEM DO
   CASE KIND OF
```

```
WORD : BEGIN
            IF NEXTITEM.KIND = PUNCTUATION
            THEN SPACENEEDED := LENGTH+2
            ELSE SPACENEEDED := LENGTH+1 ;
            IF SPACENEEDED > SPACELEFTONLINE
            THEN TAKENEWLINE
            ELSE IF SPACELEFTONLINE<>OUTPUTMAX
                THEN BEGIN
                        WRITE (' ') ;
                        SPACELEFTONLINE:=SPACELEFTONLINE-1
                     END ;
            FOR I:= 1 TO LENGTH DO WRITE (SPELLING[I]) ;
            SPACELEFTONLINE := SPACELEFTONLINE-LENGTH
        END ;
PUNCTUATION :
        BEGIN
            WRITE (SYMBOL) ;
            SPACELEFTONLINE := SPACELEFTONLINE-1
        END ;
LAYOUT :
        BEGIN
            IF SPACELEFTONLINE < OUTPUTMAX THEN TAKENEWLINE ;
            IF DEVICE=BLANKLINE
            THEN TAKENEWLINE
            ELSE BEGIN WRITE ('  ') ; SPACELEFTONLINE:=SPACELEFTONLINE-2 END
        END
    END
END ;(* WRITETHISITEM *)


BEGIN
    LINE[1]:=EOL ;  INPOINTER:=1 ;
    SPACELEFTONLINE := OUTPUTMAX ;
    READNEXTITEM ;
    REPEAT
       THISITEM := NEXTITEM ;
       READNEXTITEM ;
       WRITETHISITEM
    UNTIL NEXTITEM.KIND = ENDOFTEXT
END.
```

THE PROFILE

THE PROFILE IS AN EDITED, AUTOMATICALLY FORMATTED,
LISTING OF THE SOURCE PROGRAM WHICH DISPLAYS THE FREQUENCY
OF EXECUTION OF EACH STATEMENT OF THE PROGRAM.

TO READ OFF THE FREQUENCY OF EXECUTION OF ANY STATEMENT,
WE LOCATE THE BEGINNING OF THE STATEMENT IN THE PROFILE
LISTING. IF AN ASTERISK IS PRESENT ON THE SAME LINE, TO THE
LEFT OF THE LISTING, THEN THE DESIRED FREQUENCY WILL BE
FOUND TO THE LEFT OF THE ASTERISK. OTHERWISE, THE LINE WILL
CONTAIN ONE OR MORE UPWARD ARROWS; WE SELECT THE RIGHTMOST
ARROW, AND FOLLOW THE LINE OF ARROWS VERTICALLY UPWARDS
UNTIL AN ASTERISK IS ENCOUNTERED; AGAIN, THE DESIRED
FREQUENCY WILL BE FOUND TO THE LEFT OF THE ASTERISK.

EXERCISES

10.1 Extend Program 10 to record the goals for and against each team, and to use goal difference (goals for − goals against) to determine the league positions of teams with the same number of points.

10.2 Define a record-type, each value of which denotes a point on an x–y grid where x and y take integer values in the range 1 to 100.

Write a program which reads four pairs of values representing the vertices A, B, C, D of a quadrilateral in cyclic order, and determines whether $ABCD$ is a square, a rectangle, or otherwise.

10.3 Define a record-type enabling the name, grades, and grade total for each student processed by Program 2 to be held as a record variable. Write a procedure which reads a student's performance from one line of input and stores it as a record of this type. Use this procedure in a revised version of Program 2 which tabulates the class performance as before, but in descending order of grade total.

10.4 Define a variant record type whose values describe the shape and dimensions of geometric figures which may be circles, squares, rectangles or triangles. Write a procedure which reads a description of a geometric figure and stores it as a record of this type. Each input description is on a separate line and starts with a letter C, S, R or T denoting the shape. This is followed by one, two or three real numbers which specify the length of the radius, side or sides as appropriate, e.g.,

```
C   12.1
R   30.4   17.5
S   16.7
T   40.6   27.9   21.8
```

Write a function which determines the area of the figure described by such a record. Use the procedure and function in a program which reads a sequence of descriptions of figures, and prints out the description of the figure of largest area.

11

Sets

THE SET CONCEPT

In Chap. 3 we defined the concept of type as the set of values which a data item of that type may take. Each item has at any moment a value which is exactly one of the members of this set. In many practical situations data items arise whose values are themselves sets of the values of some other type.

Consider the familiar phenomenon of mixing colors from monochromatic sources, such as occurs on the screen of a color television set. We might have primary sources for three colors—red, yellow and blue, say—which we consider as the possible values of a type:

primarycolor = (*red,yellow,blue*)

These primary colors can be mixed in any combination. For example at some point we might use a mix of all three colors, and denote this as follows:

[*red,yellow,blue*]

(Since the order of mixing is not important, the order in which we write the primary colors is not important. We might have written [*yellow,red,blue*], or [*blue,yellow,red*] or any of the other possible orderings—there are six possible ways of denoting this mix of three sources, all of which are equivalent.)

Alternatively, we might use a mix of only two of the three primary colors, i.e., one of the following:

[*red,yellow*]
[*red,blue*]
[*yellow,blue*]

(In this case there are two equivalent ways of denoting each distinct mix of two colors.)

Again we might use a "mix" of only one of the three possible sources (i.e. use that primary color on its own), i.e., one of the following:

[*red*]
[*yellow*]
[*blue*]

Finally, at some point we may require no coloring at all, i.e., a "mix" involving none of the three primary colors, which we denote as

[   ]

The eight possible mixes which we have listed are the only possible *sets* or unordered combinations of the three primary colors *red,yellow,blue*, and are in fact the possible values of a type which we might define as

mix = **set of** *primarycolor*

where *primarycolor* is said to be the *base-type* of the *set-type mix*.

PASCAL allows the description of such set types, for a restricted range of base-types, as follows

set-type = "**set**" "**of**" *base-type* .
base-type = *type* .

The base type must be an ordinal type. In the past implementations of PASCAL have imposed additional restrictions on the base types of sets, but the PASCAL standard admits no such restriction. In practice, however, implementations may still impose some restriction on sets of integers, usually restricting the base type to be an integer subrange that lies within some limited range of the non-negative integers $0 .. N$.

As a further example of a set-type consider the data required by the control mechanism of a lift in a multistorey building. At any moment the mechanism must be aware of the outstanding calls for the lift from all floors, which may vary from no calls at all (when no-one wants the lift) to calls from all floors (at a rush period). The outstanding calls can be thought of as a value of the set-type *liftcalls* defined as follows

floor = 1 .. *top* ;
liftcalls = **set of** *floor* ;

Variables of type *liftcalls* may then be declared, e.g.,

thisjourney,callsnow : *liftcalls*

MANIPULATING SETS

Once a set-type has been defined, variables of that type may be declared and manipulated in a PASCAL program. Besides copying or assignment, PASCAL provides a number of special operations which may be applied to values of set-types.

Construction

A value of set-type may be constructed by specifying its elements, or members. This is done using the syntactic form *set*, which was noted in Chap. 4 as one alternative for a *factor* within an *expression*. This is defined as follows

> *set* = "[" *element-list* "]" .
> *element-list* = [*element* { "," *element* }] .
> *element* = *expression* [".." *expression*] .

The form "[ ]" denotes a set of no elements, and is known as the *empty set*.

A non-empty set consists of one or more element specifications, separated by commas, and enclosed in square brackets. All expressions appearing in the element specifications must be of the same type, which is the base-type of the set.

An element specification consists either of a single expression whose value determines the corresponding element of the set, or of two expressions which determine a consecutive range of elements for the set.

For example,

> [*red*]   denotes the set of type *mix* containing one element *red*
> [*red..blue*]   denotes the set of type *mix* containing all three elements, *red, yellow, blue*
> [1..3,*f,top*]   denotes the set of type *liftcalls* containing floors 1, 2, 3, *top*, and the current value of *f*, where *f* is a variable of type *floor*.

Note that two distinct element specifications may indicate the same element value. By definition an element may occur at most once in a set. Thus a constructed set [*I,J*], where the values of *I* and *J* are found to be equal, yields a set of one element.

An element specification $I . . J$, where the values of I and J are such that $I > J$, is interpreted as specifying no elements. Thus $[I . . J]$ would yield the empty set in this case.

Constructed sets are commonly used to initialize set variables, e.g.

```
callsnow := [' ]
mix 1 : = [red,blue]
```

However the empty set [ ] also plays a frequent role in set comparison, and the singleton sets (sets of one element) are used in set updating as described below.

Because a constructed set does not indicate the precise range of values that forms its base type, special rules of type apply to set assignment and the set operations defined in following sections. These are

(a)   In an expression a factor of type **set of** S, where S is a subrange of some host type T, is considered to be of type **set of** T.

(b)   A set value of type **set of** T is assignment compatible with a type of the form **set of** S if each member value that occurs within it is assignment compatible with type S.

Membership testing

PASCAL provides five relational operators by which the membership of set values can be investigated. Four of these are the familiar operators $=$, $<>$, $<=$, $>=$, which are used with two operands of the same set type. The fifth is the operator **in**, which is used with one operand of a base type and a second operand of the corresponding set type.

The operators $=$ and $<>$ are used to test set equality. Two sets are equal if they each contain exactly the same elements. Thus

```
[red,blue] = [ ]                  gives   false
[red] <> [blue]                   gives   true
[red,yellow,blue] = [red.. blue]  gives   true
```

The operators $<=$ and $>=$ are used to test set containment or inclusion. A set a is contained, or included, by a set b, written $a <= b$, if each member of a is also a member of b. Thus

$[red,blue] <= [red,yellow,blue]$ gives   *true*
$[red,blue] <- [red,blue]$ gives   *true*
$[red,blue] <= [red,yellow]$ gives   *false*
$[red,blue] <= [blue]$ gives   *false*

Note that the empty set [ ] is included by *any* other set, so

[ ] $<= b$ gives   *true*

whatever the value of the set *b*.

The relation $a >= b$ is read as *a includes b*, and is *true* if each member of *b* is a member of *a*, and *false* otherwise. Thus

$[red,blue] >= [red,yellow,blue]$ gives   *false*
$[red,blue] >= [red,blue]$ gives   *true*
$[red,blue] >= [red,yellow]$ gives   *false*
$[red,blue] >= [blue]$ gives   *true*

Note that both operators may give *false* for the same operand pair. In this respect they differ from their arithmetic counterparts—if *a* and *b* are integers, then $((a <= b)$ **or** $(a >= b))$ must be *true*, but when *a* and *b* are sets it may be *false*.

The operator **in** is used to test the presence of an individual member in a set. If *x* is a value of the base type and *a* is a value of the corresponding set type then

x **in** *a*   gives   *true* if *x* is a member of *a* ,
                           false otherwise

For example

red **in** $[red,yellow]$ gives   *true*
red **in** $[red]$ gives   *true*
red **in** $[yellow,blue]$ gives   *false*
red **in** [ ]   gives   *false*

As we shall see, the membership testing operators are commonly used to control the processing of set data, e.g.

if *thisfloor* **in** *callsnow* **then** ... **else** ...
while *callsnow* = [ ] **do** ...

However, the **in** operator is often useful in contexts where explicit set manipulation is not involved, as a means of expressing an equality test with several alternatives. Thus writing

if *d* **in** $[Monday,Wednesday,Friday]$ **then** ...

is clearer, and for most implementations more efficient, than the clumsy

if (d = *Monday*) **or** (d = *Wednesday*) **or** (d = *Friday*) **then** ...

Similarly the operator **in** provides a convenient means of expressing the commonly required test

is c a letter

where c is a variable of type *char*. If the letters form a coherent subsequence of the values of *char* this can be written as

if c **in** ['A' .. 'Z'] **then** ...

or, if they do not, as

if c **in** ['A', 'B', 'C', 'D', 'E', 'F', 'G', 'H', 'I', 'J', 'K', 'L', 'M',
          'N', 'O', 'P', 'Q', 'R', 'S', 'T', 'U', 'V', 'W', 'X', 'Y', 'Z']
then ....

Set arithmetic

Mathematical manipulation of sets is commonly expressed in terms of three operations, each of which takes two set operands and yields a set result, namely *union, intersection,* and *set difference* or *relative complement.* PASCAL also provides these operations, denoting them by the operators +, * and −. When used with two operands of a common set type these produce a result of the same set type, as follows:

$a + b$ gives the union of a and b, i.e. the set of all values which are either in a, or in b, or in both

$a * b$ gives the intersection of a and b, i.e. the set of all values which are in a, and also in b

$a - b$ gives the relative complement of a and b, i.e. the set of values which are in a but not in b.

For example,

[*red,blue*] + [*red,yellow*]   gives   [*red,yellow,blue*]
[*red,blue*] * [*red,yellow*]   gives   [*red*]
[*red,blue*] − [*red,yellow*]   gives   [*blue*]

The operators + and − are often used with singleton sets as a means of adding or removing a given member to an existing set. Thus

$a := a + [x]$ adds member x to set a—if a already contains x the operation has no effect;

$a := a - [x]$ removes member x from set a—if a does not contain x the operation has no effect.

The function (1) accepts a positive integer N as parameter and counts the number of distinct digits in its decimal representation.

```
function distinctdigits (N : nonnegativeinteger) : positiveinteger ;
var digit : 0 . . 9 ;    count : positiveinteger ;
    previousdigits : set of 0 . . 9 ;
begin
    previousdigits := [ ] ; count := 0 ;
    repeat
        digit := N mod 10 ;
        if not (digit in previousdigits)
        then begin                                                    (1)
                count := count+1 ;
                previousdigits := previousdigits + [digit]
            end ;
        N := N div 10
    until N = 0 ;
    distinctdigits := count
end
```

PROGRAM 12   (Computer-dating service)

A computer-dating service records data on each of its clients as a punched card with the following format:

columns 1–60   name and address
column 61   sex (punched as M or F)
columns 62–63 age (punched as two decimal digits)
columns 64–69 interests (an X punched in the corresponding column denotes an interest in art, books, music, theatre, politics, sport)

A program is required which will read one card representing a new client, followed by a deck of cards representing all existing clients. For example, the first few cards of the input might be as shown in (2).

ALEX ANDERSON	26 CALIFORNIA AVENUE, HUYTON.	M24 X X	
ANNE ENGLISH	21 HOME GARDENS, HUYTON.	F 19 XX	
JULIA MONTEITH	35 HEATH AVENUE, BURY.	F 33 X X	(2)
MAURICE SHORT	21 GREEN STREET, WIGAN.	M18X XX	
KATHLEEN BRYANS	3 BLUE AVENUE, WARRINGTON.	F 21 XX	

The program should print out a list of all existing clients who are 'compatible' with the new client, i.e. of opposite sex, with an age difference less than ten years, and with at least one common interest.

```
begin
    read new client ;
    repeat
        read next client ;
        if compatible with new client                              (3)
        then print name and address
    until eof(input)
end
```

The overall form of the program required is as shown in (3). To refine this further we must decide how the data on each client is to be represented. Clearly the overall form is a record, with fields representing the name and address, sex, age and interests of the client concerned. The name and address can be held as a string of length 60, the sex as a value of some suitable two-valued type, and the age as a suitable integer subrange. Since the interests are any combination of a predefined list of topics, a convenient representation is as a *set* over a corresponding base-type *topics*. The complete representation is then as shown in (4).

```
type sexes = (male,female) ;
     topics = (art,books,music,theatre,politics,sport) ;
     client = record
                identity : packed array [1 .. 60] of char ;     (4)
                sex : sexes ;
                age : 16 .. 99 ;
                interests : set of topics
              end ;
```

With this representation the process of reading the data on any client can be expressed as the procedure (5)

```
procedure readcard (var c:client) ;
var i : 1 .. 60 ; ch : char ; t : topics ;                        (5)
begin
    with c do
```

```
     begin
          for i := 1 to 60 do read (identity[i]) ;
          read(ch) ; if ch = 'M' then sex := male else sex := female ;
          read(age) ;
          interests := [ ] ;                                      (5 cont.)
          for t := art to sport do
          begin
               read(ch) ; if ch = 'X' then interests := interests + [t]
          end
     end ;
     readln
end
```

Note how the set of interests is accumulated by adding a new member
to an initially empty set for each 'X' found in a corresponding column
position. The final *readln* ensures that the input is correctly aligned at
the first column of the next card for the next call to *readcard*, or at the
end of file condition when the last card has been read. In a realistic
data-processing environment the procedure *readcard* might also validate
the data read, i.e., check that the sex is punched as an 'M' or 'F' and
nothing else, and likewise for other fields.

How is the compatibility of two clients tested? The sex and age tests
are easily programmed. To determine that the two clients have at least
one common interest we form the intersection of their sets of interests,
and test that this is not empty. Compatibility can thus be expressed as
the function (6).

```
     function compatible (c1,c2 : client) : boolean ;
     begin
          compatible := (c1.sex<>c2.sex) and
                        (abs(c1.age−c2.age)<10) and            (6)
                        (c1.interests*c2.interests<>[ ])
     end
```

Listing 12 shows the complete program and the output produced.

```
                    LISTING 12

PROGRAM COMPUTERDATINGSERVICE (INPUT,OUTPUT) ;

TYPE  SEXES = (MALE, FEMALE) ;
      TOPICS= (ART, BOOKS, MUSIC, THEATRE, POLITICS, SPORT);
      CLIENT = RECOR,
                IDENTITY : PACKED ARRAY[1..60] OF CHAR ;
                SEX : SEXES ;
                AGE : 16..99 ;
                INTERESTS : SET OF TOPICS
              END ;
```

```
VAR   NEWCLIENT, NEXTCLIENT : CLIENT ;

PROCEDURE READCARD (VAR C : CLIENT) ;
VAR   I : 1..60 ;
      CH : CHAR ;   T : TOPICS ;
BEGIN
   WITH C DO
   BEGIN
      FOR I:= 1 TO 60 DO READ (IDENTITY[I]) ;
      READ (CH) ; IF CH='M' THEN SEX:=MALE ELSE SEX:=FEMALE ;
      READ (AGE) ;
      INTERESTS := [ ] ;
      FOR T:= ART TO SPORT DO
      BEGIN
         READ (CH) ;
         IF CH='X' THEN INTERESTS:=INTERESTS+[T]
      END
   END ;
   READLN
END ; (* READCARD *)

FUNCTION COMPATIBLE (C1,C2 : CLIENT) : BOOLEAN ;
BEGIN
   COMPATIBLE := (C1.SEX<>C2.SEX) AND
                 (ABS(C1.AGE - C2.AGE)<10) AND
                 (C1.INTERESTS * C2.INTERESTS <> [ ])
END ; (* COMPATIBLE *)

BEGIN
   READCARD (NEWCLIENT) ;
   REPEAT
      READCARD (NEXTCLIENT) ;
      IF COMPATIBLE (NEWCLIENT, NEXTCLIENT)
      THEN WRITELN (NEXTCLIENT.IDENTITY)
   UNTIL EOF (INPUT)
END.


JULIA MONTEITH     35 HEATH AVENUE, BURY.
KATHLEEN BRYANS    3  BLUE AVENUE, WARRINGTON.
LINDA SMYTH        29 YELLOW STREET, BOLTON.
MARY STEWART       23 IDAHO GARDENS, BURNLEY.
```

PROGRAM 13   (Coloring a map)

A continent comprises N countries each of which borders one or more of the others. A map of the continent showing these countries must be colored such that no two countries with a common border are the same color. A computer program is required which will find a suitable coloring. (It has been shown that four colors are always sufficient to color any possible arrangement of countries.)

	1	2	3	4	5	6	7	8	9	10	11	12	13	14	15	16	17	18	19	20	21	22	23	24	25	26	27	28	29	30
1 ALBANIA												1																	1	
2 ANDORRA											1													1						
3 AUSTRIA						1							1		1	1									1				1	1
4 BELGIUM											1						1	1										1		
5 BULGARIA												1									1						1			1
6 CZECHOSLOVAKIA			1						1				1							1			1						1	
7 DENMARK																													1	
8 EAST GERMANY						1													1										1	
9 EIRE																												1		
10 FINLAND																			1				1		1					
11 FRANCE			1		1										1	1							1	1		1			1	
12 GREECE	1																										1			
13 HUNGARY			1			1															1	1	1							
14 ICELAND																														

15 ITALY	1				1												1		1
16 LIECHTENSTEIN	1													1			1		
17 LUXEMBOURG	1			1														1	
18 NETHERLANDS	1																	1	
19 NORWAY			1			1							1					
20 POLAND		1	1			1												
21 PORTUGAL										1								
22 ROMANIA		1		1	1							1				1		
23 U.S.S.R.		1	1	1			1	1						1				
24 SPAIN	1			1	1				1									
25 SWEDEN			1					1										
26 SWITZERLAND	1		1	1	1					1					1			
27 TURKEY		1	1			1					1							
28 U.K.			1															
29 WEST GERMANY	1 1	1 1 1	1	1	1		1 1	1							1			
30 YUGOSLAVIA	1 1	1	1	1	1	1			1								

203

The problem is typical of a wide class of problems which are solved by *trial and error*. The method involves successively improving a partial solution by considering one country at a time, picking a suitable color for that country, and then proceeding to consider the next. If it proves impossible to find a suitable color for the current country the method must *backtrack* to the last country for which a further alternative exists and restart from that point. This backtracking process is conveniently expressed as a recursive procedure which for the map coloring problem has the general form shown in (7).

```
procedure colorcountry (i : country) ;
begin
      for each available color do
      if this color has not been chosen for
            a country bordering country i then
            begin                                                        (7)
                  choose this color for country i ;
                  if i = N then printsolution
                              else colorcountry (i+1) ;
                  reject this color for country i
            end
end
```

The procedure must be used by a program sequence which initializes the data to indicate that no colors have been chosen so far and then calls the procedure to color country number 1.

As it stands this procedure is capable of finding all possible solutions, since it continues to consider alternative colorings even after a complete solution has been printed. If only one solution is required, resumption of the recursive process can be avoided by a goto-statement in the *printsolution* procedure which exits to the program sequence which originally called the recursive procedure.

To refine the procedure further we must decide how the data on which it operates are to be represented.

The countries which border each country of the continent are conveniently represented as a table

countriesbordering : **array** [country] **of** setofcountries

where the types *country* and *setofcountries* are defined as

country = 1 .. N ;
setofcountries = **set of** country ;

A possible coloring scheme for the continent can then be represented as a table

　　colored : **array** [*color*] **of** *setofcountries*

where the type *color* is defined, say, as

　　color = (*red,blue,green,yellow*)

The unrefined steps in our recursive procedure are easily expressed in terms of this representation. To test whether a color *c* has already been chosen for a country bordering country *i* we form the intersection of the countries which border *i* and the countries colored *c*, and test the non-emptiness of the result. The other steps are trivially programmed to give a final version of the procedure as shown in (8).

```
procedure colorcountry (i:country) ;
var c:color ;
begin
    for c := red to yellow do
        if countriesbordering[i]*colored[c]=[ ] then
        begin                                               (8)
            colored[c]:=colored[c]+[i] ;
            if i=N then printsolution
                else colorcountry(i+1) ;
            colored[c]:=colored[c]-[i]
        end
end
```

Listing 13 shows a complete program using this procedure together with a suitable means of input for the border table and output for the solution found. It also shows the output produced for input data corresponding to the table on pp. 202–3 representing the continent of Europe. If a country A has a border with some other country B, then a '1' appears in column number B of the border relationships for country A, otherwise the column is blank. Thus, Albania (country 1) borders only Greece (country 12) and Yugoslavia (country 30). The border relationships are duplicated, i.e., the entries for Greece and Yugoslavia both indicate that those countries have a border with Albania.

The actual data input to the program consist of a sequence of lines, one for each country in the above table. Each line consists of a two-digit integer numbering the country, the name of the country (18 characters), and then 30 characters (either '1' or a blank) representing the border relationships between that country and the other countries.

LISTING 13

```
PROGRAM MAPCOLORING (INPUT, OUTPUT) ;

LABEL 99 ;

CONST N = 30 ;
      CONTINENT = 'EUROPE' ;

TYPE  COUNTRY = 1..N ;
      SETOFCOUNTRIES = SET OF COUNTRY ;
      COLOR = (RED, BLUE, GREEN, YELLOW) ;

VAR   COUNTRIESBORDERING : ARRAY[COUNTRY] OF SETOFCOUNTRIES ;
      COLORED : ARRAY [COLOR] OF SETOFCOUNTRIES ;
      NAME : ARRAY [COUNTRY] OF PACKED ARRAY[1..18] OF CHAR ;
      C : COLOR ;

PROCEDURE READBORDERTABLE ;
VAR   I, J, M : COUNTRY ;
      K : 1..18 ;
      CH : CHAR ;
BEGIN
   FOR I:=1 TO N DO
   BEGIN
      READ (J) ; FOR K:=1 TO 18 DO READ (NAME[J][K]) ;
      COUNTRIESBORDERING[J]:=[ ] ;
      FOR M:=1 TO N DO
      BEGIN
         READ (CH) ;
         IF CH='1' THEN COUNTRIESBORDERING[J]:=COUNTRIESBORDERING[J]+[M]
      END;
      READLN
   END
END ; (* READBORDERTABLE *)

PROCEDURE PRINTSOLUTION ;
VAR   I : COUNTRY ;
      C : COLOR ;
BEGIN
   WRITELN ('COLORING OF MAP OF ',CONTINENT) ;
   WRITELN ('----------------------------') ;   WRITELN ;
   FOR I:=1 TO N DO
   BEGIN
      WRITE (NAME[I], '      ') ;
      C := RED ;
      WHILE NOT (I IN COLORED[C]) DO C := SUCC(C) ;
      CASE C OF
      RED    : WRITELN('RED') ;
      GREEN  : WRITELN('GREEN') ;
      YELLOW : WRITELN('YELLOW') ;
      BLUE   : WRITELN('BLUE')
      END
   END ;
   GOTO 99
END ;  (* PRINTSOLUTION *)
```

```
PROCEDURE COLORCOUNTRY (I : COUNTRY) ;
VAR   C : COLOR ;
BEGIN
   FOR C:= RED TO YELLOW DO
      IF COUNTRIESBORDERING[I] * COLORED[C] = [ ]
      THEN BEGIN
               COLORED[C] := COLORED[C] + [I] ;
               IF I=N THEN PRINTSOLUTION
                      ELSE COLORCOUNTRY (I+1) ;
               COLORED[C] := COLORED[C] - [I]
            END
END ; (* COLORCOUNTRY *)


BEGIN
   READBORDERTABLE ;
   FOR C:= RED TO YELLOW DO COLORED[C] := [ ] ;
   COLORCOUNTRY (1) ;
   WRITELN ('NO SOLUTION EXISTS') ;
99 :
END .
```

```
COLORING OF MAP OF EUROPE
----------------------------

   ALBANIA              RED
   ANDORRA              RED
   AUSTRIA              RED
   BELGIUM              RED
   BULGARIA             RED
   CZECHOSLOVAKIA       BLUE
   DENMARK              RED
   EAST GERMANY         RED
   EIRE                 RED
   FINLAND              RED
   FRANCE               BLUE
   GREECE               BLUE
   HUNGARY              GREEN
   ICELAND              RED
   ITALY                GREEN
   LIECHTENSTEIN        BLUE
   LUXEMBOURG           YELLOW
   NETHERLANDS          BLUE
   NORWAY               BLUE
   POLAND               GREEN
   PORTUGAL             RED
   ROMANIA              BLUE
   U.S.S.R.             YELLOW
   SPAIN                GREEN
   SWEDEN               GREEN
   SWITZERLAND          YELLOW
   TURKEY               GREEN
   U.K.                 BLUE
   WEST GERMANY         GREEN
   YUGOSLAVIA           YELLOW
```

EXERCISES

11.1 Given type definitions

> *countries* = (*Austria, Belgium, Denmark, Eire, France, Germany,*
> *Italy, Luxembourg, Netherlands, Norway, Portugal,*
> *Spain, Sweden, Switzerland, UK*) ;
> *setofcountries* = **set of** *countries* ;

and a variable declaration

> *Alpine, Mediterranean, Atlantic, Northsea, EEC* : *setofcountries* ;

write assignment statements to assign appropriate values to the variables. Use the variables to construct expressions which denote the following sets:

(a) the countries with both Atlantic and Mediterranean coastlines;
(b) EEC countries with Atlantic or North Sea coastlines;
(c) Alpine countries which are not in the EEC.

Write down boolean expressions which determine whether

(a) a country *c* is in the EEC;
(b) a country *c* has a Mediterranean, but not an Atlantic, coastline;
(c) all Alpine countries with a Mediterranean coastline are in the EEC.

11.2 Modify the computer-dating service program shown in Listing 12 to require at least *two* common interests for compatibility.

11.3 Write a program which reads two sentences, each terminated by a period, and prints out a list of all letters which appear in both sentences.

11.4 A college offers ten final-year courses in Art, English, French, German, History, Geography, Mathematics, Physics, Chemistry and Biology. Each student's enrolment is recorded as a punched card with the student's name in columns 1–20. Each course to be taken by the student is shown by an X punched in the corresponding column of columns 21–30. Write a program which reads the enrolment cards and prints a student list for each course. You may assume that there are not more than 100 final-year students.

11.5 A factory produces steel bars whose exact length is unknown until after production. Its cutting shop receives orders for cut lengths of bar which must be met by cutting up the manufactured bars. For a given manufactured bar of length *L* a set *C* of orders is chosen from the order list, which can be met by cutting up this bar, and with minimum wastage. Design a recursive back-tracking procedure which will construct *C* for given *L* and order list.

Incorporate the procedure in a program which constructs C from the following order list

order 1	773 mm
order 2	548 mm
order 3	65 mm
order 4	929 mm
order 5	548 mm
order 6	163 mm
order 7	421 mm
order 8	37 mm

and a manufactured bar length $L = 1848$ mm.

12

Files

THE FILE CONCEPT

Many computer applications involve the storage of very large volumes of data, perhaps in semi-permanent form. Because the data must be retained from one program execution to another, or because they are too numerous to be held in the main store of the computer, they are usually held on some secondary storage device, relevant data items being read in by the computer as required. Any stream of information which is held on some external storage medium for input to, or output by, a computer is called a *file*.

A file used by a computer program may be either an *external file* or an *internal file*. An external file is one whose contents outlive the execution of the program itself. It may be used to store data which are produced by one program for subsequent input to another program, or for input to a subsequent run of the same program. Information which is used to communicate between the computer and its human users may also be thought of as an external file—the standard input and output streams introduced in Chap. 5 are special cases of external files in PASCAL. As we shall see, the operations which are used on input and output, such as *read*, *write*, etc., are applicable to other files as well.

We have thus been using the concept of files implicitly in each of the programs developed so far, for the input of data and the output of results. Some of these could be improved by the explicit introduction of files. Consider the computer-dating service implemented as Program 12. The data on each client were held as a punched card, and for each new client a card deck, consisting of the new client's data followed by the data on all existing clients, was read (as the standard input file). A more convenient and economic solution would be to hold the data on existing clients as an external file on some storage medium such as magnetic disk or tape, and to input only the data on the new client for each program run. The program would read the data on existing clients from the client file, selecting compatible clients as before. Another program might be run at regular intervals to add new clients to the file for subsequent selection. We will outline these revised programs in describing the manipulation of files in PASCAL.

An internal file is one used to store data which are too large to fit in the computer's main store, but which are not required beyond the end of execution of the program. Consider Program 9, which produced a sorted concordance of all the words found in an input text by accumulating them in an array. A large input text might produce more words than could be held in any main-store array. An alternative program might accumulate the words in a backing-store file, sort the contents of this file in some appropriate manner, and then print out the sorted file contents as the final concordance. The contents of the file itself are irrelevant once this has been done.

In PASCAL a file is defined as a sequence of component values of the same component type, where the length of the sequence is undetermined. Each file used by a program is represented as a *file-variable* of a corresponding *file-type*. The syntax for describing a *file-type* is

> *file-type* = "**file**" "**of**" *file-component-type* .
> *file-component-type* = *type* .

Thus the component values of a file may be unstructured values, or structured values such as arrays, records or sets. However, the component values of a file cannot be, nor have components that are, of a file type.

Given a file type

> F = **file of** T

one declares file variables in the usual manner, e.g.

> f, g : F

f and g then denote files containing components of type T.

If a file is to be used as an external file it must also appear in the program heading, as well as in a file declaration in the outermost program block. We have already seen that the standard files *input* and *output* must appear in the program heading if they are used but since they are standard file identifiers it is not necessary to declare them as variables also. Thus, if we want to write a program which uses the standard files *input* and *output* and one other external file called *clientfile*, the program must take the form

> **program** *dates* (*input, output, clientfile*) ;
> ⋮
> **var** *clientfile* : **file of** *client* ;
> ⋮

A PASCAL file is constructed by writing, or appending, new values to the end of the file, which may be initially empty. When this file is subsequently read the components are read in the same order as they were written to the file. The construction of a file thus imposes a strict sequential order on its components which may be subsequently accessed only in this order. A PASCAL file is therefore called a *sequential file.*

During the sequential access of the components of a file it is not possible to alternate between reading and writing—in any one scan the file is either being written or being read. Thus an individual component of an existing file cannot be altered, leaving others unchanged, by writing just that component. This can only be done by making a copy of the entire file, altering the required component as it is copied.

A PASCAL file normally resides on some secondary storage medium but at any moment exactly one component is accessible to the program. The declaration of a file f in a block automatically introduces an additional variable which is of the same type as the file components. This variable is called the *file-buffer*, and is denoted by $f \uparrow$

file-buffer = *file-variable* " $\uparrow$ " .
file-variable = *variable* .

We might depict a file f and its associated file-buffer as shown in Fig. 12.1.

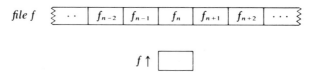

$$\text{file } f \quad \{ \ \cdots \ | \ f_{n-2} \ | \ f_{n-1} \ | \ f_n \ | \ f_{n+1} \ | \ f_{n+2} \ | \ \cdots \ \}$$

$$f \uparrow \ \boxed{}$$

Fig. 12.1   A file and its file-buffer.

The file-buffer is not part of the file itself but is the means by which component values are transmitted between the file and the program. Being an allowed form of *component-variable*, a file-buffer may be used in any context permitted for a *component-variable.*

Consider first the construction, or writing, of a file. To prepare a file f for writing, the standard procedure statement

rewrite(f)

is used. Its action is effectively to erase the contents of the file f, i.e., f becomes an empty file containing zero components. The next value written to f then becomes the first component of f, and subsequent values will be written to the end of file f. The value of the standard boolean function

    eof(*f*)

remains true throughout the time the file *f* is used for writing, although *eof* is not normally tested in the writing process.

    To write, or append, the value *x* of type *T* to the end of file *f*, the value *x* must first be assigned to the file-buffer variable *f* ↑ , i.e.,

    f ↑ := *x*

To physically append the value to the end of file *f* the standard procedure statement

    put(*f*)

is used. Its action is to append the current value of the file-buffer variable *f* ↑ to the end of file *f*; the value of the predicate *eof*(*f*) remains true, and the value of *f* ↑ becomes undefined. The normal scheme for constructing an output file *f* is as shown in (1).

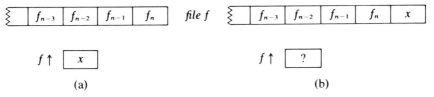

Fig. 12.2 Action of *put*(*f*): (a) before execution; (b) after execution

```
begin
    rewrite(f) ;
    while further output is necessary do
    begin                                           (1)
        f ↑ := next value to be output ;
        put(f)
    end
end
```

Consider the file-based computer-dating service suggested earlier. A program is first required to create the file of existing clients from the previously used punched cards. This would be as shown in (2). Note that the file buffer *clientfile* ↑ may be passed as a parameter, like any other variable of type *client*, to the procedure *readcard*.

```
program createclients (input,clientfile) ;
type ...
      client = ... {as in Program 12} ;
var   clientfile : file of client ;
      ⋮
procedure readcard (var c : client) ;
      ... {as in Program 12} ...
begin
      rewrite (clientfile) ;
      repeat
            readcard (clientfile ↑ ) ;
            put (clientfile)
      until eof(input)
end.
```
(2)

The combination of actions

$f \uparrow := $ *next value to be output* ;
$put(f)$

is so common in the construction of files that an extended form of the
standard PASCAL procedure *write* (which was introduced in Chap. 5
for delivering values to the standard output stream) is used to denote
these actions. The write statement used for this purpose is

write $(f,x1,x2,x3,\dots,xn)$

The values in the expression list $x1,x2,\dots$ must be assignment compatible
with the component type of the named file f (except in the case of a text file,
which is a special case discussed later in this chapter).
    The form

write $(f,x1,x2,\dots,xn)$

is equivalent to

begin write $(f,x1)$; write $(f,x2)$;...; write (f,xn) **end**

and the action of the procedure statement

write (f,x)

is defined in terms of file operations as

begin $f \uparrow := x$; $put(f)$ **end**

Introducing an extra variable

nextclient : *client*

the statement part of our program *createclients* can be written as in (3).

In this case use of the *write* procedure avoids explicit reference to the file buffer variable in the program.

> **begin**
>   *rewrite* (*clientfile*) ;
>   **repeat**
>   *readcard* (*nextclient*) ;   (3)
>   *write* (*clientfile,nextclient*)
>   **until** *eof* (*input*)
> **end**.

Now consider the operations involved in inspecting the contents of a previously constructed file. To prepare a file g for reading the standard procedure statement

> *reset* (g)

is used. Its effect depends on whether or not the file g is empty, i.e., whether or not it contains zero components. If g is not empty then the value of its first component is assigned to the file buffer variable $g \uparrow$; the value of the end-of-file predicate $eof(g)$ becomes *false*. However, if g is an empty file, then $eof(g)$ becomes *true* and the value of $g \uparrow$ is undefined.

Provided that g was not empty the contents of $g \uparrow$ may be processed. In order to read the next component value from file g the standard procedure statement

> *get* (g)

is used. Its action is to assign the value of the next available component of g to the file buffer variable $g \uparrow$. If no such component exists, i.e., the end of file g has been reached, $eof(g)$ becomes true and the value of $g \uparrow$ is undefined.

Note that the end-of-file condition does not become true until an attempt is made to get the supposed component after the last component. However, only one such attempt may be made—the effect of $get(g)$ is only defined if $eof(g)$ is false prior to its execution. Implementations may trap any subsequent execution of $get(g)$ as a programming error.

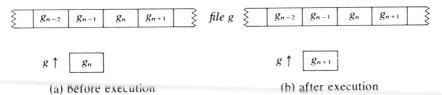

(a) before execution   (b) after execution

Fig. 12.3   Action of $get(g)$: (a) before execution; (b) after execution

Since the *reset* operation makes the first component of a file available for access, file inspection processing normally takes the form shown in (4). We can now write the revised computer-dating service program as in

```
begin
    reset(g) ;
    while not eof(g) do
    begin
        process g ↑ ;                               (4)
        get(g)
    end
end
```

(5) to print a list of compatible clients for a new client whose data are input as a single card.

```
program dates (input,output,clientfile) ;
type ...
    client = ...
var   clientfile : file of client ;
      newclient : client ;
procedure readcard (var c : client) ; ... {as before} ... ;
function compatible (c1,c2 : client) : boolean ; .... {as before} ... ;
begin {main program}
    readcard (newclient) ;                          (5)
    reset (clientfile) ;
    while not eof (clientfile) do
    begin
        if compatible (clientfile ↑ ,newclient)
        then writeln (clientfile ↑ .identity) ;
        get (clientfile)
    end
end.
```

The sequence of actions

assign value of g ↑ to a variable ;
get(g)

occurs frequently in the processing of an input file and a special form of the standard procedure *read* is used to denote these actions. The form of the read statement used for this purpose is

read (g,v1,v2, . . . ,vn)

where *v*1, *v*2, . . . are variables.

The general form

   $read\ (g,v1,v2,\ldots,vn)$

is equivalent to

   begin $read(g,v1)$; $read(g,v2)$; . . . ; $read(g,vn)$ **end**

where the action of the procedure statement

   $read\ (g,v)$

is defined (except in the case of a text file—see later in this chapter) as

   begin $v := g \uparrow$; $get(g)$ **end**

Thus the value of the file buffer $g \uparrow$ must be assignment compatible with the type of the variable v when $read(g, v)$ is executed.
Introducing an additional variable

   $nextclient$: $client$

we can rewrite the statement part of our program *dates* as in (6).

```
begin
      readcard (newclient) ;
      reset (clientfile) ;
      while not eof (clientfile) do
      begin                                                    (6)
            read (clientfile,nextclient) ;
            if compatible (nextclient,newclient)
            then writeln (nextclient.identity)
      end
end.
```

Components can be written to a PASCAL file only after preparing the file by a *rewrite* operation. It is, therefore, impossible to add the new client to the end of the existing client file, as the final action of the above program. Instead, we must write a separate program that copies the old client file to a new file, by reading and writing each component, and then appends any new clients to the end of the new file, as in (7).

```
program update (input, oldfile, newfile) ;
type . . .
  client = . . .
var oldfile, newfile : file of client ;
  nextclient : client ;
procedure readcard (var c : client) ; . . . {as before} . . . ;
begin
  reset (oldfile) ; rewrite (newfile) ;
  {first copy oldfile to newfile}
  while not eof (oldfile) do
  begin
    read (oldfile, nextclient) ;
    write (newfile, nextclient)
  end ;
  {then append new clients to new file}
  while not eof (input) do
  begin
    readcard (nextclient) ;
    write (newfile, nextclient)
  end
end.
```

If a file value were to be passed as a value parameter to a procedure then, upon entry to the procedure, a copy would have to be made of the contents of the entire file. Obviously, for a large file, this would be a very time-consuming operation. For this reason PASCAL stipulates that all file parameters must be passed as *variable* parameters. The function (8) takes a file of real numbers (of a type *realfile*) as parameter and returns, as its result, the sum of the numbers in the file.

```
function sumfile (var f : realfile) : real ;
var sum,x : real ;
begin
    sum := 0 ;
    reset(f) ;
    while not eof(f) do                                    (8)
    begin
        read(f,x) ;
        sum := sum + x
    end ;
    sumfile := sum
end
```

PROGRAM 14   (Updating a stock file)

A wholesale distribution firm maintains a file, known as the stock file, in which there is one record for each type of item stored in its warehouses. Each record contains information as follows:

stockitem = **record**
           itemnumber : 0 . . 99999 ;
           instock,targetstock,onorder,
           reorderpoint : 0 . . *maxint*
     end

When the quantity in stock plus the quantity on order for any item falls below its reorder point, an order for further supplies of the item must be raised to restore the quantity available to the value *targetstock*. The records in the stock file are ordered in ascending sequences of *item-number*.

Each day the stock file must be updated, i.e., a new stock file must be produced which reflects the transactions (deliveries and dispatches) which have taken place since the last update. These transactions are accumulated on another file, each transaction representing one delivery or dispatch of items of a given type, as in (9). The records on the transaction file are also sorted in ascending item-number order. (Program 15 shows how such a sorted file might be obtained from the unsorted data collected each day.)

transaction = **record**
           itemnumber : 0 . . 99999 ;
           transactiontype : (*delivery,dispatch*) ;   (9)
           amount : 1 . . *maxint*
     end

A program is required which updates the current stock file, according to the contents of the transaction file, to produce a new stock file. Items which are below their reorder point after that day's transactions are to be printed as an output order list.

Since both files are sorted the process required is one which deals with each item in the old stock file in turn, making amendments as indicated by the next records in the transaction file. In programming this process we must remember that

(a)   there may be no transactions for many of the records in the stock file;

(b)   there may be several transactions for the same record in the stock file;

(c)   errors may occur such as a transaction for a stock item which does not exist.

Assuming that the files involved are named *oldstock*, *newstock* and *transactions*, the basic program form required is as shown in (10).

> *reset (oldstock)* ; *reset (transactions)* ; *rewrite (newstock)* ;
> **while not** *eof (oldstock)* **do**
> **begin**
>> *currentitem* := *oldstock* ↑ .*itemnumber* ;
>> *newstock* ↑ := *oldstock* ↑ ;
>> *reject transactions with itemnumber<currentitem* ;   (10)
>> *amend newstock* ↑ *according to any transactions for*
>> *current item* ;
>> *raise order if necessary* ;
>> *put (newstock)* ; *get (oldstock)*
> **end** ;
> *reject any remaining transactions*

Rejecting transactions with an *itemnumber* less than *currentitem* is expressible as a while-loop. However, at each point where the transaction file is inspected we must guard against it being exhausted. The loop required is thus as shown in (11) (introducing a boolean variable

> *smalleritemnumber* := *true* ;
> **while not** *eof (transactions)* **and** *smalleritemnumber* **do**
> **if** *transactions* ↑ .*itemnumber* < *currentitem* **then**
> **begin**   (11)
>> *reject transaction* ;
>> *get (transactions)*
> **end else** *smalleritemnumber* := *false*

smalleritemnumber to avoid the problems of boolean expression evaluation described in Chap. 4). Likewise the step *amend newstock* ↑ *according to transactions for current item* must be programmed as in (12).

> *sameitemnumber* := *true* ;
> **while not** *eof (transactions)* **and** *sameitemnumber* **do**
> **if** *transactions* ↑ .*itemnumber* = *currentitem* **then**
> **begin**   (12)
>> *amend newstock* ↑ *according to transactions* ↑ ;
>> *get (transactions)*
> **end else** *sameitemnumber* := *false*

The step *amend newstock* ↑ *according to transactions* ↑ is easily programmed as shown in (13).

```
with newstock ↑ , transactions ↑ do
    case transactiontype of
    delivery : begin
                    instock := instock + amount ;                    (13)
                    onorder := onorder − amount
              end ;
    dispatch : instock := instock − amount
    end
```

The step *raise order if necessary* is also easily programmed as shown in (14).

```
with newstock ↑ do
    if instock + onorder < reorderpoint
    then begin
            writeln ('order', targetstock − instock − onorder,   (14)
                    ' of item', itemnumber : 6) ;
            onorder := targetstock − instock
        end
```

The final step of the program, *reject any remaining transactions*, is expressible as a simple while-loop, as in (15).

```
while not eof(transactions) do
begin
    reject transaction ;                                           (15)
    get(transactions)
end
```

In our simple program we will express the step *reject transaction* as a call to a procedure which simply prints out a rejection message incorporating the item number involved, as shown in (16).

```
procedure rejecttransaction ;
begin writeln ('transaction rejected for item ' ,
            transactions ↑ .itemnumber : 6)                        (16)
end
```

In a realistic system each transaction record would include information on the time and place of the transaction, so that those rejected can be traced back to their source. Other checks on the validity of transaction data might also be included in a real system, complicating the data manipulation involved. However, the program structure, and its file handling characteristics, would not differ from that developed here.

Listing 14 shows the final program—the output of the program execution lists the contents of a sample master file before the update, the transactions used to update this file, error messages and orders produced during the updating, and the contents of the new master file.

LISTING 14

```
PROGRAM STOCKUPDATE (TRANSACTIONS, OLDSTOCK, NEWSTOCK, OUTPUT) ;

TYPE  STOCKITEM = RECORD
                      ITEMNUMBER : 0..99999 ;
                      INSTOCK, TARGETSTOCK, ONORDER,
                      REORDERPOINT : 0..MAXINT
                  END ;
      STOCKFILE = FILE OF STOCKITEM ;
      TRANSITEM = RECORD
                      ITEMNUMBER : 0..99999 ;
                      TRANSTYPE : (DELIVERY, DISPATCH) ;
                      AMOUNT : 1..MAXINT
                  END ;
      HEADING = PACKED ARRAY[1..9] OF CHAR ;

VAR   TRANSACTIONS : FILE OF TRANSITEM ;
      OLDSTOCK, NEWSTOCK : STOCKFILE ;
      CURRENTITEM : 0..99999 ;
      SMALLERITEMNUMBER, SAMEITEMNUMBER : BOOLEAN ;

PROCEDURE LISTSTOCK (NAME : HEADING ; VAR F : STOCKFILE) ;
BEGIN
   RESET (F) ;
   WRITELN ; WRITELN ; WRITELN ('**', NAME, '**') ;
   WRITELN ('ITEM NUMBER   INSTOCK   ONORDER   TARGETSTOCK   REORDERPOINT');
   WHILE NOT EOF(F) DO WITH F^ DO
   BEGIN
      WRITELN (ITEMNUMBER, INSTOCK:12, ONORDER:10,
               TARGETSTOCK:12, REORDERPOINT:15) ;
      GET (F)
   END
END ;  (* LISTSTOCK *)

PROCEDURE LISTTRANSACTIONS ;
BEGIN
   RESET (TRANSACTIONS) ;
   WRITELN ; WRITELN ;
   WRITELN('**TRANSACTIONS**') ;
   WHILE NOT EOF(TRANSACTIONS) DO
   WITH TRANSACTIONS^ DO
   BEGIN
      IF TRANSTYPE=DELIVERY THEN WRITE('DELIVERY') ELSE WRITE('DISPATCH');
      WRITELN (ITEMNUMBER, AMOUNT) ;
      GET (TRANSACTIONS)
   END
END ;  (* LISTTRANSACTIONS *)
```

```
PROCEDURE REJECTTRANSACTION ;
BEGIN
   WRITELN ('TRANSACTION REJECTED FOR ITEM ',
            TRANSACTIONS^.ITEMNUMBER :6)
END ;   (* REJECTTRANSACTION *)




BEGIN
   LISTSTOCK ('OLD STOCK', OLDSTOCK) ;
   LISTTRANSACTIONS ;
   RESET (OLDSTOCK) ; RESET (TRANSACTIONS) ; REWRITE (NEWSTOCK) ;
   WHILE NOT EOF(OLDSTOCK) DO
   BEGIN
      CURRENTITEM := OLDSTOCK^.ITEMNUMBER ;
      NEWSTOCK^ := OLDSTOCK^ ;
      (* REJECT TRANSACTIONS WITH ITEMNUMBER < CURRENTITEM *)
      SMALLERITEMNUMBER := TRUE ;
      WHILE NOT EOF (TRANSACTIONS) AND SMALLERITEMNUMBER DO
      IF TRANSACTIONS^.ITEMNUMBER<CURRENTITEM THEN
      BEGIN
         REJECTTRANSACTION ;
         GET (TRANSACTIONS)
      END ELSE SMALLERITEMNUMBER := FALSE ;
      (* AMEND NEWSTOCK^ WITH ANY TRANSACTIONS FOR CURRENTITEM *)
      SAMEITEMNUMBER := TRUE ;
      WHILE NOT EOF (TRANSACTIONS) AND SAMEITEMNUMBER DO
      IF TRANSACTIONS^.ITEMNUMBER=CURRENTITEM THEN
      BEGIN
         WITH NEWSTOCK^, TRANSACTIONS^ DO
         CASE TRANSTYPE OF
         DELIVERY : BEGIN
                         INSTOCK := INSTOCK + AMOUNT ;
                         ONORDER := ONORDER - AMOUNT
                    END ;
         DISPATCH : INSTOCK := INSTOCK-AMOUNT
         END ;
         GET (TRANSACTIONS)
      END ELSE SAMEITEMNUMBER := FALSE ;
      (* RAISE ORDER IF NECESSARY *)
      WITH NEWSTOCK^ DO
      IF INSTOCK + ONORDER < REORDERPOINT
      THEN BEGIN
              WRITELN ('ORDER', TARGETSTOCK-ONORDER-INSTOCK,
                       ' OF ITEM', ITEMNUMBER :6 ) ;
              ONORDER := TARGETSTOCK - INSTOCK
           END ;
      PUT (NEWSTOCK) ; GET (OLDSTOCK)
   END ;
   (* REJECT ANY REMAINING TRANSACTIONS *)
   WHILE NOT EOF(TRANSACTIONS) DO
   BEGIN
      REJECTTRANSACTION ;
      GET (TRANSACTIONS)
   END ;
   LISTSTOCK ('NEW STOCK', NEWSTOCK)
END.
```

```
**OLD STOCK**
```

ITEM NUMBER	INSTOCK	ONORDER	TARGETSTOCK	REORDERPOINT
11081	5450	0	7000	5000
11202	5430	2500	8000	6000
23934	6230	2500	9000	7000
28454	1270	3500	5000	4000
36666	9090	0	9500	7000
37775	820	1000	2000	1500
39399	4620	0	6000	4500
42000	3550	1400	5000	4000
42111	4460	3500	8000	6000
42281	3750	1500	6000	4500
43327	8260	0	9000	7000
53553	8000	0	9000	7000
55376	2800	2000	5000	4000
57862	1370	1150	3000	2000
59097	3540	1460	5000	4000

```
**TRANSACTIONS**
DELIVERY   10754   1000
DISPATCH   11081    350
DISPATCH   11081   1240
DISPATCH   11081   2000
DISPATCH   11202   1500
DISPATCH   23934   2000
DELIVERY   28454   3500
DISPATCH   28454    500
DELIVERY   29334    500
DISPATCH   36666   2000
DISPATCH   37775     50
DISPATCH   42000    500
DISPATCH   42000    300
DISPATCH   42111    500
DELIVERY   42111   3500
DISPATCH   42281    450
DISPATCH   55376    520
DISPATCH   55376    470
DELIVERY   57862   1150
DISPATCH   59907    540
TRANSACTION REJECTED FOR ITEM  10754
ORDER    5140 OF ITEM 11081
ORDER    2270 OF ITEM 23934
TRANSACTION REJECTED FOR ITEM  29334
ORDER    1190 OF ITEM 55376
TRANSACTION REJECTED FOR ITEM  59907
```

```
**NEW STOCK**
```

ITEM NUMBER	INSTOCK	ONORDER	TARGETSTOCK	REORDERPOINT
11081	1860	5140	7000	5000
11202	3930	2500	8000	6000
23934	4230	4770	9000	7000
28454	4270	0	5000	4000
36666	7090	0	9500	7000
37775	770	1000	2000	1500
39399	4620	0	6000	4500

42000	2750	1400	5000	4000
42111	7460	0	8000	6000
42281	3300	1500	6000	4500
43327	8260	0	9000	7000
53553	8000	0	9000	7000
55376	1810	3190	5000	4000
57862	2520	0	3000	2000
59097	3540	1460	5000	4000

PROGRAM 15   (Sorting a file)

In Program 14 we saw a need to produce a transaction file whose components were sorted in order of ascending item number, from an initially unsorted transaction file. Such a file sort is a common requirement in file manipulation and may be stated more generally.

Given a file of records defined as in (17), a program is required which will sort the records in the unsorted file *datafile* so that the records are stored in ascending order of the value of the field key of each record.

$$
\begin{aligned}
&\textbf{type } item \; = \; \textbf{record} \\
&\qquad\qquad\quad key : keytype \; ; \\
&\qquad\qquad\quad restofrecord : sometype \qquad\qquad\qquad (17)\\
&\qquad\quad \textbf{end} \; ; \\
&\textbf{var } datafile : \textbf{file of } item
\end{aligned}
$$

We shall use the method known as the *natural merge sort* to carry out the process. In order to describe the operation of this method we define several terms.

Given a sequence $k_1, \ldots, k_n$ of key values, an ordered ascending subsequence, or *run*, $k_i, \ldots, k_l$ is such that

$$
\begin{aligned}
&k_{i-1} > k_i \\
&k_j \; \le \; k_{j+1} \qquad \text{for all } j = i, \ldots, l-1 \\
&k_l \; > \; k_{l+1}
\end{aligned}
$$

Merging is the combination of two or more such runs into a single run. Runs have the obvious property that if 2 sequences of N runs are merged, then a single sequence of N runs emerges. So the total number of runs is halved in each *pass* during the merge sort.

Let us assume that the initial sequence of unsorted records is held on a file C, that the sorted output is to appear on C, and that A and B are two auxiliary files to be used in the sort. In a real data-processing environment the actual data are first copied onto C from the original file *datafile* before sorting and, when the sort is complete, the data on C are copied back to *datafile*. This is for security reasons, in case any

unforeseen event occurs during execution of the sort program that
would result in the original data being lost.

Each pass of the sort consists of a *distribution phase* that distributes
runs from C onto A and B alternately, and a *merge phase* that merges
runs from A and B back again to C. For example, Fig. 12.4 shows the
key value of each record of an example file C in its original state, A and
B after each distribution phase, and C after each merge phase. (The end
of a run is marked by a prime.)

Note that, in this example, three passes are needed and that the sort
terminates when there is just one run on C following a merge phase.

Introducing the global definition

> **type** *filetype* = **file of** *item*

C	82′ 48′ 14 15 84′ 25 77′ 13 72′ 4 51′ 19 27 43 57′ 53′
	distribute
A	82′ 14 15 84′ 13 72′ 19 27 43 57′
B	48′ 25 77′ 4 51 53′
	merge
C	48 82′ 14 15 25 77 84′ 4 13 51 53 72′ 19 27 43 57′
	distribute
A	48 82′ 4 13 51 53 72′
B	14 15 25 77 84′ 19 27 43 57′
	merge
C	14 15 25 48 77 82 84′ 4 13 19 27 43 51 53 57 72′
	distribute
A	14 15 25 48 77 82 84′
B	4 13 19 27 43 51 53 57 72′
	merge
C	4 13 14 15 19 25 27 43 48 51 53 57 77 72 82 84′

Fig. 12.4 Operation of natural merge sort

we can formulate a procedure to carry out the natural merge sort of C, as shown in (18).

```
procedure naturalmergesort (var C : filetype) ;
var        numberofruns : integer ;
           A,B : filetype ;
begin
    repeat
        reset(C) ; rewrite(A) ; rewrite(B) ;                    (18)
        distribute ;
        reset(A) ; reset(B) ; rewrite(C) ;
        numberofruns := 0 ;
        merge
    until numberofruns = 1
end
```

We now proceed to refine each of the phases *distribute* and *merge* as local procedures of *naturalmergesort*. The action of *distribute*, shown in (19), is to copy runs from C to A and B alternately until C has been completely read (we assume that C is not empty).

```
procedure distribute ;
begin
    repeat
        copyarun(C,A) ;                                         (19)
        if not eof(C) then copyarun(C,B)
    until eof(C)
end
```

The procedure *copyarun*, developed below, copies a run of records from its first parameter file to the second parameter file.

Although it appears that the number of runs distributed onto A and B differ by at most 1, in fact this is not necessarily true since consecutive runs distributed on to a file may in fact combine to form a single run on that file (see the example where 4, 51 and 53 are distributed as distinct runs onto B but then form a single run on B). Hence the merge phase (20) combines runs from each of A and B until the end of either file is reached, following which the tail of the other file must be copied onto C.

```
procedure merge ;
begin                                                           (20)
    while not (eof(A) or eof(B)) do
```

```
    begin
        mergearunfromAandB ;
        numberofruns := numberofruns + 1
    end ;
    while not eof(A) do
    begin
        copyarun (A,C) ;
        numberofruns := numberofruns + 1                    (20 cont.)
    end ;
    while not eof(B) do
    begin
        copyarun (B,C) ;
        numberofruns := numberofruns + 1
    end
end
```

The actions of the procedure *copyarun* (21) are expressed in terms of calls of a procedure *copy* whose action is to transfer a value of type *item* from its first parameter file to its second parameter file, and determine when the end of a run has been reached. Thus a global boolean variable *endofrun* is introduced which indicates whether or not the end of a run has been reached. The value of this variable will be set by each call of *copy*. Note that both file parameters must be specified as variable parameters.

```
procedure copyarun (var source,destination : filetype) ;
begin
    repeat copy (source,destination) until endofrun          (21)
end
```

The procedure *mergearunfromAandB* (22) produces a single merged run on C formed from a run from each of A and B. It operates by comparing the key fields of records in corresponding runs on A and B, and calls *copy* to transfer the selected records to C. This process will terminate when one of the two runs is exhausted, at which point the tail of the other run is copied to C. Provided that *keytype* is an unstructured type or a string type (which we assume here) the comparison operation is expressed trivially by the $<$ operator; for a structured type there are a number of key fields and the comparison operation would be expressed rather less simply.

```
procedure mergearunfromAandB ;
begin
    repeat                                                   (22)
        if A ↑ .key < B ↑ .key then
```

$$\textbf{begin } copy(A,C) \text{ ; } \textbf{if } endofrun \textbf{ then } copyarun(B,C) \textbf{ end}$$
$$\textbf{else}$$
$$\textbf{begin } copy(B,C) \text{ ; } \textbf{if } endofrun \textbf{ then } copyarun(A,C) \textbf{ end}$$
$$\textbf{until } endofrun$$

$$\textbf{end} \hspace{4cm} (22 \ cont.)$$

The procedure *copy* (23) is readily expressible in terms of basic PASCAL file operations. In order to determine the end of a run, the key

```
procedure copy (var source,destination : filetype) ;
var copieditem : item ;
begin
    copieditem := source ↑  ; get (source) ;
    {read(source,copieditem)}                              (23)
    destination ↑  := copieditem  ; put(destination) ;
    {write(destination,copieditem)}
    if eof(source) then endofrun := true
                    else endofrun := copieditem.key > source ↑ .key
end
```

of the last record copied from a file must be retained for comparison with its successor. Thus the natural merge sort procedure has been fully developed and can be simply incorporated in a program which copies the file to be sorted on to the file *C*, calls *naturalmergesort*, and finally copies the sorted file *C* back on to the original file, as indicated in (24). The procedure *copyfile* transfers records between its two parameter files and also lists out the value of the key field for each record transferred.

```
begin
    copyfile (datafile,C) ;
    naturalmergesort (C) ;                                 (24)
    copyfile (C,datafile)
end
```

Listing 15 shows the complete program together with the list of key fields generated by the procedure *copyfile*, verifying that the sort has been successfully completed.

```
                    LISTING 15

PROGRAM SORT (DATAFILE, OUTPUT) ;

TYPE  KEYTYPE = 0..99999 ;
      SOMETYPE = RECORD
                      TRANSTYPE : (DELIVERY, DISPATCH) ;
                      AMOUNT : 1..MAXINT
                 END ;
```

```
        ITEM = RECORD
                 KEY : KEYTYPE ;
                 RESTOFRECORD : SOMETYPE
               END ;
      FILETYPE = FILE OF ITEM ;

VAR   DATAFILE : FILETYPE ;
      C : FILETYPE ;


PROCEDURE NATURALMERGESORT (VAR C : FILETYPE) ;
VAR   NUMBEROFRUNS : 0..MAXINT ;
      A, B : FILETYPE ;
      ENDOFRUN : BOOLEAN ;


  PROCEDURE COPY (VAR SOURCE, DESTINATION : FILETYPE) ;
  VAR  COPIEDITEM : ITEM ;
  BEGIN
     COPIEDITEM := SOURCE^ ; GET (SOURCE) ;
     DESTINATION^ := COPIEDITEM ; PUT (DESTINATION) ;
     IF EOF (SOURCE) THEN ENDOFRUN := TRUE
                     ELSE ENDOFRUN := COPIEDITEM.KEY > SOURCE^.KEY
  END ;  (* COPY *)


  PROCEDURE COPYARUN (VAR SOURCE , DESTINATION : FILETYPE) ;
  BEGIN
     REPEAT COPY (SOURCE, DESTINATION) UNTIL ENDOFRUN
  END ;  (* COPYARUN *)


  PROCEDURE DISTRIBUTE ;
  BEGIN
     REPEAT
        COPYARUN (C,A) ;
        IF NOT EOF(C) THEN COPYARUN (C,B)
     UNTIL EOF(C)
  END ;  (* DISTRIBUTE *)


  PROCEDURE MERGE ;

     PROCEDURE MERGEARUNFROMAANDB ;
     BEGIN
        REPEAT
           IF A^.KEY < B^.KEY THEN
           BEGIN COPY (A,C) ; IF ENDOFRUN THEN COPYARUN (B,C) END
           ELSE
           BEGIN COPY (B,C) ; IF ENDOFRUN THEN COPYARUN (A,C) END
        UNTIL ENDOFRUN
     END ;  (* MERGEARUNFROMAANDB *)

  BEGIN
     WHILE NOT (EOF(A) OR EOF(B)) DO
     BEGIN
        MERGEARUNFROMAANDB ;
        NUMBEROFRUNS := NUMBEROFRUNS + 1
     END ;
     WHILE NOT EOF(A) DO
```

```
        BEGIN
          COPYARUN (A,C) ;
          NUMBEROFRUNS := NUMBEROFRUNS + 1
        END ;
        WHILE NOT EOF(B) DO
        BEGIN
          COPYARUN (B,C) ;
          NUMBEROFRUNS := NUMBEROFRUNS + 1
        END
    END ;   (* MERGE *)


BEGIN  (* NATURALMERGESORT *)
   REPEAT
      RESET (C) ;  REWRITE (A) ;  REWRITE (B) ;
      DISTRIBUTE ;
      RESET (A) ;  RESET (B) ; REWRITE (C) ;
      NUMBEROFRUNS := 0 ;
      MERGE
   UNTIL NUMBEROFRUNS = 1
END ;  (* NATURALMERGESORT *)


PROCEDURE COPYFILE (VAR F, G : FILETYPE) ;
BEGIN
   RESET (F) ; REWRITE (G) ;
   WHILE NOT EOF(F) DO
   BEGIN
      WRITELN (F^.KEY) ;
      G^ := F^ ;
      PUT (G) ;  GET (F)
   END
END ; (* COPYFILE *)


BEGIN   (* MAINPROGRAM *)
   WRITELN ('** UNSORTED RECORD KEYS **') ;
   COPYFILE (DATAFILE, C) ;
   NATURALMERGESORT (C) ;
   WRITELN ; WRITELN ;
   WRITELN ('** SORTED RECORD KEYS **') ;
   COPYFILE (C, DATAFILE)
END.



** UNSORTED RECORD KEYS **
    57862
    29334
    42111
    42000
    36666
    11202
    11081
    55376
    28454
    23734
    42111
    11081
```

```
        11081
        55376
        28454
        42281
        42000
        37775
        10754
        59907


    ** SORTED RECORD KEYS **
        10754
        11081
        11081
        11081
        11202
        23934
        28454
        28454
        29334
        36666
        37775
        42000
        42000
        42111
        42111
        42281
        55376
        55376
        57862
        59907
```

TEXT FILES

To enable convenient manipulation of character text PASCAL provides a standard file type *text*. Files declared to be of the standard type *text* are known as *text files*.

A text file is structured as a sequence of lines—each line containing values of type *char*—separated by special line control characters. Each line may contain 0 or more character values. The standard input and output data streams described in Chap. 5 are structured in this way and the identifiers *input* and *output* used to denote these data streams are in fact pre-declared text file identifiers in every PASCAL implementation, thus

    input,output : text

Hence the procedures *write, writeln, read, readln, page* and the functions *eoln* (end of line) and *eof* (end of file), which were used in Chap. 5

with the data streams *input* and *output*, are in fact particular cases of the use of more general standard facilities for handling text files. The complete range of procedures and functions which may be applied to text files is summarized below, with reference to Chap. 5 as appropriate.

reset and rewrite

Like other files, text files must be prepared for reading or writing by use of the standard procedures *reset* or *rewrite*. However the procedure statements

> *reset(input)*
> *rewrite(output)*

are automatically assumed at the beginning of execution of each program that uses the standard files, and they need not be written there. The effect of applying *reset* or *rewrite* to the standard file *input* or *output* at any point in a program is implementation-defined, and may be an error.

eof, get and put

The standard function *eof* and the standard procedures *get* and *put* may be applied to a text file, in the same way as to any other file. Likewise a text file f has an associated file buffer $f \uparrow$ which is a variable representing the currently accessible character of the file. It differs from the file buffer of a non-text file, only as explained under *eoln* below.

As we saw in Chap. 5, use of the predicate *eof* without a file parameter is assumed to apply to the standard file *input*. Thus

> *eof*   and   *eof(input)*

are equivalent.

The existence of the file buffer for the standard input file allows a greater flexibility in the input of character information than is possible with the standard procedure *read* alone. The next available character of the input stream can be inspected, as *input* $\uparrow$, before it is to be copied to a variable c, and the input stream advanced, by a statement *read(c)*.

eoln

When the current character available from a text file f is a line-control character, the standard boolean function

> *eoln(f)*

returns the value *true*, and the character value given by the file buffer $f \uparrow$ is blank. At all other times the result of *eoln(f)* is false.

As we saw in Chap. 5, use of *eoln* without a file parameter is assumed to apply to the standard file *input*. Thus

    eoln   and   *eoln(input)*

are equivalent.

read and readln

The standard procedure statements

    read(f,v1,v2,...,vn)
    readln(f,v1,v2,...,vn)
    readln(f)

may be used with any text file *f*.
The form

    read(f,v1,v2,...,vn)

is defined to be equivalent to

    begin *read(f,v1)* ; *read(f,v2)* ; ... *read(f,vn)* **end**

The form

    readln (f, v1, v2, ..., vn)

is defined to be equivalent to

    begin *read(f, v1, v2, ..., vn)* ; *readln (f)* **end**

The form

    readln(f)

is defined to be equivalent to the basic text file operations shown in (25).

$$
\begin{aligned}
&\textbf{begin} \\
&\quad \textbf{while not } eoln(f) \textbf{ do } get(f) \text{ ;} \\
&\quad get(f) \\
&\textbf{end}
\end{aligned}
\qquad (25)
$$

Thus $f \uparrow$ is advanced to the first character of the next line.
For a text file *f* the effect of the form

    read(f,v)

depends on the type of the variable *v*, as follows:

(a)   if *v* is of type *char* the effect is defined, as for other non-text files, thus

       $v := f \uparrow$; *get(f)*

(b) if *v* is of type *real* or *integer*, or any subrange thereof, the effect is
as defined for the standard input file in Chap. 5. A sequence of
characters is input from the file *f* such that the sequence denotes
an optionally signed real or integer value (as defined in Chap. 3)
preceded by any number of blank (or line control) characters. The
value denoted by the sequence is assigned to *v*, and the first
character following the sequence is left as *f* ↑ . If the characters read
do not denote a suitable value, or if the end-of-file condition, *eof(f)*,
arises before a sufficient sequence of characters is obtained, the effect
of *read(f, v)* is a program error.

As we saw in Chap. 5, use of *read* or *readln* without a file parameter *f*
implies the standard file *input*.

write and writeln

The standard procedure statements

*write(f,x*1,*x*2, . . . ,*xn*)
*writeln(f,x*1,*x*2, . . . ,*xn*)
writeln(f)

may be used with any text file *f*.
The form

*write(f,x*1,*x*2, . . . ,*xn*)

is defined to be equivalent to

begin *write(f,x*1) ; *write(f,x*2) ; . . . *write(f,xn)* **end**

The form

*writeln(f,x*1,*x*2, . . . ,*xn*)

is defined to be equivalent to

begin *write(f,x*1,*x*2, . . . ,*xn*) ; *writeln(f)* **end**

The effect of the form

writeln(f)

is to append a line-control character to the file *f*. It is defined only for
text files. If the file is printed, the characters written after the line-
control character will appear on a line following those written before. If
the file is re-input to a PASCAL program the end of line condition, as
described above, will arise when the line control character is encountered.

The effect of the form

   $write(f,x)$

where f is a text file, is to write to f a sequence of characters which denotes the value specified by the parameter x. This parameter must take the form of an *output-value*, as defined in Chap. 5, determining the value to be output and the format in which it is to be represented.

As we saw in Chap. 5, use of *write* or *writeln* without the file parameter f implies the use of the standard file *output*.

page

The standard procedure call

   $page(f)$

may be used on any text file f which is being output on a device which allows pagination, such as a line printer. Its only effect is to cause a skip to the top of a new page on the device. Use of page without a file parameter, thus

   page

is assumed to apply to the standard file *output*.

```
procedure copyfile (var f,g : text) ;
var c : char ;
begin
    reset(f) ; rewrite(g) ;
    while not eof(f) do
    begin {copy a line from f to g}                    (26)
        while not eoln(f) do
        begin read(f,c) ; write(g,c) end ;
        readln(f) ; writeln(g)
    end
end
```

The procedure (26), given two text files f and g as parameters, will copy the contents of f onto g in such a way as to maintain the line structure of the text of file f. Note that the effect of this procedure, when called with either of the standard files *input* or *output* as an actual parameter, is implementation-defined, since it attempts to *reset* and *rewrite* its parameters. On some implementations such calls may produce an error. For these implementations a special, less general, procedure would have to be written to deal with copying to *output*, or copying from *input*.

As explained in Chap. 5 for *input*, a text file being read is assumed to consist of an integral number of lines. When a text file is being written, if the last action on the file before a *reset* operation or before execution of the program finishes is not a *writeln* operation, an implicit *writeln* is assumed. This ensures that the file has the correct line structure in any subsequent reading of its contents.

PROGRAM 16   (A text editor)

Most computer systems provide their users with a standard program known as an "editor". An editor program assists the user in the development of files of textual information. Corrections and amendments to the data in an existing file are specified by means of simple, but powerful, editing instructions. The editor obeys these instructions in editing the contents of an existing "oldfile" to produce a new "newfile".

We shall describe the construction of a simple editor. This editor makes use of four types of editing command—the *T* (transcription), *D* (delete), *I* (insert) and *E* (end) commands. Each of these instructions performs an action on the contents of the oldfile to produce information in the newfile. The instructions make use of a conceptual line-number counter which references a particular line in the oldfile. The lines of a file are considered to be numbered from zero upwards. The conceptual line-number counter is assumed initially to be zero, i.e., it points to the first line. The editing instructions are presented to the editor from the standard input file.

For the purposes of illustrating the actions of these instructions below we assume the existence of an oldfile containing the following five lines of data:

> *JIM SHORT*
> *DAVE ANDERSON*
> *JOHN HUGHES*
> *PETER HALLIDAY*
> *FRED DAVIES*

The *T* instruction appears on a line by itself and has the following format:

> *T   linenumber*

Its action is to copy text, without alteration, from the oldfile to the newfile. This copying begins at the line indicated by the current value of the conceptual line counter and continues up to, but not including, line *linenumber*. Hence, if

> *T*2

is the first edit command supplied to the editor, then the lines

JIM SHORT
DAVE ANDERSON

of the oldfile will be copied across to the newfile, and the value of the line counter becomes 2.

The *D* instruction also appears on a line by itself and has the format

D   n

where *n* is a positive integer. Its action is to increment the line counter value by *n*, i.e., the next *n* lines of the oldfile are to be skipped over. Thus the *D* instruction is used for deleting lines from a file.

After execution of the following three instructions on the given oldfile

*T*1
*D*1
*T*3

the newfile will contain

JIM SHORT
JOHN HUGHES

and the value of the line counter will be 3.

The *I* instruction is used to insert new lines of text into the newfile. Its format is

I   n

on a separate line, where *n* is a positive integer indicating the number of lines of text to be inserted, followed by the *n* lines of text. Thus, applying the series of instructions

*T*1
*D*1
*I*2
BILL COOK
COLIN JAMES

to the oldfile will result in the newfile containing

JIM SHORT
BILL COOK
COLIN JAMES

and the value of the line counter will be 2.

The *E* instruction denotes the end of the edit instructions and appears on a line by itself. Its action is to copy the remainder of the oldfile, from the position given by the current value of the line counter, to the newfile.

Hence, after execution of

> T2
> D2
> E

the newfile will contain

> *JIM SHORT*
> *DAVE ANDERSON*
> *FRED DAVIES*

We now construct a PASCAL program to implement such an editor. The oldfile and newfile will be external text files of the program and the editing instructions will be obtained from the standard input data stream, i.e., the file *input*. The editing instructions will be echoed to the file *output*, together with details of any errors in the editing instructions that may be detected by the editor program. If an error is detected the editor program should halt. Five kinds of error can occur and are indicated by the following messages:

1. ＊＊＊＊ *edit command not recognized*
2. ＊＊＊＊ *specified line number less than current line counter*
3. ＊＊＊＊ *old file exhausted prematurely*
4. ＊＊＊＊ *not enough input for insertion command*
5. ＊＊＊＊ *end of edit command missing*

Error 1 arises when an edit command other than *T,I,D*, or *E*, is issued. Error 2 arises when the *T* command specifies a line whose number is less than the current line counter. Error 3 refers to an attempt to transcribe or delete more lines than are actually present in the oldfile. Error 4 arises when an *I* command specifies more lines of new data than are available from the input file. Error 5 is due to an end command *E* not having been issued—this may indicate that the user has not issued all the editing commands that he intended.

The program heading specifies the files involved, i.e.,

> **program** *editor* (*oldfile,newfile,input,output*)

where *oldfile* and *newfile* are text files declared in the program block

> **var** *oldfile,newfile* : *text*

The basic action of the program is a loop which recognizes and executes the editing instructions supplied by the user, as shown in (28).

> **begin**
>   *initialize files and current line pointer* ;   (28)
>   *endofedit* := *false* ;

```
        repeat
            read and echo command ;
            if legal command then obey edit command          (28 cont.)
                                   else error (1)
        until endofedit
    end
```

endofedit is a boolean variable used to denote when the edit is to be terminated, either normally or due to the detection of an error. *error* is a procedure which prints the error message appropriate to the detected error and causes the edit to be abandoned (by setting the value of *endofedit* to true). Its value parameter indicates the error found.

The statement *initialize files and current line pointer* is immediately expressible as

> *reset (oldfile)* ; *rewrite (newfile)* ;
> *currentlinepointer* := 0

where

> *currentlinepointer* : 0 .. *maxint*

For *read and echo command*, we need to introduce a variable

> *operator* : *char*

and the statement is then expressible as

> *read (operator)* ; *write (operator)*

A command is legal if the set operation

> *operator* **in** ['T','I','D','E']

gives the value *true*.

The statement *obey edit command* is expressed as a case-statement discriminating between the different actions associated with the four edit commands, as in (29).

```
    case operator of
        'T' : execute transcription ;
        'D' : execute deletion ;
        'I' : execute insertion ;                           (29)
        'E' : end the edit
    end
```

The actions of *execute transcription* are summarized as shown in (30). The transcription process must ensure that an attempt to read past the end of the oldfile does not occur (error 3). Otherwise it copies from the oldfile, beginning at the line given by *currentlinepointer*, up to the

```
begin
    readln (linenumber) ; writeln (linenumber) ;
    if linenumber < currentlinepointer
    then error(2)                                          (30)
    else transcribe from oldfile to newfile
end
```

specified *linenumber*. The refinement necessary for this is shown in (31).

```
begin
    while not eof (oldfile) and (currentlinepointer<linenumber) do
    begin
        copyline (oldfile) ;                                (31)
        currentlinepointer := currentlinepointer + 1
    end ;
    if currentlinepointer<linenumber then error(3)
end
```

The procedure *copyline* copies the next line from the specified parameter file to *newfile*.

Note that the test that the end of the file has not been passed is expressed as

$$currentlinepointer < linenumber$$

and not

$$eof (oldfile)$$

since it is possible for *eof (oldfile)* and *currentlinepointer* $>=$ *linenumber* to become *true* simultaneously, i.e., when a command is issued to transcribe to the end of the file—which is not an error.

The statement *execute deletion* determines the number of lines to be deleted and skips over the required number of lines in *oldfile*. It must also check against the possibility of reading past the end of the *oldfile*. The skipping is programmed as for the transcription operation above except that the call of *copyline* is replaced by the call

$$readln (oldfile)$$

The process *execute insertion* determines the number of lines of data to be inserted into the newfile and copies the required number of lines from the input file to *newfile*—however, it must check against any attempt to read past the end of the input file (error 4), as shown in (32).

```
begin
    readln (numberoflinestobeinserted) ;
    i := 0 ;
    while (i<numberoflinestobeinserted) and not eof (input) do
    begin                                                          (32)
        copyline (input) ; i := i+1
    end ;
    if i<numberoflinestobeinserted then error (4)
end
```

The ending of the edit consists of two actions, i.e.,

```
begin
    copy remainder of oldfile to newfile ;
    endofedit := true
end
```

If the user fails to supply an E command then the main program loop will fail to terminate normally and the input stream will become exhausted. To allow for, and check against, this possibility the loop

```
repeat
    ⋮
until endofedit
```

has its terminating condition amended and becomes

```
repeat
    ⋮
until endofedit or eof (input)
```

If the loop has not been terminated by an E command, then error situation 5 must be diagnosed, i.e.,

```
if not endofedit then error (5)
```

The construction of the procedure *error* is straightforward. Its heading is

```
procedure error (number : errorrange) ;
```

and its action is to output the error message corresponding to the value of its parameter. It also sets the value of *endofedit* to *true* so that the edit will subsequently be terminated.

The procedure

```
procedure copyline (var f : text)
```

simply reads the next line of f, character by character, and transfers it to *newfile*.

Listing 16 shows the complete editor program. It has been augmented with a procedure *list* which is called to output the contents of the *oldfile* prior to the edit, and the *newfile* after completion of the edit. The reader may thus verify the correctness of the editor program for the given set of edit commands.

```
                   LISTING 16

PROGRAM EDITOR (OLDFILE, NEWFILE, INPUT, OUTPUT) ;

TYPE  ERRORRANGE = 1..5 ;

VAR   OLDFILE, NEWFILE : TEXT ;
      CURRENTLINEPOINTER, NUMBEROFLINESTOBEINSERTED, LINENUMBER ,
      N, I : 0..MAXINT ;
      ENDOFEDIT : BOOLEAN ;
      OPERATOR : CHAR ;

PROCEDURE LIST (VAR F:TEXT) ;
VAR   CH : CHAR ;
      LINE : 0..MAXINT ;
BEGIN
   RESET (F) ;
   LINE := 0 ;
   WHILE NOT EOF(F) DO
   BEGIN
      WRITE (LINE :4) ;  LINE := LINE+1 ;
      WHILE NOT EOLN(F) DO
      BEGIN
         READ (F,CH) ; WRITE(CH)
      END ;
      READLN (F) ; WRITELN
   END
END ; (* LIST *)

PROCEDURE COPYLINE (VAR F:TEXT) ;
VAR   CH : CHAR ;
BEGIN
   WHILE NOT EOLN(F) DO
   BEGIN
      READ (F,CH) ; WRITE (NEWFILE,CH)
   END ;
   READLN (F) ; WRITELN (NEWFILE)
END ;  (* COPYLINE *)

PROCEDURE ERROR (NUMBER : ERRORRANGE) ;
BEGIN
   WRITELN ; WRITE ('****    ') ;
   CASE NUMBER OF
   1 : WRITELN ('EDIT COMMAND ',OPERATOR, ' NOT RECOGNIZED') ;
   2 : WRITELN ('SPECIFIED LINE NUMBER LESS THAN CURRENT LINE NUMBER');
   3 : WRITELN ('OLDFILE EXHAUSTED PREMATURELY') ;
   4 : WRITELN ('NOT ENOUGH INPUT TO PERFORM INSERTION') ;
   5 : WRITELN ('END OF EDIT COMMAND MISSING')
   END ;
```

```
      WRITELN ('****     EDIT ABORTED') ;
      ENDOFEDIT := TRUE
   END ;  (* ERROR *)

BEGIN
   WRITELN ; WRITELN ('**** CONTENTS OF OLDFILE') ;
   LIST (OLDFILE) ; WRITELN ;
   CURRENTLINEPOINTER := 0 ;  ENDOFEDIT := FALSE ;
   RESET (OLDFILE) ; REWRITE (NEWFILE) ;
   WRITELN ('**** LISTING OF EDIT COMMANDS') ;
   REPEAT
      READ (OPERATOR) ;  WRITE (OPERATOR) ;
      IF NOT ((OPERATOR='T')OR(OPERATOR='I')OR(OPERATOR='D')OR(OPERATOR='E'))
      THEN ERROR(1) ELSE
      CASE OPERATOR OF
      'T'  : BEGIN  (* TRANSCRIPTION *)
                READLN (LINENUMBER) ;  WRITELN (LINENUMBER :4) ;
                IF LINENUMBER < CURRENTLINEPOINTER THEN ERROR(2) ELSE
                BEGIN
                   WHILE NOT EOF(OLDFILE) AND(CURRENTLINEPOINTER < LINENUMBER)DO
                   BEGIN
                      COPYLINE (OLDFILE) ;
                      CURRENTLINEPOINTER := CURRENTLINEPOINTER + 1
                   END ;
                   IF CURRENTLINEPOINTER < LINENUMBER THEN ERROR(3)
                END
             END ;
      'D'  : BEGIN  (* DELETION *)
                READLN (N) ;  WRITELN (N:4) ;
                LINENUMBER := CURRENTLINEPOINTER + N ;
                WHILE NOT EOF(OLDFILE) AND(CURRENTLINEPOINTER < LINENUMBER)DO
                BEGIN
                   READLN (OLDFILE) ;
                   CURRENTLINEPOINTER := CURRENTLINEPOINTER + 1
                END ;
                IF CURRENTLINEPOINTER < LINENUMBER THEN ERROR(3)
             END ;
      'I'  : BEGIN  (* INSERTION *)
                READLN (NUMBEROFLINESTOBEINSERTED) ;
                WRITELN (NUMBEROFLINESTOBEINSERTED :4) ;
                I := 0 ;
                WHILE NOT EOF(INPUT) AND(I < NUMBEROFLINESTOBEINSERTED) DO
                BEGIN
                   COPYLINE (INPUT) ;  I := I+1
                END ;
                IF I < NUMBEROFLINESTOBEINSERTED THEN ERROR(4)
             END ;
      'E'  : BEGIN  (* END OF EDIT *)
                READLN ;
                WHILE NOT EOF(OLDFILE) DO COPYLINE (OLDFILE) ;
                ENDOFEDIT := TRUE
             END
      END
   UNTIL ENDOFEDIT OR EOF(INPUT) ;
   WRITELN ; WRITELN ; WRITELN ('**** CONTENTS OF NEWFILE') ;
   LIST (NEWFILE) ; WRITELN ;
   IF NOT ENDOFEDIT THEN ERROR(5)
END.
```

```
**** CONTENTS OF OLDFILE
    0    JIM SHORT
    1    DAVE ANDERSON
    2    JOHN HUGHES ·
    3    PETER HALLIDAY
    4    FRED DAVIES

**** LISTING OF EDIT COMMANDS
 T    1
 D    1
 I    2
 T    4
 D    1
 E

**** CONTENTS OF NEWFILE
    0    JIM SHORT
    1    BILL COOK
    2    COLIN JAMES
    3    JOHN HUGHES
    4    PETER HALLIDAY
```

EXERCISES

12.1 Using the record type and input procedure required by Exercise 10.3, write a program which reads an unspecified number of student names and grades, and stores them as an external file of records, *Class*1.

12.2 Adapt the natural merge sort procedure given in Program 15 to sort the file *Class*1, created in Exercise 12.1, into alphabetic order by student name.

12.3 Write a program to read the student records from the sorted file *Class*1 created by Exercise 12.2, and tabulate them in the format used by Program 2.

12.4 Use the programs developed in Exercises 12.1 and 12.2 to create a second sorted file of records, *Class*2, for another class of students. Write a program to read the sorted files *Class*1 and *Class*2, and create a single sorted file *Classes* containing all the student records.

12.5 Write a program which

(a) reads a sequence of student names and stores them in an internal file *Queries*;

(b) sorts the file *Queries* into alphabetic order;

(c) tabulates the records from the student record file *Classes* created by Exercise 12.4, for those students whose names appear in the *Queries* file.

12.6 Write a program which reads two text files *Page*1 and *Page*2 and prints them side by side in the form:

Page1   Page2

```
. . . . . . . . . . . . . . . . . . . . . . . . . .        . . . . . . . . . . . . . . . . . . . . . . . . . . .
. . . . . . . . . . . . . . . . . .                        . . . . . . . . . . . . . . . . . .
. . . . . . . . . . . . . . . . . .                        . . . . . . . . . . . . . . . . . .
. . . . . . . .                                            . . . . . . . . . . . .
. . . . . . . . . . . . . . . .                            . . . . . . . . . . . . . .
                                                           . . . . . . . . . . . . . . .
```

Each printed file should retain the line structure of the corresponding
input file. You may assume that no line in either file is longer than half the
maximum length for printed lines in your implementation.

13

Pointers

THE POINTER CONCEPT

The array, record, and set types introduced in Chaps. 9–11 permit the description of data structures whose form and size are predetermined and whose components are accessed in a standard way. A file as described in Chap. 12 is a data structure which varies in size, but whose form and means of access are predetermined to allow a particular means of implementation. Many programming situations give rise to data structures which vary in size and form during their lifetime and whose means of access is particular to the programming problem involved.

Such structures are often realized as *linked data structures* in which the individual components of the structure are *linked to*, or *point to*, other related components of the structure. Some typical linked structures are illustrated in Fig. 13.1.

Such structures usually grow and contract dynamically during the execution of a program. Because the number of components in the structure is not fixed and the connections between the components are also not fixed, the component data items of the structure must be created and linked dynamically during the execution of the program.

It is impractical for a general-purpose language such as PASCAL to provide a range of data types which cover each of the possible classes of linked structures. Instead, PASCAL provides a single mechanism, called the *pointer*, which allows the programmer to realize such structures himself, and to program the operations applicable to them.

Whereas variables of all the PASCAL data types we have considered so far are *static* variables in the sense that they are declared in the program, denoted by means of their declared identifier, and their associated storage remains in existence throughout the lifetime of the block

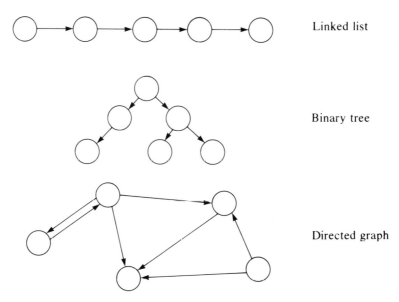

Fig. 13.1   Linked data structures

in which they are declared, this is not the case for the component variables of linked structures. These component variables are generated and destroyed *dynamically* during the execution of the program, and are not referred to by a user-declared identifier. Instead, they are referenced by means of auxiliary *pointer variables* which point to the dynamically created variables. For example, the pointer variable p in Fig. 13.2 is said to *point to*, or *reference*, the variable whose value is x. The means of dynamically creating the variable with value x is described later.

A *pointer-type* is defined in PASCAL as follows

$$pointer\text{-}type \ = "\uparrow"type\text{-}identifier \ .$$

Thus, a PASCAL program may include a type definition of the form

$$P = \ \uparrow T$$

Values of the type P so defined are said to reference, or point to, variables of the type denoted by T, which must be a type identifier defined elsewhere. The type P is said to be *bound* to the type T.

Consider the example of a list of integers in which each component of the list points to its successor in the list, as in Fig. 13.3. This structure

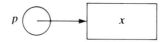

Fig. 13.2   A pointer variable

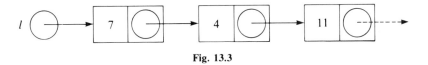

Fig. 13.3

consists of a pointer *l* to the first component of the list and a number of components linked together by means of pointers. Thus each component of the list consists of two data items, a value of type *integer* and a pointer value which refers to another component of the list. Hence the components of the list belong to a record type, which we shall choose to name *listcomponent*, consisting of two fields, an integer *i* and a pointer *next*. Choosing to name the pointer type as *listpointer* we may thus define it as in (1).

> **type** *listpointer* = ↑ *listcomponent* ;
>   *listcomponent* = **record**
>   *i* : *integer* ;   (1)
>   *next* : *listpointer*
>   **end**

Note that the definition of the type *listcomponent* follows that of the type *listpointer* even though the definition of type *listpointer* refers to *listcomponent*. This situation generally arises in the definition of pointer-types and pointed-to types and for this reason PASCAL allows the use of a type identifier before its definition in these circumstances. The definition must appear later in the same type definition part. This is the only case in PASCAL where an identifier may be used before it is defined.

Thus, in our example above, the inclusion of a pointer field of type *listpointer* in each record of type *listcomponent* enables a linear chain of records to be established, with an item component *i* held in each. As we shall see, inclusion of two or more pointers in a component enables a variety of non-linear structures to be realized in the same way.

The variable *l* which points to the first component of the list is declared as a static variable—like any other type a pointer type may be used to declare a static pointer variable, thus:

> **var** *p* : *P* ;
>   ⋮

However, the declaration of a pointer variable *p* does not create any variable to which *p* points, only the capability to do so. Creation of such a variable is achieved by use of the standard procedure *new*, called as follows

> *new* (*p*)

The effect of such a call is to create a new variable of type T, and to set the pointer variable p to point to it.

Variables created in this way are subsequently denoted as *referenced-variables*, which are defined as follows:

> *referenced-variable* = *pointer-variable* " ↑ " .
> *pointer-variable*   = *variable* .

A *referenced-variable*, i.e., a *pointer-variable* followed by an upward arrow ↑ , denotes the variable to which the pointer variable points.

Suppose l is a variable of type *listpointer* as above. After a call $new(l)$

> l ↑   denotes the variable of type *listcomponent* created,
> l ↑ .i denotes the integer component of that variable, and
> l ↑ .*next*   denotes the pointer component (see Fig. 13.4).

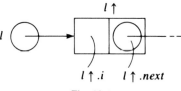

Fig. 13.4

Pointer values, and the variables which they reference, are thus created by means of the procedure *new*. They are used thereafter to reference these variables. Pointer values may also be copied, by assignment to another pointer variable.

Suppose p and q are pointer variables pointing to different list components, as shown in Fig. 13.5(a). Execution of the assignment

> $q := p$

would produce the situation in Fig. 13.5(b). Note the difference between this and assignment of the referenced variables. With the same initial situation, execution of

> q ↑ := p ↑

would result in the situation shown in Fig. 13.5(c).

Several pointer-variables may thus have the same value, i.e., point to the same referenced variable. To test whether two pointers reference the same variable they may be compared using the equality and inequality operators =, <>, e.g.,

> **if** $p = q$ **then** p ↑ .$i := 0$

> In Fig. 13.5(b) $p = q$ is *true*
> In Fig. 13.5(c) $p = q$ is *false*

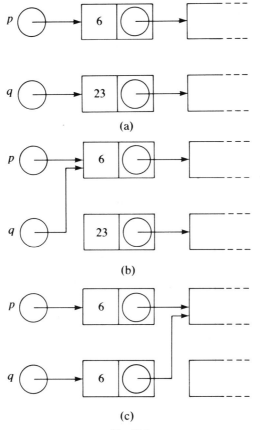

Fig. 13.5

In some cases it is necessary to indicate explicitly that a pointer does not point to anything. For this purpose PASCAL provides a special value, **nil**, which may be assigned to any pointer variable, thus

p := **nil**

For example, the value **nil** might be used in the final list component of a list of integers, to indicate that no further integers follow, as in Fig. 13.6(a), or it might be assigned to the variable l itself, to indicate that the list is empty, as in Fig. 13.6(b).

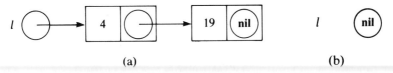

         (a)   (b)

Fig. 13.6

In processing a list, the occurrence of a **nil** value must be tested for, e.g.,

    if $l <>$ **nil then** . . .

The effect of attempting to access the variable referenced by a pointer-variable whose value is **nil** is undefined in PASCAL, but is clearly a programming error. Implementations may provide a means of detecting any such attempt during the execution of a program.

Once created by *new* a referenced-variable remains in existence until it is destroyed explicitly by a call to the built-in procedure *dispose*, thus

    dispose(p)

where *p* is a pointer to the variable to be destroyed.

Note that the lifetime of a variable created by *new* is not related either to the block in which it is created, or to the block in which pointer variables referencing it are declared. To maintain storage economy it is the programmer's responsibility to ensure that all such unwanted variables are disposed of, before the pointers to them are lost.

After a referenced-variable has been disposed of, the values of any pointer-variables which pointed to it are undefined. It is a serious programming error to use such a 'dangling' pointer value in any way. For the same reason it is an error to dispose of a referenced variable while it, or any of its components, is in use as a variable parameter, or as the record variable of a with-statement. However, implementations are often unable to detect such errors, so extreme care must be taken by the programmer to ensure that these errors are not made.

PROGRAMMING A STACK

To illustrate the use of these pointer facilities, consider the organization of a *stack*. A stack is a data structure consisting of a variable number of components of the same type. A new component may be *pushed* onto the stack, or an existing component *popped* off the stack, such that the component popped off is always that most recently pushed onto the stack.

To represent a stack, of characters say, we use a chain of record variables, each of which holds one character and a pointer to the next record in the chain. The necessary type definitions are given in (2).

    stackpointer = ↑ *stackcomponent* ;
    stackcomponent = **record**
                    c : *char* ;   (2)
                    next : *stackpointer*
        end

The records will be chained in the order in which the characters are to be popped off the stack, with a pointer variable *stack* pointing to the next record for popping at all times

   stack : stackpointer ;

Thus, if characters *'A'*, *'B'*, and *'C'* have been pushed onto the stack in that order the representation will be as shown in Fig. 13.7. Note that the value **nil** is held in the pointer field of the last record to indicate that no further records exist in the chain. An *empty* stack, i.e., one containing no components, is represented by assigning the value **nil** to the variable *stack* itself.

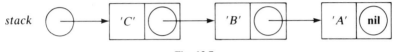

Fig. 13.7

The operation of pushing a new character *x* onto the stack can be expressed as a procedure, as given in (3).

```
procedure push (x : char) ;
var newcomponent : stackpointer ;
begin
    new (newcomponent) ;
    with newcomponent ↑ do begin
                    c := x ;                              (3)
                    next := stack
               end ;
        stack := newcomponent
end
```

Assuming a stack representation as shown in Fig. 13.7, execution of the call *push ('D')* would produce the representation shown in Fig. 13.8.

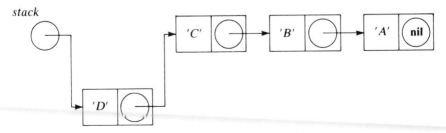

Fig. 13.8

The operation of popping a character value off the stack and assigning it to a character variable x can be expressed as a procedure, as shown in (4). Executing this procedure on the stack representation shown in

```
procedure pop (var x : char) ;
var oldcomponent : stackpointer ;
begin
    oldcomponent := stack ;
    x := oldcomponent ↑ .c ;                               (4)
    stack := oldcomponent ↑ .next ;
    dispose (oldcomponent)
end
```

Fig. 13.8 would restore that shown in Fig. 13.7. The procedure *pop* should only be executed when *stack* $<>$ **nil**, i.e., when the stack is not empty. Execution of any equal number of *pushes* and *pops* on an initially empty stack will restore the empty condition *stack* = **nil**.

Use of this stack is illustrated in the following fragment of program which reads a sequence of characters up to a period and prints out the sequence in reverse order.

```
stack := nil ;
repeat read(ch) ; push(ch) until ch = '.' ;
repeat pop(ch) ; write(ch) until stack = nil
```

Using records linked by pointers to realize a stack in this way ensures that only as much storage is used by the stack at any moment as its current number of components, or height, requires. Using an array for the same purpose would involve setting aside a fixed amount of storage throughout the stack's lifetime, which is sufficient for the maximum height of stack expected. This flexible use of storage is one advantage of the pointer mechanism. Program 17, which follows, illustrates two further situations in which this flexibility is exploited.

PROGRAM 17   (Cross-reference program)

Program 9 produced a sorted concordance of the words found in an input text. Program 11 produced a reformatted printout of an input text by scanning the words, punctuation symbols, etc., from which it was composed. Let us now extend the specification of Program 11 as follows:

(a)   each printed line is to be prefixed by a line number;

(b) the completed printed text is to be followed by a cross-referenced concordance which lists all the words used, sorted in dictionary order, and gives, for each word, a list of all the lines on which it occurs.

The overall program structure now required is an extension of that conceived for Program 11, as shown in (5).

```
begin
      readnextitem ;
      repeat
            thisitem := nextitem ;
            readnextitem ;
            writethisitem ;                                              (5)
            if thisitem is a word
            then record its occurrence
      until nextitem is endoftext ;
      print sorted table of words and occurrences
end.
```

The development of the procedures *readnextitem* and *writethisitem* and the data structures which support them remains as before, with two exceptions:

1. since word spellings now have to be stored and compared at other points in the program it is convenient to introduce a named type to represent them, thus:

   wordspelling = **packed array** $[1 .. 16]$ **of** *char*

   and to use this within the type *textitem* as well. To facilitate subsequent comparison it is also convenient to fill out each spelling with blanks as it is created in the procedure *readnextitem*.

2. The procedure *writethisitem* must now prefix each line printed with an appropriate line number. This is easily accomplished by:

   (a) introducing a global variable

        thisline : *linenumber*

   to represent the number of the line being printed at any moment, where

        linenumber = $0 .. 99999$;

   (b) initializing this variable to zero;

   (c) amending the procedure *takenewline* as in (6).

```
procedure takenewline ;
begin
    writeln ;
    thisline := thisline + 1 ;
    write (thisline : 5, '    ') ;
    spaceleftonline := outputmax - 7
end
```
(6)

Now consider the additional processes of recording and printing the cross-reference of words occurring in the text. Clearly a data structure is required in which word occurrences are recorded during text printing for subsequent printout.

A logical structure for this table is to create one record for each distinct word encountered, each record holding a list of occurrences for that word. The process of recording each occurrence of a word in the table then breaks into two steps

locate word in table ;
add this line to its list of occurrences

where *locate word in table* is assumed to create a new record for a word not previously recorded, and initialize its list of occurrences as empty.

In Program 9 we used a simple one-dimensional array to record the distinct words found in the input text. This had the disadvantage that some limit had to be set on the number of distinct words which might occur, and an array of this size had to be used, whatever the number of distinct words in the actual input might be. With pointers we can now construct an alternative form of table in which the number of entries provided is exactly that required by the input at any moment.

```
wordpointer =  ↑ wordrecord ;
wordrecord = record
                spelling : wordspelling ;
                occurrences : listofoccurrences ;
                next : wordpointer
             end
```
(7)

We might use a linear list of word records by defining the types given in (7). The complete list of words is then represented by a single pointer-variable pointing to the first word in the list:

wordlist : wordpointer

Since the words have to be printed out in dictionary order it is logical to build the list in this order. The process of locating a given word in the list is then expressible as a call to the procedure (8).

```
procedure locateword (wordsought : wordspelling ;
                      var wordfound : wordpointer) ;
begin
    search word list until either a word ≥ wordsought        (8)
    is encountered or the end of the list is reached ;
    create a new word record if necessary
end
```

Searching the list involves a repetition which terminates when either a word spelling ≥ *wordsought* is encountered, or the list is exhausted. In either case a pointer to the previous word may be needed for the subsequent insertion, so a suitable coding is as shown in (9).

```
thisword := wordlist ; previousword := nil ;
positionfound := false ;
while not positionfound and (thisword <> nil) do
    if thisword ↑ .spelling >= wordsought
    then positionfound := true                               (9)
    else begin
             previousword := thisword ;
             thisword := thisword ↑ .next
         end
```

Create a new word record if necessary is then expressible as in (10).

```
if positionfound
then if thisword ↑ .spelling = wordsought
    then wordfound := thisword                               (10)
    else insert a new record (before thisword)
else insert a new record at end of list
```

In either case the entries to precede and follow the new record are indicated by *previousword* and *thisword*, so each insertion process is expressible as a call to the local procedure (11).

```
procedure insertword ;
var newword : wordpointer ;
begin
    new (newword) ;
    with newword ↑ do                                        (11)
    begin
        spelling := wordsought ;
        occurrences := none ;
        next := thisword
    end ;
```

```
     if previousword = nil
     then wordlist := newword
     else previousword ↑ .next := newword ;                          (11 cont.)
         wordfound := newword
end
```

Note that the insertion of a new record in the ordered list is achieved without any movement or copying of existing records—a significant advantage of the linked-list representation. Also, the informal statement

occurrences := none

cannot be programmed until we determine a representation for the list of occurrences.

How should we represent the list of occurrences held for each word? The length of these lists may vary considerably—for some words only one or two occurrences may be recorded, while for other commonly used words long lists may be built up. This variation in length can again be accommodated in a representation based on pointers. The components of each list of occurrences (which are simply line numbers) are added to the list in the same order as they are to be printed, i.e., in order of ascending line number. Such a linear list is known as a *queue*, and can be represented as a chain of records with pointers leading from the first to the last, and two auxiliary pointers which indicate these first and last records at all times. Such a list of occurrences can be realized in PASCAL by (12).

```
listpointer = ↑ linerecord ;
linerecord = record
                    line : linenumber ;
                    nextline : listpointer
               end ;                                                  (12)
listofoccurrences = record
                         first,last : listpointer
                    end
```

The list of occurrences for a word occurring on lines 3, 21 and 247 would be represented as shown in Fig. 13.9. The process of adding the current line to a given list of occurrences is then expressible as the procedure (13).

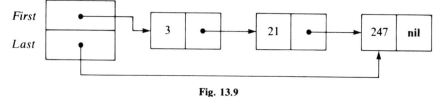

Fig. 13.9

```
procedure addthislineto (var list : listofoccurrences) ;
var occurrence : listpointer ;
begin
    new (occurrence) ;
    with occurrence ↑ do begin
                            line := thisline ;
                            nextline := nil
                        end ;                                    (13)
    with list do begin
                    if first = nil
                    then first := occurrence
                    else last ↑ .nextline := occurrence ;
                    last := occurrence
                end
end ;
```

The process of printing out a sorted list held in linked list format is also a simple list traversal loop. In our case the list may also be disposed of as it is printed, so the process required is as shown in (14).

```
procedure printtable ;
var thisword,nextword : wordpointer ;
begin
    page ;
    writeln ('crossreference of words and occurrences') ;
    writeln ; writeln ;
    nextword := wordlist ;
    while nextword <> nil do                                    (14)
    begin
        thisword := nextword ;
        print spelling and occurrences of thisword ↑ ;
        nextword := thisword ↑ .next ;
        dispose (thisword)
    end
end
```

Printing (and disposing of) the list of occurrences is in principle a simple loop process of the form (15). However, we cannot assume that

```
nextoccurrence := occurrences.first ;
repeat
    thisoccurrence := nextoccurrence ;
    write (thisoccurrence ↑ .line) ;                            (15)
    nextoccurrence := thisoccurrence ↑ .nextline ;
    dispose (thisoccurrence)
until nextoccurrence = nil
```

the list of line numbers for any word fits on a single printed line. In using second and subsequent lines we wish to indent the first number so as not to obscure the ordered list of words themselves, as shown in Fig. 13.10.

```
:
TAMELY      9     113
THE         1      5     11    . . .
           93     99    106    . . .
          111
TOWN       46
:
```

Fig. 13.10

The reformatted text printout with line numbers still uses a total print width of *outputmax* characters. Using the same width for the cross-reference printout, we have *wordmax* characters for the words themselves and *listmax* (= *outputmax* − *wordmax*) characters for the occurrence lists. Using a variable *spaceleftonline*, as in Program 11, to indicate the number of remaining print positions on the current line of the printout, the complete task of printing one word and its list of occurrences is as shown in (16).

```
procedure printoccurrences (spelling : wordspelling ;
                            occurrences : listofoccurrences) ;
var spaceleftonline : 0 .. listmax ;
    thisoccurrence,nextoccurrence : listpointer ;
begin
    write (spelling) ;
    spaceleftonline := listmax ;
    nextoccurrence := occurrences.first ;
    repeat
        thisoccurrence := nextoccurrence ;                    (16)
        if spaceleftonline < 6 then
        begin
            writeln ;
            write (' ' : wordmax) ;
            spaceleftonline := listmax
        end ;
        write (thisoccurrence ↑ .line : 6) ;
        spaceleftonline := spaceleftonline − 6 ;
        nextoccurrence := thisoccurrence ↑ .nextline ;
        dispose (thisoccurrence)
```

```
        until nextoccurrence = nil ;
        writeln                                              (16 cont.)
   end
```

Listing 17 shows the complete program, and the output produced by it
for the same input as was used for Programs 9 and 11.

```
                    LISTING 17

PROGRAM CROSSREFERENCE (INPUT, OUTPUT) ;

CONST INPUTMAX = 81 ;
      EOL = '^' ;
      OUTPUTMAX = 60 ; WORDMAX = 16 ; LISTMAX = 44 ;

TYPE  ITEMKIND = (WORD, PUNCTUATION, LAYOUT, ENDOFTEXT);
      WORDSPELLING = PACKED ARRAY [1..WORDMAX] OF CHAR ;
      TEXTITEM = RECORD
                     CASE KIND : ITEMKIND OF
                     WORD : (LENGTH : 1..WORDMAX ;
                             SPELLING : WORDSPELLING) ;
                     PUNCTUATION : (SYMBOL : CHAR);
                     LAYOUT : (DEVICE : (BLANKLINE, PARAGRAPH));
                     ENDOFTEXT : ( )
                  END ;
      LINERANGE = 1..INPUTMAX ;
      LINENUMBER = 0..9999 ;
      LISTPOINTER = ^LINERECORD ;
      LINERECORD = RECORD
                       LINE : LINENUMBER ;
                       NEXTLINE : LISTPOINTER
                   END ;
      LISTOFOCCURRENCES = RECORD
                              FIRST, LAST : LISTPOINTER
                          END ;
      WORDPOINTER = ^WORDRECORD ;
      WORDRECORD = RECORD
                       SPELLING : WORDSPELLING ;
                       OCCURRENCES : LISTOFOCCURRENCES ;
                       NEXT : WORDPOINTER
                   END ;

VAR   THISITEM, NEXTITEM : TEXTITEM ;
      LINE : ARRAY [LINERANGE] OF CHAR ;
      INPOINTER : LINERANGE ;
      SPACELEFTONLINE : 0..OUTPUTMAX ;
      THISLINE : LINENUMBER ;
      WORDLIST, THISWORD : WORDPOINTER ;

PROCEDURE READNEXTITEM ;

   PROCEDURE READLINE ;
   VAR I : LINERANGE ;
   BEGIN
      I:=1 ;
      WHILE NOT EOLN(INPUT) DO
```

```
      BEGIN READ (LINE[I]); I:=I+1 END ;
      READLN ;
      LINE[I]:=EOL ;  INPOINTER:=1
   END ; (* READLINE *)



   PROCEDURE SCANNONBLANKITEM ;
   VAR  L : 0..WORDMAX ;
   BEGIN
      WITH NEXTITEM DO
      CASE LINE[INPOINTER] OF
      'A','B','C','D','E','F','G',
      'H','I','J','K','L','M','N',
      'O','P','Q','R','S','T','U',
      'V','W','X','Y','Z' :
         BEGIN
            KIND:=WORD;  L:=0;
            REPEAT
               L:=L+1;  SPELLING[L]:=LINE[INPOINTER] ;
               INPOINTER := INPOINTER+1
            UNTIL (LINE[INPOINTER]<'A')OR(LINE[INPOINTER]>'Z') ;
            LENGTH:=L ;
            WHILE L<WORDMAX DO BEGIN L:=L+1; SPELLING[L]:=' ' END
         END ;
      ',','.',';' :
         BEGIN
            KIND:=PUNCTUATION ;
            SYMBOL:= LINE[INPOINTER] ;
            INPOINTER := INPOINTER+1
         END
      END
   END ; (* SCANNONBLANKITEM *)



BEGIN (* READNEXTITEM *)
   WHILE LINE[INPOINTER] = ' ' DO INPOINTER:=INPOINTER+1 ;
   IF LINE[INPOINTER] = EOL
   THEN IF EOF(INPUT)
        THEN NEXTITEM.KIND := ENDOFTEXT
        ELSE BEGIN
                READLINE ;
                WHILE LINE[INPOINTER]=' ' DO INPOINTER:=INPOINTER+1;
                WITH NEXTITEM DO
                IF LINE[INPOINTER]=EOL
                THEN BEGIN KIND:=LAYOUT; DEVICE:=BLANKLINE END
                ELSE IF INPOINTER>2
                     THEN BEGIN KIND:=LAYOUT ; DEVICE:=PARAGRAPH END
                     ELSE SCANNONBLANKITEM
             END
   ELSE SCANNONBLANKITEM
END ; (* READNEXTITEM *)



PROCEDURE WRITETHISITEM ;
VAR   SPACENEEDED : 1..18 ;
      I : 1..16 ;
```

```
    PROCEDURE TAKENEWLINE ;
    BEGIN
       WRITELN ;
       THISLINE := THISLINE+1 ;
       WRITE (THISLINE :5, '  ') ;
       SPACELEFTONLINE := OUTPUTMAX-7
    END ;  (* TAKENEWLINE *)



BEGIN
    WITH THISITEM DO
    CASE KIND OF
    WORD : BEGIN
              IF NEXTITEM.KIND = PUNCTUATION
              THEN SPACENEEDED := LENGTH+2
              ELSE SPACENEEDED := LENGTH+1 ;
              IF SPACENEEDED > SPACELEFTONLINE
              THEN TAKENEWLINE
              ELSE IF SPACELEFTONLINE<>OUTPUTMAX
                   THEN BEGIN
                          WRITE (' ') ;
                          SPACELEFTONLINE:=SPACELEFTONLINE-1
                        END ;
              FOR I:= 1 TO LENGTH DO WRITE (SPELLING[I]) ;
              SPACELEFTONLINE := SPACELEFTONLINE-LENGTH
           END ;
    PUNCTUATION :
           BEGIN
              WRITE (SYMBOL) ;
              SPACELEFTONLINE := SPACELEFTONLINE-1
           END ;
    LAYOUT :
           BEGIN
              IF SPACELEFTONLINE < OUTPUTMAX THEN TAKENEWLINE ;
              IF DEVICE=BLANKLINE
              THEN TAKENEWLINE
              ELSE BEGIN WRITE (' ') ; SPACELEFTONLINE:=SPACELEFTONLINE-2 END
           END
    END
END ;(* WRITETHISITEM *)



PROCEDURE LOCATEWORD (WORDSOUGHT : WORDSPELLING ;
                      VAR WORDFOUND : WORDPOINTER ) ;
VAR  THISWORD, PREVIOUSWORD : WORDPOINTER ;
     POSITIONFOUND : BOOLEAN ;



PROCEDURE INSERTWORD ;
VAR  NEWWORD : WORDPOINTER ;
BEGIN
    NEW (NEWWORD) ;
    WITH NEWWORD DO
    BEGIN
       SPELLING := WORDSOUGHT ;
```

```
            WITH OCCURRENCES DO BEGIN FIRST:=NIL ; LAST:=NIL END
            NEXT := THISWORD
      END ;
      IF PREVIOUSWORD = NIL
      THEN WORDLIST := NEWWORD
      ELSE PREVIOUSWORD^.NEXT := NEWWORD ;
      WORDFOUND := NEWWORD
END ;   (* INSERTWORD *)


BEGIN
   THISWORD := WORDLIST ;  PREVIOUSWORD := NIL ;
   POSITIONFOUND := FALSE ;
   WHILE NOT POSITIONFOUND AND (THISWORD<>NIL) DO
      IF THISWORD^.SPELLING >= WORDSOUGHT
      THEN POSITIONFOUND := TRUE
      ELSE BEGIN
              PREVIOUSWORD := THISWORD ;
              THISWORD := THISWORD^.NEXT
           END ;
   IF POSITIONFOUND
   THEN IF THISWORD^.SPELLING = WORDSOUGHT
        THEN WORDFOUND := THISWORD
        ELSE INSERTWORD
   ELSE INSERTWORD
END ; (* LOCATEWORD *)



PROCEDURE ADDTHISLINETO (VAR LIST : LISTOFOCCURRENCES) ;
VAR   OCCURRENCE : LISTPOINTER ;
BEGIN
   NEW (OCCURRENCE) ;
   WITH OCCURRENCE^ DO BEGIN
                          LINE := THISLINE ;
                          NEXTLINE := NIL
                       END ;
   WITH LIST DO BEGIN
                   IF FIRST = NIL
                   THEN FIRST := OCCURRENCE
                   ELSE LAST^.NEXTLINE := OCCURRENCE ;
                   LAST := OCCURRENCE
                END
END ; (* ADDTHISLINETO *)



PROCEDURE PRINTTABLE ;
VAR   THISWORD, NEXTWORD : WORDPOINTER ;

   PROCEDURE PRINTOCCURRENCES (SPELLING : WORDSPELLING ;
                               OCCURRENCES : LISTOFOCCURRENCES )
   VAR  SPACELEFTONLINE : 0..LISTMAX ;
        THISOCCURRENCE, NEXTOCCURRENCE : LISTPOINTER ;

BEGIN
   WRITE (SPELLING) ;
   SPACELEFTONLINE := LISTMAX ;
```

```
            NEXTOCCURRENCE := OCCURRENCES.FIRST ;
            REPEAT
               THISOCCURRENCE := NEXTOCCURRENCE ;
               IF SPACELEFTONLINE < 6 THEN
               BEGIN
                  WRITELN ;
                  WRITE (' ': WORDMAX) ;
                  SPACELEFTONLINE := LISTMAX
               END ;
               WRITE (THISOCCURRENCE^.LINE :6) ;
               SPACELEFTONLINE := SPACELEFTONLINE-6 ;
               NEXTOCCURRENCE := THISOCCURRENCE^.NEXTLINE ;
               DISPOSE (THISOCCURRENCE)
            UNTIL NEXTOCCURRENCE = NIL ;
            WRITELN
         END ; (*  PRINTOCCURRENCES  *)

   BEGIN
      PAGE ;
      WRITELN ('CROSSREFERENCE OF WORDS AND OCCURRENCES') ;
      WRITELN ; WRITELN ;
      NEXTWORD := WORDLIST ;
      WHILE NEXTWORD <> NIL DO
      BEGIN
         THISWORD := NEXTWORD ;
         WITH THISWORD^ DO PRINTOCCURRENCES (SPELLING, OCCURRENCES) ;
         NEXTWORD := THISWORD^.NEXT ;
         DISPOSE (THISWORD)
      END
   END ; (*  PRINTTABLE *)


BEGIN
   LINE[1]:=EOL ;  INPOINTER:=1 ;
   SPACELEFTONLINE := 0 ;
   WORDLIST := NIL ;
   THISLINE := 0 ;
   READNEXTITEM ;
   REPEAT
      THISITEM := NEXTITEM ;


      READNEXTITEM ;
      WRITETHISITEM ;
      IF THISITEM.KIND = WORD
      THEN BEGIN
              LOCATEWORD (THISITEM.SPELLING, THISWORD) ;
              ADDTHISLINETO (THISWORD^.OCCURRENCES)
           END
   UNTIL NEXTITEM.KIND = ENDOFTEXT ;
   PRINTTABLE
END.
```

```
 1   THE PROFILE
 2
 3
 4
 5
 6       THE PROFILE IS AN EDITED, AUTOMATICALLY FORMATTED,
 7   LISTING OF THE SOURCE PROGRAM WHICH DISPLAYS THE
 8   FREQUENCY OF EXECUTION OF EACH STATEMENT OF THE
 9   PROGRAM.
10
11
12       TO READ OFF THE FREQUENCY OF EXECUTION OF ANY
13   STATEMENT, WE LOCATE THE BEGINNING OF THE STATEMENT
14   IN THE PROFILE LISTING. IF AN ASTERISK IS PRESENT ON
15   THE SAME LINE, TO THE LEFT OF THE LISTING, THEN THE
16   DESIRED FREQUENCY WILL BE FOUND TO THE LEFT OF THE
17   ASTERISK. OTHERWISE, THE LINE WILL CONTAIN ONE OR
18   MORE UPWARD ARROWS; WE SELECT THE RIGHTMOST ARROW,
19   AND FOLLOW THE LINE OF ARROWS VERTICALLY UPWARDS
20   UNTIL AN ASTERISK IS ENCOUNTERED; AGAIN, THE DESIRED
21   FREQUENCY WILL BE FOUND TO THE LEFT OF THE ASTERISK.
22
23
```

CROSSREFERENCE OF WORDS AND OCCURRENCES

WORD						
AGAIN	20					
AN	6	14	20			
AND	19					
ANY	12					
ARROW	18					
ARROWS	18	19				
ASTERISK	14	17	20	21		
AUTOMATICALLY	6					
BE	16	21				
BEGINNING	13					
CONTAIN	17					
DESIRED	16	20				
DISPLAYS	7					
EACH	8					
EDITED	6					
ENCOUNTERED	20					
EXECUTION	8	12				
FOLLOW	19					
FORMATTED	6					
FOUND	16	21				
FREQUENCY	8	12	16	21		
IF	14					
IN	14					
IS	6	14	20			
LEFT	15	16	21			
LINE	15	17	19			
LISTING	7	14	15			
LOCATE	13					
MORE	18					
OF	7	8	8	8	12	12	13
	15	16	19	21			

OFF	12						
ON	14						
ONE	17						
OR	17						
OTHERWISE	17						
PRESENT	14						
PROFILE	1	6	14				
PROGRAM	7	9					
READ	12						
RIGHTMOST	18						
SAME	15						
SELECT	18						
SOURCE	7						
STATEMENT	8	13	13				
THE	1	6	7	7	8	12	13
	13	14	15	15	15	15	16
	16	17	18	19	20	21	21
THEN	15						
TO	12	15	16	21			
UNTIL	20						
UPWARD	18						
UPWARDS	19						
VERTICALLY	19						
WE	13	18					
WHICH	7						
WILL	16	17	21				

NON-LINEAR STRUCTURES

In our use of pointers so far we have illustrated three forms of linear-list structure:

(a) a *stack*, which is extended and reduced at one end only;
(b) a *queue*, which is extended at one end and reduced at the other;
(c) an *ordered list*, whose extension may involve an insertion at any point in the list.

All of these structures can be realized as a sequence of records, each of which contains a single pointer to the next record in the list.

However, each record of the ordered list of words built by Program 17 also contained a pointer (or rather two pointers) to the corresponding queue of occurrences. The overall structure was thus as illustrated in Fig. 13.11. Viewed as a whole this is not a linear structure, and it shows clearly that any node or record within a linked structure which contains two or more pointers to other nodes creates a potential non-linearity. PASCAL's pointers can thus be used without further extension to realize non-linear structures of arbitrary complexity.

Program 17 provides a further opportunity to illustrate the (judicious) use of pointers in creating non-linear structures. Representation of the

Words

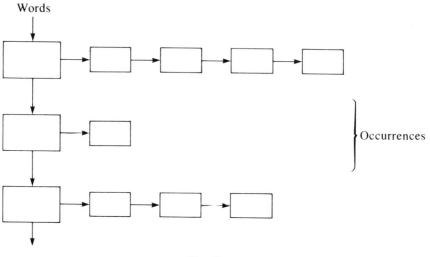

Fig. 13.11

ordered list of words as a linked linear list enabled the amount of storage used to be limited to that required by the list at any moment, and allowed insertion of new words in the ordered list without any movement or copying of existing words. However, the simple linear linkage meant that the list could oniy be searched for an existing word, or to determine the correct position for a new one, by a linear traversal of the list. For long lists such a linear search is a time-consuming process.

A faster search can be achieved, and the storage and insertion flexibility of the linked list retained, by holding the list as a *binary tree*. Figure 13.12

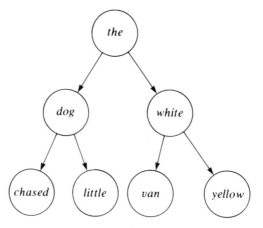

Fig. 13.12   Binary tree

shows how the words of the sentence

the white dog chased the little yellow van

might be held as a binary tree. The node for the word *the* is called the *root* of the tree, while those for *chased, little, van* and *yellow* are called its *leaves*. The tree is sorted in that for each node the words in its left subtree precede, in dictionary order, the word at that node, while the words in its right subtree succeed that word.

$$
\begin{aligned}
&\textit{wordpointer} \ = \ \uparrow \textit{wordrecord} \ ; \\
&\textit{wordrecord} \ = \ \textbf{record} \\
&\qquad\qquad\qquad \textit{spelling} \ : \ \textit{wordspelling} \ ; \\
&\qquad\qquad\qquad \textit{occurrences} \ : \ \textit{listofoccurrences} \ ; \\
&\qquad\qquad\qquad \textit{predecessors,successors} \ : \ \textit{wordpointer} \\
&\qquad\qquad \textbf{end}
\end{aligned}
\qquad (17)
$$

Such a tree can be represented in PASCAL using records connected by pointers defined as in (17). The complete word tree is then represented as a single pointer-variable which points to its root:

wordtree : wordpointer ;

An empty tree, and hence the subtrees of each leaf node, are represented by the value **nil**.

A binary tree is inherently recursive in structure, since each node is defined in terms of two further trees of the same form. The process of locating an existing entry, or creating a new entry, in such a tree is simply expressed as a recursive procedure with the outline (18).

$$
\begin{aligned}
&\textbf{procedure } \textit{locatewordin} \ (\textbf{var } \textit{thistree} \ : \ \textit{wordpointer}) \ ; \\
&\textbf{begin} \\
&\quad \textbf{if } \textit{thistree is empty} \\
&\quad \textbf{then } \textit{create a leaf node as thistree} \\
&\quad \textbf{else if } \textit{root word} > \textit{word sought} \\
&\qquad \textbf{then } \textit{locatewordin (predecessors)} \\
&\qquad \textbf{else if } \textit{root word} < \textit{word sought} \\
&\qquad\quad \textbf{then } \textit{locatewordin (successors)} \\
&\qquad\quad \textbf{else } \textit{root is word sought} \\
&\textbf{end}
\end{aligned}
\qquad (18)
$$

Each step in the searching process which this procedure implements halves the area of subsequent search, since it chooses either the predecessors or successors subtree of the current node. This halving process leads to an average searching time proportional to $\log_2 N$, where there are N words in the tree. In practice this logarithmic performance is guaranteed only if the tree is balanced, i.e., there is an equal number of words in the predecessors and successors subtrees at each node. With the simple insertion process outlined above, the balance of the tree depends on the order of insertion of the words involved. The example sentence used in Fig. 13.12 leads to an exactly balanced tree, but not all data are so well chosen. However, the words encountered in any sizeable natural text are sufficiently random in order to produce a reasonably balanced tree, and hence an average search time which is close to the ideal $\log_2 N$.

The procedure *locateword* of Program 17 may now therefore be written using a local recursive procedure of this form, as shown in (19). In this

```
procedure locateword (wordsought : wordspelling ;
                          var wordfound : wordpointer) ;
   procedure locatewordin (var thistree : wordpointer) ;
        ... as outlined above ...                                    (19)
begin
     locatewordin (wordtree)
end
```

context the details of the recursive procedure are easily settled, as in (20).

```
   procedure locatewordin (var thistree : wordpointer) ;
   begin
        if thistree = nil
        then begin
                  new (thistree) ;
                  with thistree ↑ do begin
                                      spelling := wordsought ;
                                      occurrences := none ;
                                      predecessors := nil ;
                                      successors := nil            (20)
                                  end ;
                  wordfound := thistree
              end
        else
              with thistree ↑ do
                  if spelling > wordsought
                  then locatewordin (predecessors)
                  else if spelling < wordsought
                       then locatewordin (successors)
                       else wordfound := thistree
   end ;
```

The process of printing out a sorted list held as a binary tree is also

expressible as a recursive procedure. For any non-empty tree the
predecessors in the left subtree must be printed before the word at the
root node itself, and the successors after it. Assuming the word tree is also
to be disposed of as it is printed, an appropriate recursive procedure is (21).

```
procedure printwordsin (thistree : wordpointer) ;
begin
    if thistree <> nil then
    with thistree ↑ do
    begin
        printwordsin (predecessors) ;                          (21)
        printoccurrences (spelling,occurrences) ;
        printwordsin (successors) ;
        dispose (thistree)
    end
end
```

The body of the procedure *printtable* used in Program 17 then becomes
as shown in (22).

```
begin
    page ;
    writeln ('crossreference of words and occurrences') ;
    writeln ; writeln ;                                        (22)
    printwordsin (wordtree)
end
```

The linear wordlist used in Program 17 may thus be replaced by a binary
tree, simply by redefining the record type *wordcomponent*, and rewriting
the procedures *locateword* and *printtable* which manipulate these records.
The resultant program should run faster on input texts of significant length.

The binary-tree structure was achieved simply by introducing two
components of type *wordpointer* into each *wordcomponent* rather than
one. In a similar way a variety of non-linear structures can be realized, by
including an appropriate set of linking pointers in each component node.
This power which the pointer mechanism provides should be used with
caution, however, as the complexity of the data structures realized can
quickly go beyond our intellectual grasp, and errors in the programs which
manipulate them are difficult to diagnose.

STORAGE TAILORING

The variables referenced by pointer values are often variant records.
The different variants of a variant record may require different amounts of

storage for the components of each variant. A record variable which changes its variant must therefore be allocated sufficient storage for the largest variant involved. However, it sometimes happens that the variant of a record created by a particular call of *new* is known in advance, and remains fixed throughout its lifetime. In this case it is feasible to use only the amount of storage required for that particular variant in creating the record variable. PASCAL enables this tailoring of variant record storage by means of an extended call of the standard procedure *new*, in the form

$$new\ (p,t1,t2,\ldots,tn)$$

where $t1,t2,\ldots,tn$ are constants specifying the tag values of the particular variants required. The tag values must be listed in the order of their occurrence in the record-type definition, i.e., from the outermost to the innermost nested variant. However, specifications of innermost nested variants may be omitted, implying that variation of those variants is to be allowed.

For example, suppose we have a pointer type

$$personpointer\ =\ \uparrow person$$

where the type *person* is defined, as in Chap. 10, thus:

```
person = record
              name : personname ;
              dateofbirth : date ;
              case origin : personkind of
              national : (birthplace : placename ;
                          case qualification : status of
                          bybirth : ( ) ;
                          naturalization : (number : integer ;
                                            dateofnaturalization :
                                            date)) ;
              alien     : (countryoforigin : placename ;
                          dateofentry : date ;
                          portofentry : placename )
          end
```

Given a pointer variable

$$p\ :\ personpointer$$

new(p)   creates a new record which may take either of the variants *national* or *alien*, and either of the subvariants *bybirth* or *naturalization*, as appropriate;

new(p,national)   creates a new record which must take the
                                          variant *national*, but may take either of the
                                          subvariants *bybirth* or *naturalization*;
new(p,national,bybirth)   creates a new record which must take the
                                          variant *national* and subvariant *bybirth*.

Tailoring of dynamically created variant records in this way may produce a considerable saving in the storage used by programs which manipulate large numbers of such records. However, the following must be borne in mind:

(a)   Although the extended form of the call on *new* implies the variant(s) involved, it does not assign the corresponding tag field values; this assignment remains the programmer's responsibility.
(b)   Once determined by an extended call of *new*, the variant of the record created must not be changed in any way, e.g., by assignment of a different value to the tag field.
(c)   For the same reason, assignment of the entire record variable created by an extended call of *new* is not allowed; however, individual components may be assigned.

A corresponding extended form of the standard procedure *dispose* is also provided, *viz.*

dispose (p,t1,t2, . . . ,tn)

The PASCAL standard requires that each record created by an extended call of *new* is disposed of by an extended call of *dispose* with a set of constant tag values that imply the same variant.

EXERCISES

13.1   The program shown in Listing 17 uses a single-pointer variable *wordlist*. Modify the program to use an array

wordlist : **array** [*'A' . . 'Z'*] **of** *wordpointer*

each element of which is a pointer to the head of a linked list of words beginning with the corresponding letter.

13.2   An office block accommodates employees in rooms occupied by one or more people, each room having one telephone. An internal telephone directory for the block is available on a file, each record of the file containing an employee's name (a 16 character string) and his telephone number. The file is in alphabetic order of employees' names. Write a program which will read the directory and output a series of lists of the employees in each room (together with the number of the telephone in that room). The lists are to be output in ascending order of telephone number, and the names of the employees in each room are to be output in alphabetic order.

13.3 Rewrite the program shown in Listing 10 to hold the league table as an array of pointers, each element of which points to the corresponding *teamdetails* record. What effect does this change have on the efficiency of the program?

13.4 A polynomial of arbitrary degree is representable as a sequence of coefficient–degree pairs, preferably held in descending order of degree. For example, the polynomial

$$x^8 + 5x^6 - 7x^5 + 6x + 1$$

may be represented as

(1,8) , (5,6) , (−7,5) , (6,1) , (1,0)

Define a pointer type which enables such a sequence to be held in a linked list.

Write a procedure *readpolynomial* which reads a positive integer indicating the number of terms in a polynomial, followed by the ordered coefficient–degree pairs. For example, the above polynomial would be input as

5 1 8 5 6 − 7 5 6 1 1 0

The procedure should build the linked-list representation of the polynomial.

Write two functions *sum* and *product*, each of which takes two pointers representing polynomials as parameters and returns as result a polynomial which is the sum and product, respectively, of the parameters. Use these in a program which calculates the sum and product of the following polynomials

$$3x^2 + 9x + 1$$
$$x^3 - 3x^2 - 5x$$

and outputs the results in the form

$$SUM \quad\quad = \quad X \uparrow 3 + 4X + 1$$
$$PRODUCT = 3X \uparrow 5 - 41X \uparrow 3 - 48X \uparrow 2 - 5X$$

Appendix 1

SYNTAX DIAGRAMS

The syntax of PASCAL is often described by means of syntax diagrams. The sequences of symbols allowed for a language construct may be described by a syntax diagram, which is a directed graph with one entry and one exit. Each path through the graph defines an allowable sequence of symbols.

For example, the structure of a complete PASCAL program is defined by Fig. A1. The occurrence of the name of another diagram, such as *identifier*, *identifier list* and *block* in Fig. A1, indicates that any sequence of symbols defined by the other diagram may occur at that point. Diagram names are always represented as italicized words; all other symbols occurring are symbols of the language itself.

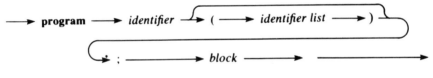

Fig. A1 *program*

Alternative or repetitive sequences of symbols are indicated by forks or loops in the corresponding syntax diagram. For example, an identifier is defined by Fig. A2. The names *letter* and *digit* are used to denote any of the 52 upper- and lower-case letters and the 10 decimal digits, respectively.

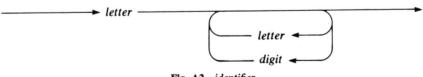

Fig. A2 *identifier*

The diagrams in Figs. A3–27 define the complete syntax of PASCAL. All names that end with *identifier*, such as *procedure identifier*, *variable identifier*, etc., are syntactically equivalent to *identifier*, and merely indicate the class of declared identifiers that may occur at that point.

275

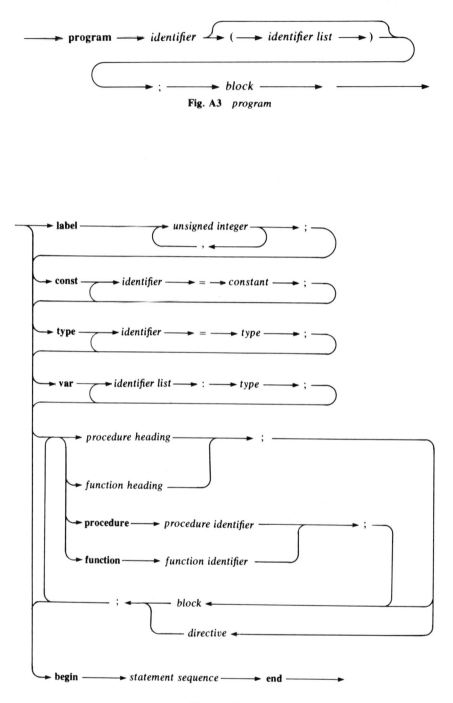

Fig. A3 *program*

Fig. A4 *block*

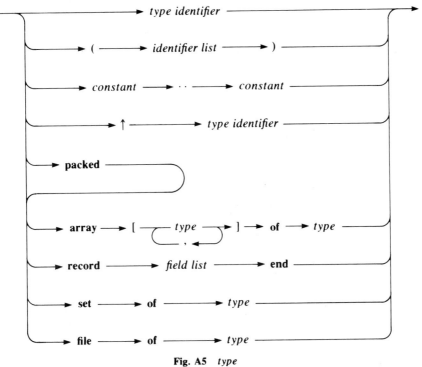

Fig. A5 *type*

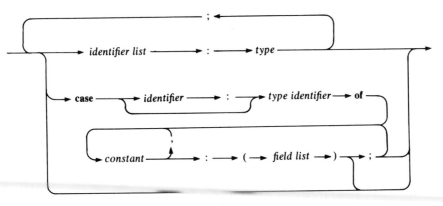

Fig. A6 *field list*

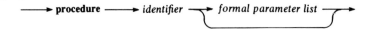

Fig. A7   *procedure heading*

Fig. A8   *function heading*

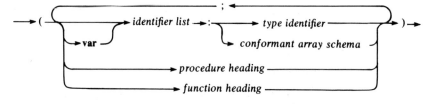

Fig. A9   *formal parameter list*

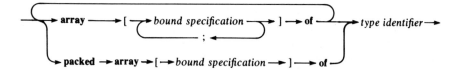

Fig. A10   *conformant array schema*

— *identifier* — · · — *identifier* — : — *type identifier* —

Fig. A11   *bound specification*

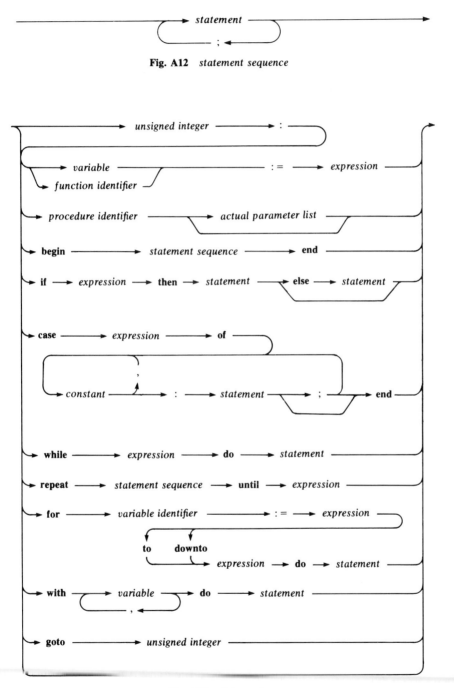

Fig. A12 *statement sequence*

Fig. A13 *statement*

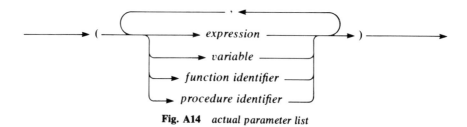

Fig. A14   *actual parameter list*

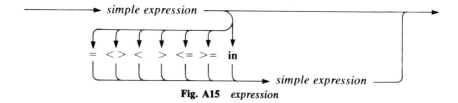

Fig. A15   *expression*

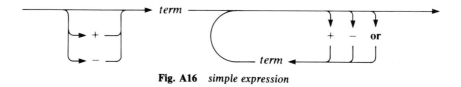

Fig. A16   *simple expression*

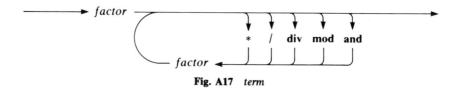

Fig. A17   *term*

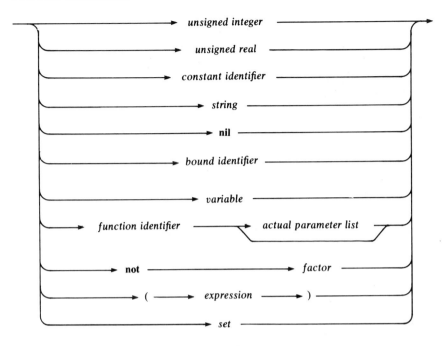

Fig. A18 *factor*

Fig. A.19 *set*

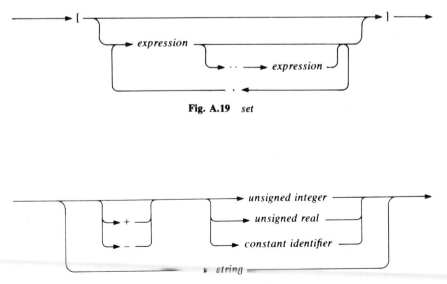

Fig. A20 *constant*

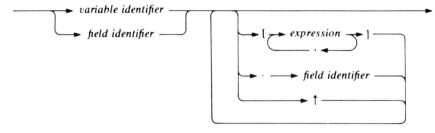

Fig. A.21 *variable*

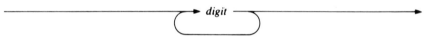

Fig. A22 *identifier list*

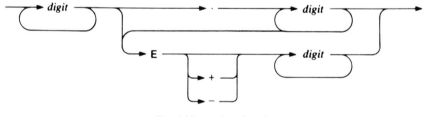

Fig. A.23 *identifier* and *directive*

Fig. A24 *unsigned integer*

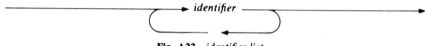

Fig. A25 *unsigned real*

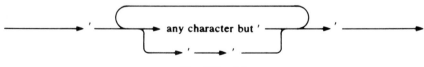

Fig. A26 *string*

Appendix 2

SELECTED EXERCISE SOLUTIONS

Exercise 2.1

Valid integers in Pascal :
       275   6000   27365982   0

Valid reals in Pascal :
       7.4   6E3   275.0   0.001
       10E-4   0.074E3 0.1E999   0.0620

Invalid numbers in Pascal :
       3,475   contains a comma
       .1475   no digits before the decimal point
       275.   no digits after the decimal point

The following numbers denote the same value :
   0.001   10E-4
The pairs
       275   275.0
       6000   6E3
are not considered to denote the same values as in each case
the first is an integer value while the second is a real value.

The following are unacceptable to many implementations for the reasons given
       27365982   integer value is too large (but acceptable as a real)
       0.1E999   real-value is too large

Exercise 2.3

The line
'SPRATT' 'S WIFE'
contains two strings, i.e., 'SPRATT' and 'S WIFE'.
The other lines contain valid strings which denote the following character
sequences :
JACK SPRATT
six + one = ninetyseven
HIS WIFE'S DOG
'''''

Exercise 3.1

       67 div 8   valid - value 8
       12*2.75   valid - value 33.0
       67 mod 8   valid - value 3
       (-3) div 8   valid - value 0
       succ (66.3)   illegal - succ is not defined for real values
       sqr (2.5)   valid - value 6.25
       'A'<'Z'   valid - value true
       pred ('7')   valid - value '6'
       67 / 8   valid - value 8.375
       6.7 div 8   illegal - div must have integer operands

283

```
sqr (10E4)        valid - value 100E8
sqr (100001)      valid - value 10000200001
sqrt (6.25)       valid - value 2.5
sqrt (4)          valid - value 2.0 (real)
succ (true)       illegal - true does not have a successor value
exp (1.0E60)      valid - an extremely large real value !
```

The values of sqr(100001) and exp(1.0E60) may lie outside the implemented range of integer and real values, respectively.

Exercise 3.2

```
constant-identifiers  :     linemax        printwanted    true
                            single         double         treble

type-identifiers      :     lineposition   spacing        char

variable-identifiers  :     thischar       lastchar       thisposition
                            spacingnow
```


Exercise 3.3

```
const
   inchespermetre    = 39.37 ;
   currencysymbol    = '$'   ;
   degreesperradian  = 57.30 ;
   speedlimit        = 60    ;   { miles per hour }
```


Exercise 3.4

```
type
   age = 0..120 ;
   sex = (male , female) ;
   height = real ;   { metres }
   weight = 0..500 ; { pounds }
   maritalstatus = (single , married , widowed , divorced) ;
```

Exercise 3.5

```
var
   bedrooms , receptionrooms : 1..10 ;
   centralheating : (oilfired, electric, solidfuel, gasfired, none) ;
   garage : boolean ;
```


Exercise 4.1

```
      Expression with brackets              Value
      -----------------------               -----
          6.75 - (12.3/3)                    2.65
         (6*11) - (42 div 5)                  58
      ((175 mod 15) div 3) * 65              195
      13 + (7*5) - ((4*5) div 2)              38
         ((11 mod 4) div 2) <> 0             true
  ('A'>='Z') or (('9'>='8') and ('A'<'I'))   true
```

Exercise 4.2

The final values of X, Y, and Z are 17, 217, and 34, respectively.

Exercise 4.3

(a)   (1<=i) and (i<=100)   { - alternatively (0<i) and (i<101) }

(b)   (j mod k = 0) or (k mod j = 0)   { neither j nor k may be zero }

(c)   (y <> 1900) and (y mod 4 = 0)

Exercise 4.4

(a)   using an additional real variable t :
      t:=x ; x:=y ; y:=t

(b)   sum := X+Y+Z ;
      product := X*Y*Z ;
      average := sum/3
      { assumes var sum, product : integer ; average : real ; }

(c)   I := 100*(ord(H)-ord('0')) + 10*(ord(T)-ord('0')) + (ord(U)-ord('0'))

Exercise 5.1

Values of variables following each sequence of input statements :

	X	Y	Z	I	J	K	c
(a)	12.75	24.7	-33E10				
(b)	12.75	-33E10	0.075				
(c)	12.75	24.7	-33E10	0			
(d)				12	-33	0	
(e)				12	75	24	'.'

Exercise 5.2

      writeln ('NUMBER   RANGE   MEAN') ;
      writeln (count:5 , min:8 , '..' , max:2 , mean:10:1)

Exercise 5.3

      program increasesum (input , output) ;
      var sum : real ;
      begin
        read (sum) ;
        writeln ('original sum =' , sum:7:2) ;
        writeln ('increased sum =' , sum*1.08:7:2)
      end.

This program only works for input of the form ddd.dd, so we modify it as
follows :

```
program increasesum (input , output) ;
var   dollars , cents : 0..maxint ;
      ch : char ;
      sum : real ;
begin
   read (dollars , ch , cents) ;
   sum := dollars + cents/100 ;
   writeln ('original sum =' , sum:7:2) ;
   writeln ('increased sum =' , sum*1.08:7:2)
end.
```

Exercise 5.4

```
program calculatechange (input , output) ;
var   cost , tendered : real ;
begin
   read (cost , tendered) ;
   writeln ('amount due' , '$':9 , cost:6:2) ;
   writeln ('amount tendered' , '$':4 , tendered:6:2) ;
   writeln ('change due' , '$':9 , tendered-cost:6:2)
end.
```

Exercise 6.2

```
PROGRAM EXERCISE62 (INPUT , OUTPUT) ;

   (* THIS PROGRAM READS IN THE AMOUNT OF A LOAN AND PRINTS   *)
   (* THE REPAYMENT TABLE SHOWING THE PAYMENT NUMBER, THE     *)
   (* MONTHLY INTEREST, THE INTEREST REPAYMENT, AND THE       *)
   (* RESIDUAL BALANCE.                                        *)

   CONST ANNUALRATE = 8 ; (* PER CENT *)

   VAR NUMBER : 1..MAXINT ;
       INTEREST, REPAYMENT,
       LOAN, PAYMENT, RESIDUE, MONTHRATE : REAL ;

   BEGIN
      READ(LOAN) ;
      WRITE ('AMOUNT BORROWED = ', LOAN:12:2) ;
      PAYMENT := LOAN/100 ;
      WRITELN (' ':10, 'MONTHLY REPAYMENT =', PAYMENT:10:2) ;
      WRITELN ; WRITELN ;
      WRITELN ('  NUMBER  INTEREST REPAYMENT   RESIDUE') ; WRITELN ;
      MONTHRATE := ANNUALRATE/100/12 ;
      NUMBER := 1 ;
      RESIDUE := LOAN ;
      REPEAT
         INTEREST := MONTHRATE*RESIDUE ;
         REPAYMENT := PAYMENT-INTEREST ;
         RESIDUE := RESIDUE-REPAYMENT ;
         WRITELN (NUMBER:7, INTEREST:10:2, REPAYMENT:10:2, RESIDUE:10:2) ;
         NUMBER := NUMBER + 1
      UNTIL RESIDUE+RESIDUE*MONTHRATE <= PAYMENT ;
      WRITELN ; WRITELN ;
      WRITELN ('LAST PAYMENT = ', RESIDUE+RESIDUE*MONTHRATE:10:2)
   END .
```

Exercise 6.3

```
PROGRAM EXERCISE63 (OUTPUT) ;

   (* THIS PROGRAM PRINTS A NUMBER PYRAMID *)

   VAR MAX, NEXT : CHAR ;

   BEGIN
     FOR MAX := '1' TO '9' DO
     BEGIN
        WRITE (' ':20-ORD(MAX)+ORD('0')) ;
        FOR NEXT := '1' TO MAX DO WRITE(NEXT) ;
        FOR NEXT := PRED(MAX) DOWNTO '1' DO WRITE(NEXT) ;
        WRITELN
     END
   END .
```

Exercise 6.6

```
PROGRAM EXERCISE66 (INPUT , OUTPUT) ;

   (* THIS PROGRAM READS AND PRINTS LINES OF TEXT, DETERMINING *)
   (* THE NUMBER OF LINES, WORDS, AND SENTENCES INVOLVED.      *)
   (* IT IS ASSUMED THAT THE LETTERS A TO Z ARE 26 CONSECUTIVE *)
   (* VALUES OF THE TYPE CHAR.                                 *)

   VAR WORDS, LINES, SENTENCES : 0..MAXINT ;
      CH : CHAR ;

   BEGIN
     SENTENCES := 0 ; LINES := 0 ; WORDS := 0 ;
     WHILE NOT EOF (INPUT) DO
     BEGIN
        WHILE NOT EOLN (INPUT) DO
        BEGIN
           READ (CH) ; WRITE (CH) ;
           IF (CH>='A') AND (CH<='Z')
           THEN BEGIN  (* SCAN A WORD *)
                   WORDS := WORDS + 1 ;
                   REPEAT
                      READ (CH) ; WRITE (CH)
                   UNTIL (CH<'A') OR (CH>'Z') OR EOLN(INPUT)
                END ;
           IF CH = '.' THEN SENTENCES := SENTENCES + 1
        END ;
        LINES := LINES + 1 ;
        READLN ; WRITELN
     END ;
     WRITELN ; WRITELN ;
     WRITELN ('TEXT CONSISTS OF :') ;
     WRITELN ;
     WRITELN (LINES, ' LINES') ;
     WRITELN (SENTENCES, ' SENTENCES') ;
     WRITELN (WORDS, ' WORDS')
   END .
```

Exercise 7.3

```
PROGRAM EXERCISE73 (INPUT , OUTPUT) ;

   (* PROGRAM TO INPUT, PRINT AND SUM A SEQUENCE OF OCTAL NUMBERS *)
   (* THE NUMBERS ARE INPUT AND OUTPUT ONE PER LINE              *)

TYPE NONNEGATIVEINTEGER = 0..MAXINT ;

VAR  NUMBER, SUM : NONNEGATIVEINTEGER ;

PROCEDURE READOCTAL (VAR I : NONNEGATIVEINTEGER) ;
   VAR CH : CHAR ;
       N : NONNEGATIVEINTEGER ;
   BEGIN
      (* SKIP CHARACTERS UP TO AN OCTAL DIGIT *)
      REPEAT  READ (CH)  UNTIL (CH >= '0') AND (CH <= '7') ;
      N := 0 ;
      REPEAT
         N := N*8 + (ORD(CH) - ORD('0')) ;
         READ (CH)
      UNTIL (CH < '0') OR (CH > '7') ;
      I := N
   END  (* READOCTAL *) ;

PROCEDURE WRITEOCTAL (I : NONNEGATIVEINTEGER) ;
   VAR  FACTOR : NONNEGATIVEINTEGER ;
   BEGIN
      FACTOR := 1 ;
      WHILE I DIV FACTOR >= 8 DO FACTOR := FACTOR * 8 ;
      REPEAT
         WRITE (CHR(I DIV FACTOR + ORD('0'))) ;
         I := I MOD FACTOR ;
         FACTOR := FACTOR DIV 8
      UNTIL FACTOR = 0
   END  (* WRITEOCTAL *) ;

BEGIN
   WRITELN('OCTAL NUMBER SEQUENCE .....') ;  WRITELN ;
   SUM := 0 ;
   WHILE NOT EOF (INPUT) DO
   BEGIN
      READOCTAL (NUMBER) ;   READLN ;
      WRITEOCTAL (NUMBER) ;   WRITELN ;
      SUM := SUM + NUMBER
   END ;
   WRITELN ;
   WRITE ('OCTAL SUM OF SEQUENCE = ') ;
   WRITEOCTAL (SUM) ;
   WRITELN
END .
```

Exercise 7.5

```
PROGRAM EXERCISE75 (INPUT , OUTPUT) ;

   (* THIS PROGRAM READS A DIGIT AND PRINTS A LIST OF     *)
   (* ALL THE NUMBERS BETWEEN 1 AND 100 SUCH THAT THE     *)
   (* DECIMAL REPRESENTATION OF THE NUMBER, ITS SQUARE    *)
   (* AND ITS CUBE ALL CONTAIN THE SPECIFIED DIGIT.       *)
```

```
TYPE DIGITS = 0..9 ;

VAR  D : DIGITS ;
     BASE, SQUARE, CUBE : 1..MAXINT ;

FUNCTION PRESENT (DIGIT : DIGITS ;  NUMBER : INTEGER) : BOOLEAN ;
   VAR NEXTDIGIT : DIGITS ;
   BEGIN
     REPEAT
        NEXTDIGIT := NUMBER MOD 10 ;
        NUMBER := NUMBER DIV 10
     UNTIL (NEXTDIGIT = DIGIT) OR (NUMBER = 0) ;
     PRESENT := NEXTDIGIT = DIGIT
   END  (* PRESENT *) ;

BEGIN
   READ (D) ;
   WRITELN ('DIGIT SPECIFIED = ', D:1) ;
   WRITELN ; WRITELN ;
   WRITELN ('NUMBER    SQUARE       CUBE') ;
   FOR BASE := 1 TO 100 DO
      IF PRESENT (D, BASE)
      THEN BEGIN
              SQUARE := SQR (BASE) ;
              IF PRESENT (D, SQUARE)
              THEN BEGIN
                      CUBE := SQUARE * BASE ;
                      IF PRESENT (D, CUBE)
                      THEN WRITELN (BASE:4, SQUARE:11, CUBE:11)
                   END
           END
END .


Exercise 7.6

PROGRAM EXERCISE76 (OUTPUT) ;

   (* THIS PROGRAM GENERATES THE NUMBER PYRAMID *)
   (* OF EXERCISE 6.3 USING ONE LOOP AND A      *)
   (* RECURSIVE PROCEDURE.                      *)

TYPE RANGE = '1'..'9' ;

VAR  MAX : RANGE ;

PROCEDURE GENERATE (M, N : RANGE) ;
   (*      GENERATES THE DIGIT STRING        *)
   (*    M,M+1,...,N-1,N,N-1,...,M+1,M       *)
   BEGIN
      IF M = N
      THEN WRITE (M)
      ELSE BEGIN
              WRITE (M) ;
              GENERATE (SUCC(M),N) ;
              WRITE (M)
           END
   END  (* GENERATE *) ;
```

```
BEGIN
   FOR MAX := '1' TO '9' DO
   BEGIN
      WRITE (' ':20-ORD(MAX)+ORD('0')) ;
      GENERATE ('1',MAX) ;
      WRITELN
   END
END .
```

Exercise 9.1

```
PROGRAM EXERCISE91 (INPUT , OUTPUT) ;

   (* AN EXTENDED VERSION OF EXERCISE 6.6 WHICH ALSO COUNTS    *)
   (* AND PRINTS THE NUMBER OF OCCURRENCES OF EACH LETTER.      *)

VAR
   WORDS, LINES, SENTENCES : 0..MAXINT ;
   CH : CHAR ;
   COUNT : ARRAY['A'..'Z'] OF 0..MAXINT ;
   INDEX : 'A'..'Z' ;
   LASTWASLETTER : BOOLEAN ;

BEGIN
   SENTENCES := 0 ;  LINES := 0 ;  WORDS := 0 ;
   FOR INDEX := 'A' TO 'Z' DO COUNT[INDEX] := 0 ;
   WHILE NOT EOF (INPUT) DO
   BEGIN
      LASTWASLETTER := FALSE ;
      WHILE NOT EOLN (INPUT) DO
      BEGIN
         READ (CH) ; WRITE (CH) ;
         IF (CH>='A') AND (CH<='Z')
         THEN BEGIN
                 IF NOT LASTWASLETTER THEN
                 BEGIN WORDS := WORDS + 1 ; LASTWASLETTER := TRUE END ;
                 COUNT[CH] := COUNT[CH] + 1
              END
         ELSE BEGIN
                 IF CH = '.' THEN SENTENCES := SENTENCES + 1 ;
                 LASTWASLETTER := FALSE
              END
      END ;
      LINES := LINES + 1 ;
      READLN ; WRITELN
   END ;
   WRITELN ; WRITELN ;
   WRITELN ('TEXT CONSISTS OF :') ;
   WRITELN ;
   WRITELN (LINES, ' LINES') ;
   WRITELN (SENTENCES, ' SENTENCES') ;
   WRITELN (WORDS, ' WORDS') ;
   WRITELN ; WRITELN ;
   WRITELN ('OCCURRENCES OF LETTERS')  ;  WRITELN ;
   FOR INDEX := 'A' TO 'Z' DO WRITELN (INDEX, ' :', COUNT[INDEX]:5)
END .
```

Exercise 9.3

```
PROGRAM EXERCISE93 (INPUT , OUTPUT) ;

    (* THIS PROGRAM READS AN INPUT TEXT AND PRINTS OUT *)
    (* THE NUMBER OF OCCURRENCES OF EACH ADJACENT      *)
    (* LETTER PAIR WHICH APPEARS WITHIN THE TEXT.      *)
    (* THIS PROGRAM ASSUMES THAT THE LETTERS A TO Z    *)
    (* ARE 26 CONSECUTIVE VALUES OF THE TYPE CHAR.     *)

TYPE LETTER = 'A'..'Z' ;

VAR COUNT : ARRAY[LETTER, LETTER] OF 0..MAXINT ;
    FIRST, SECOND : LETTER ;
    THISCH, LASTCH : CHAR ;
    LASTWASLETTER : BOOLEAN ;

BEGIN
    FOR FIRST := 'A' TO 'Z' DO
       FOR SECOND := 'A' TO 'Z' DO
          COUNT[FIRST,SECOND] := 0 ;
    WHILE NOT EOF (INPUT) DO
    BEGIN
       LASTWASLETTER := FALSE ;  (* AT THE START OF A LINE *)
       WHILE NOT EOLN (INPUT) DO
       BEGIN
          READ (THISCH) ; WRITE (THISCH) ;
          IF (THISCH >= 'A') AND (THISCH <= 'Z')
          THEN IF LASTWASLETTER
                  THEN COUNT[LASTCH,THISCH] := COUNT[LASTCH,THISCH]+1
                  ELSE LASTWASLETTER := TRUE
          ELSE LASTWASLETTER := FALSE ;
          LASTCH := THISCH
       END ;
       READLN ; WRITELN
    END ;
    WRITELN ; WRITELN ;
    WRITELN ('OCCURRENCES OF LETTER PAIRS ....') ;
    FOR FIRST := 'A' TO 'Z' DO
       FOR SECOND := 'A' TO 'Z' DO
          IF COUNT[FIRST,SECOND] <> 0
          THEN WRITELN (FIRST, SECOND, '-', COUNT[FIRST,SECOND]:4)
END .
```

Exercise 9.4

```
PROGRAM EXERCISE94 (INPUT , OUTPUT) ;

    (* THIS PROGRAM READS A SEQUENCE OF WORD PAIRS AND PRINTS *)
    (* EACH PAIR IN DICTIONARY ORDER.                         *)

CONST WORDLENGTH = 16 ;
      BLANKWORD = '                ' ; (* WORDLENGTH SPACES *)

TYPE WORD = PACKED ARRAY[1..WORDLENGTH] OF CHAR ;

VAR WORD1, WORD2 : WORD ;
```

```
PROCEDURE READIN (VAR THEWORD : WORD) ;
   VAR I : 0..WORDLENGTH ;
       CH : CHAR ;
   BEGIN
      THEWORD := BLANKWORD ;
      REPEAT READ (CH) UNTIL CH <> ' ' ;
      I := 0 ;
      REPEAT
         I := I+1 ; THEWORD[I] := CH ;  READ (CH)
      UNTIL (CH = ' ') OR EOLN (INPUT) ;
      IF EOLN(INPUT) AND (CH <> ' ') THEN THEWORD[I+1] := CH
   END  (* READIN *) ;

BEGIN
   WHILE NOT EOF (INPUT) DO
   BEGIN
      READIN (WORD1) ;
      READIN (WORD2) ;
      IF WORD1 > WORD2
      THEN WRITE (WORD2, ' ', WORD1)
      ELSE WRITE (WORD1, ' ', WORD2) ;
      READLN ; WRITELN
   END
END.



Exercise 10.2

PROGRAM EXERCISE102 ( INPUT , OUTPUT ) ;

   (* A PROGRAM WHICH READS FOUR PAIRS OF VALUES REPRESENTING *)
   (* THE VERTICES OF A QUADRILATERAL IN CYCLIC ORDER,    AND *)
   (* DETERMINES WHETHER IT IS A SQUARE, RECTANGLE, OR        *)
   (* OTHERWISE.                                              *)

TYPE COORDINATES = RECORD
                      X, Y : 1..100
                   END ;
     POINT = (A, B, C, D) ;

VAR VERTEX: ARRAY[POINT] OF COORDINATES ;
    P : POINT ;

FUNCTION SQUARELENGTH (P1,P2 : POINT) : INTEGER ;
   BEGIN
      SQUARELENGTH := SQR(VERTEX[P1].X - VERTEX[P2].X) +
                      SQR(VERTEX[P1].Y - VERTEX[P2].Y)
   END  (* SQUARELENGTH *) ;

BEGIN
   WRITE('THE POINTS .... ') ;
   FOR P := A TO D DO
   WITH VERTEX[P] DO
   BEGIN
      READ (X,Y) ;
      WRITE ('(',X:3,Y:3,')') ;
   END ;
   WRITE (' REPRESENT A ') ;
```

```
    IF  (SQUARELENGTH(A,B) = SQUARELENGTH(C,D))
    AND (SQUARELENGTH(B,C) = SQUARELENGTH(D,A))
    AND (SQUARELENGTH(A,C) = SQUARELENGTH(B,D))
    THEN
        (* OPPOSITE SIDES AND DIAGONALS ARE EQUAL *)
        IF SQUARELENGTH(A,B) = SQUARELENGTH(B,C)
        THEN WRITE ('SQUARE')
        ELSE WRITE ('RECTANGLE')
    ELSE WRITE ('QUADRILATERAL') ;
    WRITELN ; WRITELN
END .


Exercise 10.4

PROGRAM EXERCISE104 (INPUT , OUTPUT) ;

    (* THIS PROGRAM READS IN A SEQUENCE OF DESCRIPTIONS    *)
    (* OF GEOMETRIC FIGURES AND PRINTS OUT THE DESCRIPTION *)
    (* OF THE ONE WITH THE LARGEST AREA.                   *)

CONST PI = 3.14159 ;

TYPE FIGURETYPE = (CIRCLE, RECTANGLE, SQUARE, TRIANGLE) ;
     FIGURE =
         RECORD
            CASE SHAPE : FIGURETYPE OF
            CIRCLE     : (RADIUS : REAL) ;
            RECTANGLE  : (SIDE1, SIDE2 : REAL) ;
            SQUARE     : (SIDE : REAL) ;
            TRIANGLE   : (A, B, C : REAL)
         END ;

VAR THISFIGURE, LARGESTFIGURE : FIGURE ;
    FIGUREAREA, LARGESTAREA : REAL ;

PROCEDURE READFIGURE (VAR AFIGURE : FIGURE) ;
    VAR CH : CHAR ;
    BEGIN
        WITH AFIGURE DO
        BEGIN
            READ (CH) ;
            IF CH = 'C'
            THEN BEGIN
                    SHAPE := CIRCLE ;
                    READ (RADIUS)
                 END
            ELSE IF CH = 'R'
                THEN BEGIN
                        SHAPE := RECTANGLE ;
                        READ (SIDE1, SIDE2)
                     END
                ELSE IF CH = 'S'
                    THEN BEGIN
                            SHAPE := SQUARE ;
                            READ (SIDE)
                         END
```

```
                    ELSE IF CH = 'T'
                        THEN BEGIN
                                SHAPE := TRIANGLE ;
                                READ (A, B, C)
                            END
                        ELSE BEGIN
                                WRITELN ('FIGURE TYPE NOT RECOGNISED') ;
                                SHAPE := CIRCLE ;
                                RADIUS := 0.0
                            END
        END
    END ; (* READFIGURE *)

FUNCTION AREA (AFIGURE : FIGURE) : REAL ;
    VAR S : REAL ;
    BEGIN
        WITH AFIGURE DO
        CASE SHAPE OF
            CIRCLE      : AREA := PI*SQR(RADIUS) ;
            RECTANGLE   : AREA := SIDE1*SIDE2 ;
            SQUARE      : AREA := SQR(SIDE) ;
            TRIANGLE    : BEGIN
                            S := (A+B+C) / 2 ;
                            AREA := SQRT(S*(S-A)*(S-B)*(S-C))
                        END
        END
    END ; (* AREA *)

PROCEDURE WRITEFIGURE (AFIGURE : FIGURE) ;
    BEGIN
        WITH AFIGURE DO
        CASE SHAPE OF
            CIRCLE      : WRITE ('A CIRCLE OF RADIUS', RADIUS:6:1) ;
            RECTANGLE   : WRITE ('A RECTANGLE WITH SIDES', SIDE1:6:1, SIDE2:6:1) ;
            SQUARE      : WRITE ('A SQUARE WITH SIDE LENGTH', SIDE:6:1) ;
            TRIANGLE    : WRITE ('A TRIANGLE WITH SIDES', A:6:1, B:6:1, C:6:1)
        END
    END ; (* WRITEFIGURE *)

BEGIN
    LARGESTAREA := 0 ;
    WRITELN ('FIGURE SEQUENCE ....') ; WRITELN ; WRITELN ;
    WHILE NOT EOF (INPUT) DO
    BEGIN
        READFIGURE (THISFIGURE) ;
        FIGUREAREA := AREA (THISFIGURE) ;
        WRITE ('AREA =', FIGUREAREA:10:2, ' OF ') ;
        WRITEFIGURE (THISFIGURE) ;
        IF FIGUREAREA > LARGESTAREA
        THEN BEGIN
                LARGESTAREA := FIGUREAREA ;
                LARGESTFIGURE := THISFIGURE
            END ;
        READLN ; WRITELN ; WRITELN
    END ;
    WRITE ('THE LARGEST FIGURE IN THE SEQUENCE IS ') ;
    WRITEFIGURE (LARGESTFIGURE) ;
    WRITELN (' AND ITS AREA IS', LARGESTAREA:10:2)
END.
```

Exercise 11.3

```
PROGRAM EXERCISE113 (INPUT , OUTPUT) ;

   (* A PROGRAM WHICH READS TWO SENTENCES, EACH TERMINATED *)
   (* BY A PERIOD, AND OUTPUTS A LIST OF ALL LETTERS WHICH *)
   (*                 APPEAR IN BOTH SENTENCES.            *)

TYPE CHARS = SET OF CHAR ;

VAR  CHARS1, CHARS2, COMMONLETTERS : CHARS ;
     LETTER : CHAR ;

PROCEDURE SCANSENTENCE (VAR CHARSUSED : CHARS) ;
   VAR CH : CHAR ;
   BEGIN
     CHARSUSED := [] ;
     REPEAT
        READ (CH) ;
        CHARSUSED := CHARSUSED + [CH]
     UNTIL CH = '.'
   END ; (* SCANSENTENCE *)

BEGIN
   SCANSENTENCE (CHARS1) ;
   SCANSENTENCE (CHARS2) ;
   COMMONLETTERS := CHARS1 * CHARS2 * ['A'..'Z'] ;
   WRITE ('COMMON LETTERS ARE :') ;
   FOR LETTER := 'A' TO 'Z' DO
      IF LETTER IN COMMONLETTERS THEN WRITE (LETTER:2) ;
   WRITELN
END.
```

Exercise 11.4

```
PROGRAM EXERCISE114 (INPUT , OUTPUT) ;

   (* THIS PROGRAM READS THE ENROLMENT CARDS OF STUDENTS AND *)
   (* PRINTS A STUDENT LIST FOR EACH OF THE TEN SUBJECTS     *)

CONST NAMELENGTH = 20 ;
      MAXNUMBERSTUDENTS = 100 ;
TYPE SUBJECT = (ART, ENGLISH, FRENCH, GERMAN, HISTORY, GEOGRAPHY,
                MATHEMATICS, PHYSICS, CHEMISTRY, BIOLOGY) ;
     STUDENTDETAILS = RECORD
                         NAME : PACKED ARRAY[1..NAMELENGTH] OF CHAR ;
                         COURSES : SET OF SUBJECT
                      END ;
VAR THISSUBJECT : SUBJECT ;
    N, NUMBEROFSTUDENTS : 0..MAXNUMBERSTUDENTS ;
    STUDENT : ARRAY[1..MAXNUMBERSTUDENTS] OF STUDENTDETAILS ;

PROCEDURE READCARD(VAR S : STUDENTDETAILS) ;
   VAR CH : CHAR ;
       THISSUBJECT : SUBJECT ;
       I : 1..NAMELENGTH ;
   BEGIN
     WITH S DO
     BEGIN
        FOR I:=1 TO NAMELENGTH DO READ (NAME[I]) ;
```

```
            COURSES := [] ;
            FOR THISSUBJECT := ART TO BIOLOGY DO
            BEGIN
               READ (CH) ;
               IF CH = 'X' THEN COURSES := COURSES + [THISSUBJECT]
            END
        END ;
        READLN
    END (* READCARD *) ;

BEGIN
    N := 0 ;
    REPEAT
      N := N+1 ;  READCARD (STUDENT[N] )
    UNTIL EOF (INPUT) ;
    NUMBEROFSTUDENTS := N ;
    FOR THISSUBJECT := ART TO BIOLOGY DO
    BEGIN
      CASE THISSUBJECT OF
          ART          : WRITELN ('*** ART ***') ;
          ENGLISH      : WRITELN ('*** ENGLISH ***') ;
          FRENCH       : WRITELN ('*** FRENCH ***') ;
          GERMAN       : WRITELN ('*** GERMAN ***') ;
          HISTORY      : WRITELN ('*** HISTORY ***') ;
          GEOGRAPHY    : WRITELN ('*** GEOGRAPHY ***') ;
          MATHEMATICS  : WRITELN ('*** MATHEMATICS ***') ;
          PHYSICS      : WRITELN ('*** PHYSICS ***') ;
          CHEMISTRY    : WRITELN ('*** CHEMISTRY ***') ;
          BIOLOGY      : WRITELN ('*** BIOLOGY ***')
      END ;
      WRITELN ;
      FOR N:=1 TO NUMBEROFSTUDENTS DO
      WITH STUDENT[N] DO
          IF THISSUBJECT IN COURSES THEN WRITELN (NAME) ;
      WRITELN ;   WRITELN
    END
END.



Exercise 11.5

PROGRAM EXERCISE115 (INPUT , OUTPUT);

    (* THIS PROGRAM READS A BAR LENGTH AND A LIST OF OUTSTANDING *)
    (* ORDERS FOR LENGTHS TO BE CUT FROM SUCH BARS, AND CHOOSES  *)
    (* (BY RECURSIVE TRIAL AND ERROR) THE SET OF ORDERED LENGTHS *)
    (* THAT SHOULD BE CUT TO MINIMISE BAR WASTAGE.               *)

CONST MAXSIZEOFORDERLIST = 20 ;

TYPE  ORDERS = 1..MAXSIZEOFORDERLIST ;
      ORDERSET = SET OF ORDERS ;

VAR   SIZEOFORDERLIST : ORDERS ;
      BESTSET : ORDERSET ;
      BESTLENGTH, L : 0..MAXINT ;
      LENGTH : ARRAY[ORDERS] OF 1..MAXINT ;
      I:ORDERS ;
```

```
(* SETS ARE USED TO DESCRIBE THE TRIAL SOLUTION, BEST SOLUTION, AND *)
(* POTENTIAL COMPONENTS.                                            *)
(* THE LENGTHS OF THE ORDERS ARE HELD IN THE ARRAY LENGTH .         *)
(* BESTSET CONTAINS THE INDICES IN LENGTH OF THE ORDERS MAKING      *)
(* UP THE BEST SOLUTION FOUND SO FAR.                               *)
(* BESTLENGTH DENOTES THE TOTAL LENGTH OF THE ORDERS IN BESTSET.    *)

PROCEDURE CONSIDER (TRIALLENGTH : INTEGER ;
                    ORDERSCHOSEN , ORDERSREMAINING : ORDERSET);

    (* TRIALLENGTH DENOTES THE TOTAL LENGTH OF ORDERS CURRENTLY IN  *)
    (* THE SET ORDERSCHOSEN.                                        *)
    (* ORDERSCHOSEN IS A SET WHOSE MEMBERS ARE THE INDICES IN LENGTH *)
    (* OF THE ORDERS IN THE CURRENT TRIAL SOLUTION.                 *)
    (* ORDERSREMAINING IS A SET WHOSE MEMBERS ARE THE INDICES IN    *)
    (* LENGTH OF THE ORDERS AVAILABLE FOR INCORPORATION INTO THE    *)
    (* TRIAL SOLUTION.                                              *)

    VAR   X : 0..MAXSIZEOFORDERLIST ;

    BEGIN
       IF TRIALLENGTH <= L
       THEN BEGIN
              IF TRIALLENGTH > BESTLENGTH
              THEN BEGIN
                     BESTLENGTH := TRIALLENGTH ;
                     BESTSET := ORDERSCHOSEN
                   END ;
              X := 0 ;
              WHILE ORDERSREMAINING <> [] DO
              BEGIN
                 REPEAT X := X+1 UNTIL X IN ORDERSREMAINING ;
                 ORDERSREMAINING := ORDERSREMAINING - [X] ;
                 CONSIDER (TRIALLENGTH + LENGTH[X],
                           ORDERSCHOSEN + [X],
                           ORDERSREMAINING)
              END
           END
    END ; (* IMPROVE *)

BEGIN
   READ (L) ; WRITELN ('MANUFACTURED BAR LENGTH IS', L:5, ' MM');
   WRITELN ; WRITELN ('ORDER LIST IS') ;
   READ (SIZEOFORDERLIST) ;
   FOR I:=1 TO SIZEOFORDERLIST DO
   BEGIN READ (LENGTH[I]) ; WRITELN (LENGTH[I], ' MM') END ;

   BESTLENGTH:=0 ;  BESTSET := [] ;

   (* INITIALLY, TRIAL SET IS EMPTY AND ALL ORDERS ARE  *)
   (* AVAILABLE FOR INCLUSION IN THE TRIAL SOLUTION.    *)
   CONSIDER (0, [ ], [1..SIZEOFORDERLIST]) ;

   WRITELN ; WRITELN ('OPTIMAL SET OF ORDERS') ;
   FOR I:=1 TO SIZEOFORDERLIST DO
      IF I IN BESTSET THEN WRITELN (LENGTH[I]:6, ' MM') ;
   WRITELN ; WRITELN ('WASTAGE =', L DEOTLENGTH:4, ' MM')
END.
```

Exercise 12.1

```
PROGRAM EXERCISE121 (INPUT, CLASS1) ;

     (* CREATION OF THE STUDENT GRADES FILE CLASS1 *)

TYPE
   STUDENTDETAILS = RECORD
                        NAME  : PACKED ARRAY[1..30] OF CHAR ;
                        GRADE : ARRAY[1..5] OF 0..10 ;
                        TOTAL : 0..50
                    END ;
   STUDENTFILE = FILE OF STUDENTDETAILS ;

VAR
   CLASS1 : STUDENTFILE ;

PROCEDURE READCARD (VAR S : STUDENTDETAILS) ;
   VAR
      NAMELENGTH : 0..30 ;
      SUBJECT : 1..5 ;
      CH : CHAR ;
   BEGIN
      WITH S DO
      BEGIN
         NAMELENGTH := 0 ;
         REPEAT
            NAMELENGTH := NAMELENGTH+1 ;  READ (CH) ;  NAME[NAMELENGTH] := CH
         UNTIL CH = '.' ;
         WHILE NAMELENGTH<30 DO
         BEGIN
            NAMELENGTH := NAMELENGTH+1 ;
            NAME[NAMELENGTH] := ' '
         END ;
         TOTAL := 0 ;
         FOR SUBJECT := 1 TO 5 DO
         BEGIN
            READ (GRADE[SUBJECT]) ;
            TOTAL := TOTAL + GRADE[SUBJECT]
         END
      END ;
      READLN
   END  (* READCARD *) ;

BEGIN
   REWRITE (CLASS1) ;
   WHILE NOT EOF (INPUT) DO
   BEGIN
      READCARD (CLASS1^) ;
      PUT (CLASS1)
   END
END.
```

Exercise 12.3

```
PROGRAM EXERCISE123 (OUTPUT, CLASS1) ;

     (* TABULATION OF THE RECORDS IN THE FILE CLASS1 *)

TYPE
   STUDENTDETAILS = RECORD
                        NAME  : PACKED ARRAY[1..30] OF CHAR ;
                        GRADE : ARRAY[1..5] OF 0..10 ;
                        TOTAL : 0..50
                     END ;
   STUDENTFILE = FILE OF STUDENTDETAILS ,
VAR
   CLASS1 : STUDENTFILE ;

PROCEDURE PRINTDETAILS (S : STUDENTDETAILS) ;
   VAR STAR : 1..20 ;
   BEGIN
      WITH S DO
      BEGIN
         WRITE (NAME, TOTAL:10, '  ') ;
         FOR STAR := 1 TO ROUND(0.4*TOTAL) DO WRITE ('*')
      END ;
      WRITELN
   END ; (* PRINTDETAILS *)

BEGIN
   RESET (CLASS1) ;
   WHILE NOT EOF (CLASS1) DO
   BEGIN
      PRINTDETAILS (CLASS1^) ;
      GET (CLASS1)
   END
END.
```

Exercise 12.4

```
PROGRAM EXERCISE124 (CLASS1, CLASS2, CLASSES) ;

     (* MERGE OF THE SORTED STUDENT GRADES FILES CLASS1 *)
     (* AND CLASS2, TO PRODUCE A SINGLE SORTED FILE     *)
     (* CLASSES.                                        *)

TYPE
   STUDENTDETAILS = RECORD
                        NAME  : PACKED ARRAY[1..30] OF CHAR ;
                        GRADE : ARRAY[1..5] OF 0..10 ;
                        TOTAL : 0..50
                     END ;
   STUDENTFILE = FILE OF STUDENTDETAILS ;
VAR
   CLASS1, CLASS2, CLASSES : STUDENTFILE ;
   ENDOFEITHERFILE : BOOLEAN ;
```

```
BEGIN
   RESET (CLASS1) ; RESET (CLASS2) ; REWRITE (CLASSES) ;
   ENDOFEITHERFILE := EOF (CLASS1) OR EOF (CLASS2) ;
   WHILE NOT ENDOFEITHERFILE DO
   BEGIN
      IF CLASS1^.NAME < CLASS2^.NAME
      THEN BEGIN
              CLASSES^ := CLASS1^ ; GET (CLASS1) ;
              ENDOFEITHERFILE := EOF (CLASS1)
           END
      ELSE BEGIN
              CLASSES^ := CLASS2^ ; GET (CLASS2) ;
              ENDOFEITHERFILE := EOF (CLASS2)
           END ;
      PUT (CLASSES)
   END ;
   WHILE NOT EOF (CLASS1) DO
   BEGIN CLASSES^ := CLASS1^ ; PUT (CLASSES) ; GET (CLASS1) END ;
   WHILE NOT EOF (CLASS2) DO
   BEGIN CLASSES^ := CLASS2^ ; PUT (CLASSES) ; GET (CLASS2) END
END.
```

Exercise 12.6

```
PROGRAM EXERCISE126 (OUTPUT, PAGE1, PAGE2) ;

     (* THIS PROGRAM READS THE TEXT FILES PAGE1 AND    *)
     (* PAGE2, AND PRINTS THEIR CONTENTS SIDE BY SIDE *)

CONST HALFMAXLINELENGTH = 30 ;

TYPE  TEXTRANGE = 0..HALFMAXLINELENGTH ;

VAR   PAGE1, PAGE2 : TEXT ;
      LENGTH : TEXTRANGE ;

PROCEDURE PRINTALINEFROM (VAR F : TEXT ; VAR LENGTH : TEXTRANGE) ;
   VAR CH : CHAR ;
       COUNT : TEXTRANGE ;
   BEGIN
      COUNT := 0 ;
      WHILE NOT EOLN (F) DO
      BEGIN
         COUNT := COUNT+1 ;
         READ (F, CH) ; WRITE (CH)
      END ;
      READLN (F) ;
      LENGTH := COUNT
   END ; (* PRINTALINEFROM *)
```

```
BEGIN
   RESET (PAGE1) ; RESET (PAGE2) ;
   WRITELN ('  ':HALFMAXLINELENGTH DIV 2 -3, 'PAGE 1',
            '  ':HALFMAXLINELENGTH-6,         'PAGE 2') ;
   WHILE NOT (EOF (PAGE1) OR EOF (PAGE2)) DO
   BEGIN
      PRINTALINEFROM (PAGE1, LENGTH) ;
      IF LENGTH < HALFMAXLINELENGTH
      THEN WRITE ('  ':HALFMAXLINELENGTH-LENGTH) ;
      PRINTALINEFROM (PAGE2, LENGTH) ;
      WRITELN
   END ;
   WHILE NOT EOF (PAGE1) DO
   BEGIN
      PRINTALINEFROM (PAGE1, LENGTH) ;
      WRITELN
   END ;
   WHILE NOT EOF (PAGE2) DO
   BEGIN
      WRITE ('  ':HALFMAXLINELENGTH) ;
      PRINTALINEFROM (PAGE2, LENGTH) ;
      WRITELN
   END
END.



Exercise 13.2

PROGRAM EXERCISE132 (OUTPUT , EMPLOYEES) ;

   (* THIS PROGRAM READS A FILE OF EMPLOYEE/PHONE-NUMBER   *)
   (* RECORDS AND PRINTS A LIST OF PHONE/USERS RECORDS     *)


CONST NAMELENGTH = 16 ;

TYPE  SPELLING = PACKED ARRAY[1..NAMELENGTH] OF CHAR ;
      NUMBER   = 0..MAXINT ;
      LISTPOINTER = ^OCCUPANT ;
      OCCUPANT    = RECORD
                       NAME : SPELLING ;
                       NEXT : LISTPOINTER
                    END ;
      LISTOFOCCUPANTS = RECORD
                           FIRST, LAST : LISTPOINTER
                        END ;
      ROOMPOINTER = ^ROOMRECORD ;
      ROOMRECORD  = RECORD
                       PHONE : NUMBER ;
                       OCCUPIERS : LISTOFOCCUPANTS ;
                       NEXT : ROOMPOINTER
                    END ;

VAR   EMPLOYEES : FILE OF RECORD
                             NAME : SPELLING ;
                             PHONE : NUMBER
                          END ;
      ROOMLIST, ROOM : ROOMPOINTER ;
```

```
PROCEDURE LOCATEROOM (NUMBERSOUGHT : NUMBER ;
                      VAR ROOMFOUND: ROOMPOINTER) ;
   VAR  THISROOM, PREVIOUSROOM : ROOMPOINTER ;
        POSITIONFOUND : BOOLEAN ;

   PROCEDURE INSERTROOM ;
      VAR  NEWROOM : ROOMPOINTER ;
      BEGIN
         NEW (NEWROOM) ;
         WITH NEWROOM^ DO
         BEGIN
            PHONE := NUMBERSOUGHT ;
            WITH OCCUPIERS DO BEGIN FIRST:=NIL ; LAST:=NIL END ;
            NEXT := THISROOM
         END ;
         IF PREVIOUSROOM = NIL
         THEN ROOMLIST := NEWROOM
         ELSE PREVIOUSROOM^.NEXT := NEWROOM ;
         ROOMFOUND := NEWROOM
      END ;   (* INSERTROOM *)

   BEGIN
      THISROOM := ROOMLIST ;  PREVIOUSROOM := NIL ;
      POSITIONFOUND := FALSE ;
      WHILE NOT POSITIONFOUND AND (THISROOM<>NIL) DO
         IF THISROOM^.PHONE >= NUMBERSOUGHT
         THEN POSITIONFOUND := TRUE
         ELSE BEGIN
                 PREVIOUSROOM := THISROOM ;
                 THISROOM := THISROOM^.NEXT
              END ;
      IF POSITIONFOUND
      THEN IF THISROOM^.PHONE = NUMBERSOUGHT
           THEN ROOMFOUND := THISROOM
           ELSE INSERTROOM
      ELSE INSERTROOM
   END ; (*  LOCATEROOM  *)

PROCEDURE ADDEMPLOYEETO (VAR LIST : LISTOFOCCUPANTS) ;
   VAR THISOCCUPANT : LISTPOINTER ;
   BEGIN
      NEW (THISOCCUPANT) ;
      WITH THISOCCUPANT^ DO
      BEGIN
         NAME := EMPLOYEE^.NAME ;
         NEXT := NIL
      END ;
      WITH LIST DO
      BEGIN
         IF FIRST = NIL
         THEN FIRST := THISOCCUPANT
         ELSE LAST^.NEXT := THISOCCUPANT ;
         LAST := THISOCCUPANT
      END
   END ; (* ADDEMPLOYEETO *)
```

```
PROCEDURE PRINTDIRECTORY ;
   VAR THISROOM, NEXTROOM : ROOMPOINTER ;

   PROCEDURE PRINTOCCUPANTS (PHONE : NUMBER ;
                            OCCUPIERS : LISTOFOCCUPANTS) ;
      VAR FIRSTLINE : BOOLEAN ;
          THISOCCUPANT, NEXTOCCUPANT : LISTPOINTER ;
      BEGIN (* PRINTOCCUPANTS *)
         WRITELN ;
         FIRSTLINE := TRUE ;
         NEXTOCCUPANT := OCCUPIERS.FIRST ;
         REPEAT
            THISOCCUPANT := NEXTOCCUPANT ;
            IF FIRSTLINE
            THEN BEGIN WRITE (PHONE:6, '  ') ; FIRSTLINE := FALSE END
            ELSE WRITE (' ':8) ;
            WRITELN (THISOCCUPANT^.NAME) ;
            NEXTOCCUPANT := THISOCCUPANT^.NEXT
            DISPOSE (THISOCCUPANT)
         UNTIL NEXTOCCUPANT = NIL
      END ; (* PRINTOCCUPANTS *)

   BEGIN
      PAGE ;
      WRITELN ('ROOM LIST') ;
      WRITELN ('---------') ; WRITELN ; WRITELN ;
      NEXTROOM := ROOMLIST ;
      WHILE NEXTROOM <> NIL DO
      BEGIN
         THISROOM := NEXTROOM ;
         WITH THISROOM^ DO PRINTOCCUPANTS (PHONE, OCCUPIERS) ;
         NEXTROOM := THISROOM^.NEXT ;
         DISPOSE (THISROOM)
      END
   END ; (* PRINTDIRECTORY *)

BEGIN (* MAIN PROGRAM *)
   RESET (EMPLOYEES) ;
   ROOMLIST := NIL ;
   WHILE NOT EOF (EMPLOYEES) DO
   BEGIN
      LOCATEROOM (EMPLOYEE^.PHONE, ROOM) ;
      ADDEMPLOYEETO (ROOM^.OCCUPIERS) ;
      GET (EMPLOYEES)
   END ;
   PRINTDIRECTORY
END.
```

Index

This index provides an exhaustive list of the words and terms used throughout the book. Those shown in *italics* are standard identifiers in PASCAL, or standard terms used in its definition.

The page number of the defining occurrence of a word or term is shown in **heavy** type, with other significant occurrences in normal type.